Christ's Hospital

Tradition with Vision

David Taplin
&
Lizzie Ballagher

Grosvenor House
Publishing Limited

This book is published by
Grosvenor House Publishing Ltd
Link House, 140 The Broadway, Tolworth, Surrey, KT6 7HT.
www.grosvenorhousepublishing.co.uk

Permission to quote extracts from this book
should be sought directly from Professor David Taplin via email:
coliemore@hotmail.com

Permission for use / circulation of any of the poems by Lizzie Ballagher in Chapter VI
should be sought directly from the poet via email:
lizzieballagherpoetry@gmail.com

For more information on how to go about purchasing a copy of this book,
please contact Bruce Heywood:
bruceheywood@hotmail.co.uk

Purchases of hardback, paperback, and eBook copies may be made through Amazon or other e-tailers' websites.

A CIP record for this book is available from the British Library

ISBN: 978-1-83975-017-5

Also available as:

Hardback: 978-1-83975-016-8
eBooks: 978-1-83975-018-2

The Benevolent Society of Blues: Blues Supporting Blues

Since the costs for the publication of this book have been met privately, 100% of net proceeds from sales, and all royalties, will go to the BSB.

The BSB works with Old Blues and Blues alike: any who are in need, hardship, or distress. The BSB's support is practical, financial, pastoral, and social: through the widespread work of many OB volunteers; through CH's pastoral care team; and through the donations of many Old Blues.

Current Blues facing challenging circumstances at home can, through the BSB, be supported with essential grocery and travel help in school holidays, and with direct pastoral engagement during term-time.

The scheme also operates a buddies' system that allows leavers who experience difficulties after CH to receive continuing support from the Old Blue community in their local area, or in a new university setting.

Contributors to *Christ's Hospital: Tradition with Vision* are pleased to contribute through the book's sales to the BSB's excellent and ongoing work.

BSB Registered Charity Number: 207 818
President: Kathleen Duncan, OBE
Chairman: Andrew Cosedge, LLB
Deputy Chair: Robin Clarke
Treasurer: Perry D C N Kitchen MA FCA
Secretary: Julie Wilson

The Counting House
Christ's Hospital
Horsham
West Sussex
RH13 0YP

Telephone: 01403 247418
Email: julie@bluessupportingblues.net

With contributions from:

David Arnold
John Arnold
Terry Bate
Christopher Bugge
Desi Elizabeth
Bruce Heywood
Chris Johnson
Amy Lonton
Tim Parsons
Josh Reynolds
Benedict Rubbra
Roger Wickins
Sinclair Wynchank

Christ's Hospital: Tradition with Vision

David Taplin & Lizzie Ballagher

Sponsored by the British Columbia Old Blues (BCOB), an overseas section of the Christ's Hospital Old Blues Association (CHOBA)

'A Ripening' by Benedict Rubbra

When I was very young I made a painting of freshly picked vegetables.

Since then I have always enjoyed the shared process of sowing seeds and gathering the harvest. This seems to embody the idea of nature's circular movement and I try to relate this concept in my work.

A Ripening voices the beginning of a circular movement that epitomises the beginning of a child's education. The image is based on a model that I made out of clay and lengths of string. The balls of clay become the seeds of youth and the intertwining string their upward growth. And so the image becomes a ripening of youthful potential.

In 1947 I was placed in Prep A and then moved to Coleridge A until 1956. The arrival of Nell Todd as our Art Teacher marked the beginning of my awakening and education. She was an inspiration and we established a deep friendship that remained until the end of her life.

www.benedictrubbra.co.uk

Contents

Frontispiece

Anthem for the Children of Christ's Hospital

Seraphs! around th'Eternal's seat who throng
    With tuneful ecstasies of praise:
O! teach our feeble tongues like yours the song
    Of fervent gratitude to raise—
    Like you, inspired with holy flame
    To dwell on that Almighty name
Who bade the child of Woe no longer sigh,
And joy in tears o'erspread the widow's eye.

Editor's Notes: As a schoolboy, Coleridge wrote a fanciful poem called 'A Mathematical Problem' for his older brother, a vicar, sending him the poem with a short letter that gives hints of the poet's childhood difficulties with mathematics… an awkward situation to be in when, by Coleridge's time, CH had been the Royal Mathematical School's home for more than 100 years.

To the Reverend George Coleridge

Dear Brother,

I have often been surprised that Mathematics, the quintessence of Truth, should have found admirers so few and so languid. Frequent consideration and minute scrutiny have at length unravelled the cause; viz, that though Reason is feasted, Imagination is starved; while Reason is luxuriating in its proper Paradise, Imagination is wearily travelling on a dreary desert. To assist Reason by the stimulus of Imagination is the design of the following production. In the execution of it, much may be objectionable. The verse… may be accused of unwarrantable liberties… [but] I have three strong champions to defend me against the attacks of Criticism: the Novelty, the Difficulty, and the Utility of the work. I may justly plume myself that I have drawn the nymph Mathesis from the visionary caves of abstracted idea, and caused her to unite with Harmony. The first-born of this Union I now present to you.

And when, some time later, Coleridge left Christ's Hospital, he wrote the poem that follows in a less playful, more touching tone:

Sonnet on Quitting School for College

Farewell, parental scenes! a sad farewell!
To you my grateful heart still fondly clings,
The fluttering round on Fancy's burnished wings
Her tales of future Joy Hope loves to tell.
Adieu, adieu! ye much-loved cloisters pale!
Ah! would those happy days return again…
Dear haunts! where oft my simple lays I sang,
Listening meanwhile the echoings of my feet,
Lingering I quit you…

The above extracts are from *Coleridge, Poetical Works*, E H Coleridge, Editor, first published 1912; reprinted Oxford University Press, 1969 pages 5–6, 21–22, and 29.

…He brought me
to Christ's new Hospital,
spoke gentle words,
gave bread to me, and meat.

They taught me *à écrire et lire en Anglais*
how to read & write in English,
clad me in russet, then in blue & gold,
apprenticed me
to the Worshipful Company of Drapers
in fair & ancient halls on old Throgmorton Street—

all for the love of Edward, King;
for the love of God, their Lord:
true founders of the Hospital.

From 'On Cheapside, 1552'

...marching from long-past Tudor days,
they are the ones coming to be
tomorrow's hopes, those finding newer ways—
daughters & sons of Christ's Hospital.

From 'A Bronze for Christ's Hospital'

Prologue

Christ's Hospital is a school of profound and treasured traditions. For some 65,000 Old Blues (with perhaps 10,000 living Old Blues worldwide) this great school has embedded tradition and vision in its pupils ever since its auspicious foundation in 1552 in London by the boy-king Edward VI. The visionary engineer Sir Barnes Neville Wallis and the visionary poet Samuel Taylor Coleridge are ever-present influences, with other famous Old Blues to mention: Saint Edmund Campion, George Peele, Charles Lamb, Leigh Hunt, Edward Thornton, Joshua Barnes, Thomas Middleton, Alexander Cunningham, Henry Maine, Lilian Bostock, Charlotte Mitchell, Augustus Pugin, Louis Harold Gray, Ida Busbridge, Michael Stewart, Keith Douglas, Violet Green, Margaret Gowing, Norah McNaulty, Michael Wilding, Rhea Martin, Ian Trethowan, Edmund Blunden, Carol Adams, Christopher Zeeman, Colin Davis, Benedict Rubbra, Ruth Deech — the list goes on…

Science teaching has been especially strong at CH since the introduction of the heuristics system of Henry Armstrong in the 19th century through the teaching of chemistry by discovery, developed by the distinguished CH teachers Charles Browne (who taught Barnes Wallis) and Gordon Van Praagh in the 20th century, following the move of CH from London to the Sussex weald in 1902. Engineering teaching was also unusually strong throughout the 20th century, including sophisticated structural integrity testing and metallurgy (arguably the oldest profession in the technological evolution of civilisation, heralding the Bronze Age).

Mathematics teaching has also had an exceptional tradition at CH since the 17th century with the establishment of a Royal Mathematical School by Charles II oriented to navigational engineering, with the renowned William Wales as Master (following his 18th-century navigational work with James Cook aboard *Resolution* in the Southern Ocean, and indeed his mentoring of George Vancouver in Canada). We might well heed the following comment by Bertrand Russell:

'Mathematics… possesses not only truth, but supreme beauty – a beauty cold and austere … yet sublimely pure … the sense of being more than Man … the touchstone of the highest excellence … as surely as in poetry.'

(Bertrand Russell, *The Study of Mathematics,* Longman, London, 1919, p60.)

Coleridge's mathematics was in fact taught by William Wales; tradition claims that Wales inspired his *Ancient Mariner*. The Reverend James Boyer (headmaster 1778–1799) was also a major poetical influence on Coleridge, and was especially praised by him:

'I learned from him that poetry, even that of the loftiest and, seemingly, that of the wildest odes, had a logic of its own, as severe as that of science; and more difficult, because more subtle, more complex, and dependent on more fugitive causes. In the truly great poets, he would say, there is a reason assignable, not only to every word, but for the position of every word; and I well remember that, availing himself of the synonyms to the Homer of Didymus, he made us attempt to show, with regard to each, why it would not have been conveyed with equal force and dignity in plainer words.'

(*Biographia Literaria* by Samuel Coleridge, Harper and Brothers, New York, 1884)

The Newton, Boltzmann, Einstein, Dirac, Turing, and Mandelbrot equations are, in a sense, some of the most beautiful mathematical poems ever written. The Einstein equation ushered in the modern post-Newton world, while Mandelbrot's work produced wonderful fractal images. Arguably, however, the most beautiful mathematical poem of the 20th century is the Dirac Equation by 1933 Nobel Laureate Paul Dirac – opening up the field of quantum mechanics and predicting the existence of anti-matter – and on which so much of our 21st century endeavour depends.

$$\left(\beta mc^2 + c\left(\sum_{n=1}^{3} \alpha_n p_n\right)\right)\psi(x,t) = i\hbar\frac{\partial\psi(x,t)}{\partial t}$$

At CH in 1955, I was memorably introduced to the magic of literary poetry in the Lamb B dayroom through a discussion with a poetic friend on how wonderful it would be to be married, and thereafter reading Edmund Spenser's *Epithalamion* – written in 1594 to his bride Elizabeth Boyle on their wedding day (I married in 1961). Robert Graves (son of a renowned Irish poet) was the Professor of Poetry (in 1966 to be succeeded by Old Blue Edmund Blunden) when I arrived at Oxford in 1961. Subsequently, I was much influenced by Graves' book *White Goddess*, about the origins of poetry. In Ireland, I was especially moved by the poetry of William Butler Yeats (Nobel 1923) and Seamus Heaney (Nobel 1995), including Yeats' sublime 'Lake Isle of Innisfree'.

At Trinity College Dublin (founded by Edmund Spenser's 'Faerie Queene', Elizabeth I, half-sister of the boy-king, in 1592), I served as Professor of Engineering between 1982 and 1992. There, I customarily began my undergraduate lectures on 'Structural Integrity and Electron Microscopy of Materials' with William Blake's 'To see the world in a grain of sand' and with T S Eliot's 'We shall not cease from exploration'.

The values of Christ's Hospital have meant that the school is especially concerned with the diversity of human dignity and with promoting equality, as perhaps evidenced by the service of 20th century Old Blue government ministers/ peers and MPs (Baron Michael Stewart, Baron David Simon, Baroness Ruth Deech, Bryan Magee MP, Stuart Holland MP); this service is reflected in the values and insights of *Christ's Hospital: Tradition with Vision.* CH in the 20th century was forever changed by the move of the boys' school from London to Sussex – highlighted at the quatercentenary. And CH in the 21st century is forever transformed by the merger of the girls' and boys' schools in the late 20th century. Now, of course, there are the effects of the global financial crisis in the early years of the 21st century as CH looks to the great quincentenary in 2052.

I am old now and have, more than most, sailed to all corners of the world, meeting many other wandering Old Blues on my travels. Accordingly, 'The Song of Wandering Aengus' by W B Yeats now seems especially apt:

The Song of Wandering Aengus

I went out to the hazel wood,
Because a fire was in my head,
And cut and peeled a hazel wand,
And hooked a berry to a thread;
And when white moths were on the wing,
And moth-like stars were flickering out,
I dropped the berry in a stream
And caught a little silver trout.

When I had laid it on the floor
I went to blow the fire aflame,
But something rustled on the floor,
And someone called me by my name:
It had become a glimmering girl
With apple blossom in her hair
Who called me by my name and ran
And faded through the brightening air.

Though I am old with wandering
Through hollow lands and hilly lands,
I will find out where she has gone,
And kiss her lips and take her hands;
And walk among long dappled grass,
And pluck till time and times are done,
The silver apples of the moon,
The golden apples of the sun.

(William Butler Yeats, *The Wind among the Reeds,* 1899. 4th ed. (London, 1903), 15–16.)

Somehow, all these seemingly unconnected strands of life led me most fortuitously in September 2018 to invite Old Blue poet Lizzie Ballagher to write the poetry for this book – building on the tradition of Coleridge, Lamb, Douglas, Blunden, and other Old Blue poets. Lizzie's poetic work represents the deep heart's core of this book. Then, in October 2018, in Vancouver, I also met a young, world-wandering Old Blue, Desi Elizabeth, a healthcare professional, whom I asked to be project co-ordinator for this venture. Desi provided an essential, diverse, 21st century perspective for this project with her professional orientation to public health and diversity.

Thus, the present book has evolved from a curious mixture of happenstance and happy meetings. Our hope is that this book, principally of poetry and science-themed essays by Old Blues, will further the ancient charitable mission and ethos of Christ's Hospital to educate and inspire poor and disadvantaged children, and contribute to the general and governmental development of state/independent secondary education in the UK, and even internationally.

David Taplin, Summer 2019, Vancouver, BC
(*Extracts from the poetry of W B Yeats are used here and in following pages by kind permission of The Estate of W B Yeats, and United Agents/A P Watts.*)

Introduction

This book celebrates the traditional charitable mission, ethos and ideals of Christ's Hospital since its foundation by King Edward VI in 1552. As a themed collection of essays by Old Blues, *Christ's Hospital: Tradition with Vision* embodies a vision to *inspire* the furthering of these ideals in the context of the practicalities of the 21st century – to the quincentenary in 2052 and beyond. It is hoped that this book will become the first in a series of books quadrennially through to 2052, asking 'quincentenary questions' of the highly committed global CH community. With all this in mind, Yeats' poem 'The Lake Isle of Innisfree' seems apt, contrasting the earthly realm of ordinary life with the mystical world of dreams and ideals: the need to handle the practical things of life with the compulsion to follow one's ideals and dreams.

The Lake Isle of Innisfree

I will arise and go now, and go to Innisfree
And a small cabin build there, of clay and wattles made;
Nine bean-rows will I have there, a hive for the honey-bee,
And live alone in the bee-loud glade.

And I shall have some peace there, for peace comes
    dropping slow,
Dropping from the veils of the morning to where the cricket
    sings;
There midnight's all a glimmer, and noon a purple glow,
And evening full of the linnet's wings.

I will arise and go now, for always night and day
I hear lake water lapping with low sounds by the shore;
While I stand on the roadway, or on the pavements grey,
I hear it in the deep heart's core.

(William Butler Yeats)

Innisfree is to be found in County Sligo – described here as a place of tranquility and peace where the poet feels grounded. Christ's Hospital was designed by the founder in 1552 as a safe haven for 'grounding' disadvantaged girls and boys. Known as 'Housey', the school has succeeded in this great mission for nearly five centuries. Today, however, the foundation is facing unprecedented new challenges.

What brought me to Christ's Hospital?

In September 1950, at eleven years of age, I took the train from the gritty, coal, steel, and railways town of Chesterfield (home of railway entrepreneur and visionary mechanical engineer George Stephenson) to St Pancras Station in London; thence to Victoria Station, and onwards to Horsham in the rural weald of faraway Sussex. Here, I donned the long Tudor blue coat and yellow stockings of Christ's Hospital, becoming thereby the smallest 'Blue' in my Lamb B boarding house of 52 Blues, with a giant of a house captain, Nigel Nathan.

In 1950, when I entered CH, Clement Attlee, a former social worker, was the reforming UK Prime Minister. Attlee's Labour government (1945–1951) had begun to radically transform society in Britain from its unequal, racist, sexist, imperialist, class-ridden, and environmentally neglectful past. In post-war Britain, social services were improved and the exceptional National Health Service was created. Major industries were nationalised, notably the railways, coal, and steel. Attlee presided over the decolonialisation of India, and the creation of

Pakistan; Myanmar, Sri Lanka, and Jordan were decolonised; and Israel came into being. By 1950, a new social order was coming into place in Britain, albeit austerely, with food and general rationing persisting after the ravages of WW2. Under the premiership of Winston Churchill, decolonialisation was halted after 1951, and Anthony Eden was responsible for the embarrassing debacle of Suez in 1956. By 1957, further decolonialisations were again in progress; in that year, the Gold Coast became the independent Ghana. Prime Minister Harold Macmillan gave his great 'Winds of Change' speech in South Africa in 1960, heralding the final break-up of the British Empire – a process that had been foreshadowed in 1776 with the independence of the North American colonies under the leadership of Frederick North. This process was completed in 1997 when, under Prime Minister Tony Blair, Hong Kong passed into the control of China.

Attlee had worked before WWII as manager of Haileybury House – a charity in East London for poor, working-class boys – and after his experience of the poverty and deprivation, judged that private charity would never be sufficient to alleviate poverty and that only direct action by the State, with income redistribution, would have sufficient effect. Childhood deprivation was still very evident in East London in 1950, four centuries after the founding of Christ's Hospital; Old Blue Bryan Magee, one-time Labour MP and well-known BBC broadcaster on social reform and philosophy, wrote movingly about this ongoing deprivation in East London in the mid-20th century in his autobiography *Growing up in a War*. Significantly, Attlee was educated at Haileybury College – an independent school (with origins in 1806 as the College of the fabulously wealthy East India Company), which in 1858 became a public school in the wake of the 1857–8 First War of Indian Independence and the establishment of the British Raj, which indeed ended at the stroke of the midnight hour on August 15th, 1947, through the leadership of Mahatma Gandhi, Jawaharlal Nehru, and Clement Attlee.

Christ's Hospital in 1950 was an endowed, independent charity school, founded by Edward VI in 1552 for poor and disadvantaged children in the former Greyfriars' monastery in the shadow of St Paul's Cathedral. Christ's Hospital was, however, effectively in the category of privileged, independent schools in England. Schooling for those of us at Horsham was indeed privileged, set within a monastic-style, residential institution isolated in about a thousand acres of countryside, with magnificent buildings and facilities set around a great cloistered quadrangle, with pupils in Tudor clerical dress. What is revealed, as the decades pass thereafter, is the enduring impact felt by Old Blues almost universally of Christ's Hospital, and of the dedication of alumni in giving their time, talent, and support to the furtherance of the ancient ethos and charitable mission.

As Blues, we were taught, often by exceptional scholars, to be curious, radical, to think independently, sensitively, socratically, and with an evidence base; we acquired self-control, a robust social resilience; we learned science, mathematics, philosophy; and were inducted into and inspired by the great intellectual contributions of visionary, inspirational Old Blues. There were debates, plays, a music school, a great chapel choir, a famous band, an art school, an engineering school, the Dominions Library, the Royal Mathematical School, very extensive science laboratories, a cinder athletic track, a school farm, an infirmary with a resident medical doctor and nurses, a compulsory cadet force, swimming pools, fives courts, many sports fields (especially rugby and cricket, but not yet quidditch!), and opportunities to play against other great schools in a world of apparent elitism and great privilege. Yet all of us were from disadvantaged homes with a parental maximum income bar. In 1950, this represented extraordinary social engineering.

Today the situation is very different. Out of approximately 900 students at Christ's Hospital in 2019, some 75% receive means-tested bursaries, with approximately 90% of the school's main intake (Year 7) coming from state primary schools. The selection of students continues strongly to prioritise children with social and economic disadvantage. Accordingly, CH is the mirror of mainstream independent schools who may seek a modest proportion of high-attaining disadvantaged children, with the priority being academic strength. There are currently 24% full-fee payers (FFP), a percentage that will fall to 22% by 2021/22. Of the school's population, 13% pay zero fees. CH is focused on challenging social and economic disadvantage, and the full-fee payers choose Christ's Hospital specifically for its diversity and social engineering. As economic and social inequality continue to grow in the UK, the role of education as a catalyst for change has become ever more critical. Christ's Hospital has pioneered social mobility in education for nearly 500 years, with a proven model for transforming and inspiring the lives of disadvantaged children. By providing first-class, free or supported education to talented young people from disadvantaged backgrounds, Christ's Hospital helps them to reach their full potential and inspire and transform lives in a way that no other educational establishment in the UK can match. Until the first years of the 21st century, the FFP was essentially kept at <3%. Accordingly, a crucial question arises for Old Blues as stakeholders: 'What level of FFP admissions would be at variance with the ancient charitable ethos and Royal Charter?'

Fortuitously, I had won a Derbyshire County Council scholarship via good performance in the now-discredited and divisive 11+ examination, the sponsorship of Dorothy Tempest, headmistress of my state primary school, Highfield Hall in Chesterfield, and through a successful interview in Derby with Dr Jack Longland, of BBC Radio *Brain's Trust* fame, County Director of Education, to either Repton School in Derbyshire (where the inspirational Harold Abrahams of Olympic Gold Medal *Chariots of Fire* fame had been a pupil - established in 1557 in a former Augustinian Priory) or

Christ's Hospital in faraway Sussex (where the inspirational, Derbyshire-born Barnes Wallis of *Dambusters* fame had been a pupil) – founded in 1552 in a former Greyfriars' monastery.

Following further successful written examinations in the Christ's Hospital Counting House in Great Tower Street, London, and an interview with the patrician Henry Lael Oswald Flecker, headmaster of Christ's Hospital, CH was selected for me over Repton. A London cousin was already at CH on an LCC scholarship, and the 'Bluecoat' school was revered as a uniquely admirable institution – unlike any other school. To my Chesterfield relatives and boyhood friends, this even topped the prize of going to the also ancient Chesterfield Grammar School, founded in 1598.

In July 1957, now a house monitor among the science Grecians at eighteen years of age, after a science/engineering-oriented schooling, I took off my blue coat and yellow stockings and became forever an Old Blue – part of a global network of great fellowship. One of the greatest benefits of becoming a Blue is then becoming an Old Blue, with an imprinted sense of the charitable social ethos, never forgetting the Christ's Hospital Charge in the chapel after the solemn presentation of the Almoners' leaving Bible:

I charge you never to forget the great benefits that you have received in this place, and in time to come, according to your means, to do all that you can to enable others to enjoy the same advantage. And remember that you carry with you, wherever you go, the good name of Christ's Hospital.

I left CH in 1957 with good A-levels in chemistry, physics, and mathematics, and a place at King's College, London, to study for a BSc in Chemistry.

What next?

Instead of taking up the King's College offer, however, I elected on the thoughtful advice of the renowned CH Director of Science, Dr Gordon Van Praagh, to become an industrial metallurgy apprentice with ICI in Birmingham and to study for the new-fangled DipTech engineering diploma which was designed to rival the famous German DiplIng. Barnes Wallis had also followed the engineering apprenticeship route on leaving CH; and like Barnes Wallis in 1904, I had won the Willcox Engineering Prize in 1955 (now re-endowed from 2015 by BCOB as the Willcox-Wallis Engineering Prize). An interesting aside from the obituary in *The Times* of Wallis's daughter Mary Stopes-Roe (May 31, 2019) might be noted here: the fact that Barnes Wallis always insisted on being known as an engineer – only secondarily as a scientist – decrying the general failure of the English to properly respect and invest in the standing and education of engineers.

This decision was influenced by my thereby becoming a hands-on, self-supporting, salaried employee of ICI at the gritty coal-face of heavy industry in Birmingham, the machine-shop of the world, with wide-ranging worker benefits (including an innovative bonus of worker ICI shares each year). The DipTech undertaken with an iconic industrial company which had diversified from armaments, zip-fasteners, copper and aluminium alloys to focus on new metals (magnesium, titanium, zirconium, beryllium) proved a good decision for me. ICI (Metals Division), in integrated association with Birmingham College of Advanced Technology (the first 'CAT' established in 1956, later to become Aston University in 1966), provided excellent training on the shop floor and innovative teaching by industrial practitioners. These pioneering DipTech students, who mostly went on to work at the coal-face of industrial practice as senior managers, formed a lively camaraderie. And sixty years on, we still meet annually through the 'Old Cobras' (Colleges of Birmingham Rugby Association) at the Shakespeare Hotel for a Six Nations rugby weekend in Stratford-upon-Avon, while also enjoying the Bard's plays and poetry.

The great experiment of the fully sponsored, industry-based DipTech of the then ten innovative and ambitious Colleges of Advanced Technology with leading UK industries sadly disappeared into a university-based BSc, and a great opportunity was lost for world-leading technological education. However, for myself and other DipTech pioneering students, this was an exhilarating training within the 'white heat of industry'. Harold Wilson in 1963, in one of the most perceptive political speeches of the 20th century, reflected on the pace of technological change and its implications for industry, and in the closing moments Wilson uttered the lines for which it is remembered. Wilson warned his audience that if the country were to prosper, a 'new Britain' would need to be forged in the 'white heat' of this 'scientific revolution'.

Fifty and more years on from Wilson's great speech, is Britain still lagging the world in universal technological and entrepreneurial education in primary and secondary schools, and in universities – behind China, Germany, and especially Singapore – and thereby in having political leaders who lack the necessary evidence-based understanding of science in the burgeoning fourth technological revolution? Canada has an astronaut-computer scientist as Governor-General; Germany has a Chancellor with a PhD in quantum chemistry – both women. China is led by a chemical engineer. Singapore is led by a computer scientist who was the 'Senior Wrangler', i.e., the top mathematics undergraduate at Cambridge University. Is the gaping lack of professional scientists, engineers, and mathematicians in government leadership in Britain the fault of the general lack of a paramount priority of UK schools to cutting-edge, technological education – due in part, perhaps, to English snobbery and an untoward focus on the history of Britain's imperial, colonial, class-ridden past, even today?

Having been nurtured on the heuristic teaching of science by discovery at Christ's Hospital, I became oriented myself at ICI to metallurgical research rather than industrial practice.

This was initially through a UKAEA/ICI-supported DipTech dissertation on fracture micro-mechanisms in nuclear fuel magnesium canning alloys, work in a titanium factory in Waunarlwydd, and in a space-age beryllium factory in Birmingham. 'Green' nuclear (uranium) electrical energy and new materials/composites were all the rage – designed to replace fossil-fuel energy and old-fangled steel in a new 'atomic' age.

In 1961, I went on to Oxford University to study for a doctorate on the structural integrity of materials, especially on radioactive uranium alloy nuclear fuel rods, with Dr John Martin, funded by UKAEA. Two other Old Blues were remarkably also researching the structural integrity of materials in this small department: Keith Bowen and John Daniel. Life at Oxford was in many ways privileged and seamless with life at Christ's Hospital – tutorials, debating, rowing, rugby, sailing, squash – in the brand-new science-oriented St Catherine's College, headed by Alan Bullock FBA, and the brand-new Department of Metallurgy, headed by the legendary William Hume-Rothery FRS, within this medieval university.

In 1964, at 24 years of age, I obtained my DPhil degree and was appointed Lecturer in Physical Metallurgy at Melbourne University in Australia. I was welcomed there by Robin Paul, managing director of Shell, Australia – an Old Blue and President of the Victorian Society of Blues. I enjoyed my four years in Australia, but moved on in 1968 (after a transforming sabbatical at Banaras Hindu University, India, working on high temperature fracture of new Indian steels and studying Sanskrit) to the wildly ambitious University of Waterloo in Canada, becoming Professor of Physics & Materials Engineering there in 1973.

Remarkably, at Waterloo three other Old Blues were also professors: Michael Craton, distinguished for his poignant books on slavery in the West Indies; and another Oxford metallurgist, former Senior Grecian (and at CH an early

Engineering Grecian and a WW2 hero [DFC] as an RAF pilot), William Pearson; as well as my own teacher of history in my year on Science Grecians, Michael Cherniavsky, albeit an honorary Old Blue. In 1981, I was elected President of the International Congress on Fracture, and in 1982 moved to Trinity College, Dublin, to be part of the 'Celtic Tiger' revival in Ireland, for a very happy and fulfilling decade.

Jumping now to 2013, after an interesting and enjoyable career as a Professor of Structural Integrity at universities in Australia, India, Canada, USA, Ireland, Cuba, Singapore, and England, and as President/CEO/Treasurer 1981–2017 of the International Congress on Fracture, I retired to Vancouver, Canada. I was particularly welcomed here by the past president of BCOB, John Stanger (CH 1939–1945); by donation governor Terry Bate (CH 1944–1951); by the BCOB Secretary, Chris Johnson (CH 1952–1959); and by Graham Riches (CH 1952–1960). During 2013–2014, I worked with Graham on the educational legacy of Barnes Wallis, and during 2014–2016 on Petition 1552. With over one thousand Old Blue signatories, this petition called for a reduction in the proportion of full fee paying Blues (FFP) from 25% to under 10% in keeping with the 1552 mission of Housey. Together, these projects were forerunners to *Christ's Hospital: Tradition with Vision,* which evolved into its present form through collaboration with the poet and editor Lizzie Ballagher (CH 1961–1967). We hope that CHTWV2020 will endure in the archives of Christ's Hospital alongside Trollope 1834, CH1953 and CH2000 in furthering the 1552 ethos towards the great quincentenary in 2052.

David Taplin, Summer 2019, Vancouver, BC

I

Success and Diversity

'Let not ambition mock their useful toil,
Their homely joys, and destiny obscure;
Nor grandeur hear with a disdainful smile
The short and simple annals of the poor...

Full many a flower is born to blush unseen,
And waste its sweetness on the desert air.'

'Elegy Written in a Country Churchyard', Thomas Gray (1751)

'The accomplishment of an aim or purpose... the attainment of popularity or profit' – What defines success? Who defines it? Are we only successful after recognition by others?

Born from humble beginnings in the 16th century as a final legacy and manifestation of King Edward VI's vision, Christ's Hospital school has, from the very outset, sought to provide education for the most disadvantaged children. Inspired by a sermon from Nicholas Ridley, Bishop of London at the time, King Edward VI was moved to reduce the increasing number of destitute children on the streets of London following Henry VIII's dissolution of monasteries in England, Ireland, and Wales between 1536 and 1541.

The first group of 380 girls and boys stepped into Christ's Hospital in Newgate in 1552, a year before Edward VI granted and signed the Royal Charter. The school was granted a second Royal Charter in 1673 by Charles II, primarily for the creation of the Royal Mathematical School, which would go on to train and educate mathematicians such as Ida Busbridge (1908–1988 – the first woman to be appointed to an Oxford fellowship in mathematics) and Sir Alfred George Greenhill FRS (1847–1927 – the mind behind the Greenhill Formula), as well as navigators who became senior naval officers, such as Rear-Admiral Sir Bertram Cowles Allen (1875–1957) and Vice-Admiral Sir Thomas Bertie (1758–1825 – close friend of Nelson). A successful feat by the school, indeed.

But by what criteria should we measure the success of Christ's Hospital and those who have passed through the school? Exploring questions such as this can enable the school to continue to be aligned with its traditionally charitable mission, and to foster an environment for pupils that supports their development into motivated and well-adjusted adults, preparing them for life in our ever-shifting world.

Particularly for those who were financially disadvantaged growing up, success might perhaps be determined by the sums of money one makes, how prestigious the job, or how much recognition a career brings. Despite many Old Blues going on to become very affluent, however, wealth was not often a topic or theme during my time at Christ's Hospital. Instead, the culture and environment encouraged pupils to be confident, determined, independent, and self-aware; in addition, it fostered inner mental and spiritual strength. Pupils were encouraged to find strength in collaboration, in working together.

This theme of collaboration was reinforced through activities such as inter-house sports, singing competitions, and daily marching into the dining hall for lunch. Essentially, what students at Christ's Hospital learn towards the end of their time at the school is the value of community and how we only really succeed when our actions benefit others; when those around us are flourishing. Success need not be measured to scale, but can be born from small acts and gestures. Christ's Hospital is an excellent and enduring example of how true success is defined by our service to others.

In recent years, Christ's Hospital has extended its welcome, not only to those from disadvantaged backgrounds, but also to all who wish to experience an education of breadth, rich variety, and excellence. And individuals from across the globe have been drawn to the school as a result. This recent shift is a testament to how Christ's Hospital has been able to flourish for over 450 years, adapting constantly to the surrounding political and socio-economic environment, surviving the Great Fire of London in 1666; its relocations to Horsham in 1902 and from Hertford in 1985; and, more significantly, World Wars I and II, to which the school lost some 600 Old Blues. In terms of withstanding time, Christ's Hospital has proved to be especially successful and resilient. The ability of the school to successfully adapt to its surroundings is possible, in part, through its foresight and continuous engagement with the wider community. These factors have allowed the school accurately to determine social conditions and to take appropriate action to preserve the continuation of the school. This remit has extended to looking into the future to determine what role the school can play on a national and international platform.

Christ's Hospital has had a profound effect on the lives of many Old Blues through the years, nurturing children from a variety of backgrounds and supporting their successes along the way. Here, then, are just two stories – from two Old Blues who write from utterly different perspectives and different times, even though both of them have, in many of the same ways, experienced what Christ's Hospital has to offer.

Bruce

"Most of our people have never had it so good"
– Macmillan, Bedford (1957)

I was 15 when those famous words were spoken, and felt they applied to me, the free-ranging country boy from a dysfunctional home with no running water, no indoor sanitation, or electricity. My impoverished childhood memories of Christmas morning are of a stocking at the foot of the bed filled with small insignificant presents, but with the thrill of an orange at the bottom. This puts the excesses and waste of food today in sharp perspective. I was torn apart by warring parents both vying for, and giving great affection to, my sister and me. Our mother visited me from Exmoor once every term; our father, although he wrote to me every week of every term, never once came to CH in my nine years.

I was subsumed into CH after an unsettling start in Prep B, 200+ miles from home, and with a strange new life to embrace; I made it through into Lamb A, in the Upper School. A L Johnstone, our housemaster, really cared for his charges, even though it was by a regime that matched his red hair and moustache. He did his best to rid the house of bullying and instilled a good spirit which extended greatly to sport. This inspired me to give of my best in all games, together with the chapel and Big School choirs, the manual school, art school, and Corps. Through 'Johnny's' influence, which came down through the house captain and monitors, manners and respect were instilled into us. He was a great believer in discipline, which in turn gave me self-discipline that led to self-reliance, for which I have been forever grateful. His great emphasis on team and house spirit gave one an awareness of others and their needs.

CH inducted me into being socially mobile and able to mix with all manner of people in life, from tradesmen to peers of the realm. During the school holidays, I had the good fortune to be invited and included in the events and parties of those who were at other public schools. Although I always felt equal to them, I was constantly aware of the large gulf between us financially; however, several remain good friends to this day.

I was always still in touch with the countryside and the soil, whether through looking after the Lamb A House garden, going for long walks outside the ring fence, making a collection of wild flowers, or having an aquarium in Kirby's lab to fill with pond life garnered from the surrounding farm land. Here, amongst that very individual man's possessions, I felt quite at home, made some cowslip wine, and was referred to as 'Fat Friend of Flap Eagle'. No-one knew it, but the fat was myxoedema caused by a yet to be diagnosed pituitary tumour. This was surgically removed when I was 23, having been 10 years growing. After removal, there was still another decade of health ramifications, affecting everything, including my ability to study; hence my failing the National Diploma of Agriculture in 1964.

Another conduit to the soil was 'Pip' Newberry, an earthy man who took us out on geography field trips, making us feel the differences of the soils, from Gault Clay to Lower or Upper Greensand and chalk. He certainly made geography come to life. In my last year, I was haunted as to what my career path should be, until I had my lightbulb moment in the grandiose-sounding careers room – in reality, a dull and uninspiring room lined with shelves on which were booklets and prospectuses by the score. The moment I opened books on agriculture, I was transfixed, but, alas, I needed to have O-level chemistry and biology to qualify to enter any college. To give the teachers great credit, I was allowed to abandon S Level (scholarship level) geography and history, and studied hard at the back of the respective O-level classes.

I was given evening tuition by Mr Potts, and my friend David Humphreys from Barnes A set me tests, as he had already passed his A-levels. I was able to enjoy two terms with the great Van Praagh, and to experience the heuristic method of teaching for the first time, down to bringing some iron ore from near home to work out the iron content. I passed my two O-levels with good percentage points – about 80% (there were no grades back then).

After leaving CH and upon receiving the results, I set about getting into Seale-Hayne Agricultural College, and was successful. I then had to find a farm on which to work for 12 months, gaining practical experience. This is where an Old Blue in the then CH Agric Club came to help and found a farm in West Sussex where I could be a live-in working pupil. He was Phillip Mathews from Midhurst, who worked for ICI at Fernhurst. At this stage in life, I was totally unaware of the great OB farming achievers who might have inspired me, such as Rex Paterson, OBE; Adrian Scripps, Mid A 47–55; Graham Mellstrom, Mid A 41–48; or my old friend who started out in Prep B with me, Chris Lewis, MaB 52–58.

I have never had a burning ambition to make money. Having had the decade of the pituitary tumour growing and many years following its removal to find my feet, my life was about physical and financial survival. Within two years of the operation, I was floored by *salmonella typhimurium,* with a temperature nearing 105 degrees F – in effect typhoid fever (my immune system was highly compromised by lack of cortisone). It took me six months to recover.

Eventually my genes, coupled with the good fortune of marrying the daughter of a man who owned a 5,000 acre estate, ensured that my farming ambitions were at last to be realised. I married a fellow agrarian with a BSc (Hons) from Reading, who maintains that it was my having been to CH that made her find me eligible; it might well have not been the case if I had been to the local secondary modern. We started out farming on a small livestock farm in North Devon in 1971, and then moved to a bigger farm on the estate in 1974. My philosophy could well be summed up by the folk poem found on old jugs and mugs dating from 1700s:

In God Is Our Trust: The Farmer's Arms

Let the Wealthy and Great
Roll in splendour and state!
I envy them not, I declare it.
I have lawns, I have Bow'rs.

I have Fruit I've Flowrs.
The Lark is my Morning Alarmer.
So jolly Boys now
Here's God speed the Plough—
Long Life and Success to the FARMER!

This poem does not mention the headaches that go with farming, the vagaries of the seasons, physically demanding work, increasing costs and decreasing prices, tussles with banks – all coupled with layers of unnecessary bureaucracy. To counter this, the simple basic pleasure of eating a completely home-produced meal of fresh lamb, new potatoes and peas or beans from the garden, is beyond measure.

To survive and perhaps be successful as a farming food producer meant being open-minded, inquisitive, and keeping abreast of developments, not to be fainthearted but keen to try new ideas and approaches to husbandry. (Shades of Dr Van Praagh?) In 1975, the government produced the White Paper 'Food from our own resources'. This chimed with our aspirations to do well, if not better than before. We became disciples of Professor Rene Laloux of Gembloux in Belgium; we grew the magic three tons per acre of winter wheat using his revolutionary methods, whereas the norm was two tons per acre. Forty years on, most farmers now hope for four tons per acre; such is progress. With our pig farming of 120 sows, with all progeny to bacon weight and fed on home-grown grain, we tried hard to, and did, achieve very good performance figures.

Looking back, I see that CH in the 1950s was a tough environment which taught me how to overcome problems and hardships in order to survive and flourish. When faced with adversity, I have been fortunate to call on inner resilience. All this has put me in good stead for farming, with its problems and setbacks, so that I could always rise above them to appreciate the good things – the natural world, the art and beauty in nature, and the fellowship of the rural community.

When the chips were down with rain coming, I was not afraid to spend 18 hours non-stop on the tractor, drilling oil seed rape, then crawl into bed a happy man.

In 1996, we decided to leave our son behind on the farm in East Yorkshire, and moved 'home' to a 140-acre farm near Dulverton on the edge of Exmoor to farm sheep. When I eventually relinquished the physical work, others locally must have seen me as having the potential to become a district councillor and cajoled me – a small 'c' conservative with pinkish tendencies – to contest the local elections in 2011 for the Dulverton Ward of West Somerset Council. I feel sure that being a local farmer helped my election prospects. Stepping into a big organisation was almost akin to going back to school: much learning; people to meet; meetings; decisions and judgments to make. Our first leader had been headmaster of Bromsgrove School and knew of Lionel Carey, a previous head. I was able to tell him that I remembered Carey as housemaster of MaB. Fortunately, I found it relatively easy after the initial bedding-in period, ending up chairman for my final three years. It is said that once a farmer, always a farmer; even if today we annually sell off our grass-keep to other local farmers, I can still get satisfaction when their sheep look well and they make good hay.

Although it is 59 years since the leaving service, I remember the powerful words of St Paul to the Philippians (Chapter 4: 4–8), and I have not forgotten the great benefits that I received at CH, for they have given my life a stable thread and sense of purpose.

How can one ever forget that you carry with you the good name of Christ's Hospital?

On my way to CH in the Summer of 2001, I had the sudden urge to visit Itchingfield churchyard. As I walked around, I was overwhelmed with emotion at seeing the names of teachers whom I remembered so clearly, and on returning to my car, I wrote:

Itchingfield

Walking slowly in the warming sun
Along mown paths, peering
At names behind the oxeye daises,
On gravestones.
Already time and nature
Have done their work:
Lichens, mosses and stains,
Yet the faces come flooding back
To fill the names –
Headmaster, housemaster, maths and music –
And O how fresh the voices
Booming in classroom, corridor,
Dayroom or chapel
As if it were yesterday.
Now all is changed. Time moved on.
No more familiar faces, old friends.
We have become
Just older men scattered to the winds,
Whilst our character-formers lie
Altogether unchanged
Amongst the oxeye daises and long grass,
Still to yield their influence
From the hallowed ground
Of Itchingfield churchyard.

Bruce Heywood, Dulverton, West Somerset, May 2019

Amy

When I tell new friends of the life I led prior to joining CH, aged 15, I'm met with disbelieving, puzzled expressions. It's hard for those who know me now – a professional, well-spoken woman with two degrees and a stable relationship – to marry up this Amy with the girl who arrived at her new boarding house in 2005, in the middle of a cold November week, mid-term, terrified, and exhausted.

Socially, I quickly felt at home. Something infrequently talked about was the pattern of experiences that many of my fellow Blues and I shared. Our worlds were shaped by single-parent households, absent dads, breadline living, and growing up in under-resourced communities where toughness was capital. Britain's supposed 'meritocracy' didn't seem to have space for us, for our experiences or our values.

Like many Blues, I've always been an odd blend of cultural influences. I was brought up in a rough, multicultural corner of London, enjoying Ghanaian cooking and Bangladeshi family life at friends' houses, and a bohemian, arty, cash-strapped life at home with my half-German, half-Cockney actor mother and working-class Mancunian poet father. My father struggled with mental health problems through most of my life, and Mum and I finally moved away when I was nine.

Mum worked hard to cope financially as a single parent, and I found increasingly inappropriate ways to abuse the freedoms I was afforded by her busy life. Lacking the nuclear family, generous pocket money and nice house required to be allowed into 'It' crowds, I spent my early teens searching for acceptance, attention, and love in the wrong places: bad, older boys; risky behaviour; and alcohol. With undiagnosed dyslexia and teachers failing to manage the chaos of needy and overcrowded classes, missing school or acting out became easier than trying. I fell massively behind at school. The only thing that truly engaged me, and in many ways gave me hope for my future, was music.

The big turning point in my life arrived when I was aged 15. I was coming home late after choir when I witnessed a friend of mine being brutally attacked by a group of teenagers I knew. The 'stand up against injustices' mentality, instilled in me by my parents, kicked in and took over my fear. I turned around, went back to school, and gave a statement to the police. A few weeks later, my name was accidentally released by a teacher; I ended up under police protection, stuck in my house for months. My mum had just left an abusive relationship, and the two of us rattled round the house, shell-shocked, sad, de-energised by life, and with no clue of what direction to take next.

One thing that brought a weekly hour of respite in that time, some humour and escapism, was watching *Rock School*. Gene Simmons took a bunch of kids – exactly my age, in long navy coats and yellow socks, who marched into lunch – and turned them into a rock band. I loved how innocent their lives seemed compared to my school life; how happy and confident, and how easy life looked in those glorious cloisters. At the end of one episode, we looked up CH online and were surprised to find that it was a school for people like me. We called them the next day.

Having been told there was no space, that expulsions were rare, and that we needed to come up with a Plan B, we got a call a fortnight later asking if I could come to the school for an interview. As Dad and I arrived into the quad for the first time, we both burst into tears, confronted by the gravity and privilege of the opportunity to live here! I was set an exam and couldn't answer any of the questions… but I did manage to write a song. A week later, I was told to pack a suitcase. I was going to be a Blue. On my first night at the school, I sat in my common room in Housey, and in a state of disbelief, watched the final episode of *Rock School*.

Joining CH was tough. I suddenly had rules to follow and schedules to adhere to. I rowed with my house mum on the first night, as she tried to turn my light out for bedtime before I was ready to sleep. I had siblings for the first time in my life, borrowing my clothes and emulating family relationships. By far the greatest struggle was academic. I didn't know how to learn: how to take notes; how to follow instructions; how to motivate myself; how to ask for help; how to be organised;

how to read complex sentences; how to multiply and divide; how to write an essay.

But I did know how to sing. And as I threw myself into music at CH, my confidence slowly grew, and the impossibly murky challenge in front of me started to morph into a bright, electric future. From day one, music school was where I felt belonging, where I knew how to succeed, where I felt motivated by the challenge rather than defeated, where I felt I had something of worth to contribute.

I joined everything: gospel choir, jazz singers, Scholar, chapel choir, big band, talent shows, musical theatre productions… the list goes on. The more I sang, the more I asked for and accepted help. The more full my week was with musical engagements, the more focused and organised I was in my homework hours. The more feedback I got on my music-making, the more my ambition exploded in all areas of school life. At the end of my first term, I went home for Christmas and announced that I – that kid who one month ago had seriously been losing her way – was going to get GCSEs. And nothing was going to stop me.

A particular musical highlight at CH was becoming choir captain, and being able to really encourage others to delight in the magnificence of sacred choral music in our beautiful chapel. The thing about music-making is that it is so much bigger than you. When you get your notes right, you are a vital, powerful, perfect spoke in a beautifully symmetrical wheel. When the choir or band reach peak performance, it's a unifying of minds, the sound erupting and changing the minds of listeners, making people feel things they might not have been expecting but that somehow alters their perspective forever. For both singer and listener, it's a potent tool of persuasion and healing, of reflection and memory, of empathy and relief.

At CH, I learned that singing is about breathing. Your control and aptitude come from your control of your breath. It's a whole-body experience that creates muscle memory, so that when you sing something ten years later, you not only remember the words and the melody, but somehow your body recalls how it felt to sing those notes, your diaphragm contracting as you remember, your shoulders loosening at those moments of release.

Over a decade later, I would train as a multi-systemic therapist, working with families about to lose their child into care or prison due to complex needs within the child, family, and community. Part of my training involved helping parents to de-escalate situations by learning how to first calm and steady themselves. I was delighted to find my trainer advising the exact same breathing exercises I learnt in singing lessons and chapel choir at CH, explaining how slowing and deepening one's breathing creates a physiological and chemical shift in the body, helping us feel safe, calm, focused, and in control. This was something I taught parents to great effect.

Singing certainly had that impact on me as a teen at CH, giving me the reassurance and focus I needed to turn GCSEs into AS levels, and A-levels into an Oxbridge interview, and finally, gain a place at Cambridge University – something my family and I have still not quite got our heads around.

Looking back, I owe an awful lot to music at CH beyond a lifelong love of singing and the ability to breathe deeply. It gave me the cultural capital I needed to navigate elites at university, yet it also gave me the swagger, playfulness, and resolve I've greatly relied on as a social worker and therapist working in Liverpool with those on the margins. It has helped me find my voice when I have felt intimidated, and allowed me to express my biggest emotions in a constructive way.

Music at CH was there when I most needed it. It gave me permission and encouragement to make something of my life, and for that I will always be so grateful.

Amy Lonton, July 2019
CH 2005–09 (Col A/ Thorn B/ Gre W)

So, is success always an outcome? Many people determine that success is achieved when a goal has already been completed. What about the journey itself? Few of us can deny the sense of relief after finishing an arduous project, or the pride and joy we might feel upon obtaining a promotion, or the acknowledgement of our achievements. But what about the little successes we achieved along the way? It's these small successes and pockets of learning on the journey to our main goals that I believe are the true success stories; after all, goals and visions are often achieved, manifested in steps as opposed to giant leaps. Ida Winifred Busbridge could not have been awarded an Oxford fellowship for mathematics without first overcoming the obstacle of quadratic equations while studying at Christ's Hospital's Royal School of Mathematics; or John Robert Arnold being appointed priest in the Anglican Church without first strengthening his religious beliefs in Christ's Hospital's chapel.

Parallels can be drawn with the Christ Hospital that we see today. The school exists now in a world that looks significantly different from the one in which it was created over 450 years ago; even so, it is thriving. Just as the Christ's Hospital we see today is a sum of all its small victories and successes over the years, we too are a sum of our own small successes. These successes are not limited to material or financial gain. In fact, some will argue that these accomplishments are by no means the most noteworthy. Rather, fostering relationships with others, developing ourselves spiritually and emotionally, and supporting our community and those in our lives – qualities that are nurtured particularly well at Christ's Hospital – are also worthy of recognition as successes. It is these qualities and types of success which endure and transcend time which also contribute to the success of others, just as Christ's Hospital has supported the small and large successes of up to 65,000 Old Blues since its foundation in 1552.

Desi Elizabeth, Vancouver, May 2019

II

Some Memories and Reflections

This chapter is made up of three parts. The first section is about life in Barnes A as the Second World War was coming to an end, and is a chapter from my autobiography, *From Hackney to Horsham, a Schoolmaster's Life*. The second section, which quotes a later chapter from the same book, concerns the Old Blue poet, Keith Douglas, who was killed in the war at the age of twenty. In the third and final section, which is extracted from another of my books, *Education and Politics: a History of Unintended Consequences and the Case for Change*, I say something about what has happened to arrangements for English secondary education during my lifetime.

In order to put these things in context, it may be helpful to provide the reader with a brief summary of my life, particularly as it relates to Christ's Hospital. My twin brother, John – who is another contributor to this volume – and I were born in Hackney in 1933, and were in Barnes A together from 1944 until 1952. My National Service, mostly in a Polish tank transporter unit in Germany, was followed by three years as a scholar of Pembroke College, Oxford, reading history. I then taught at Clifton College, and while there I married a girl whom I had met at St Catherine's, Bramley, at a Grecians' dance, when I was a History Grecian. For sixteen years, from 1967 until 1976, I was a head of a history department, first at a former London grammar school and then at Stowe; and from 1976 until 1983 was Headmaster of King George V School, Southport.

After my first wife died in 1982, I moved to be the principal of Collyer's, the sixth-form college in Horsham, and while there married the niece of David Roberts, who had taught me history while I was at school. So, in a way, I owe both of my wives partly to Christ's Hospital. I became a governor of CH in 1991, retired from Collyer's in 1999 at the age of 65, after forty-two years as a schoolteacher, and was then an almoner of CH from 2002 until 2007.

The CH I knew

Christ's Hospital was, above all, an academic institution, a 'Religious, Royal and Ancient Foundation', where godliness and good learning were promoted. Quite a large part of the day was spent in lessons, and unlike my elementary school, in which we had stayed in the same classroom all day, we went to different classrooms for different subjects. English and history might be taught by the same teacher in the same room, but German or French were on another floor; geography was in a separate building, and so were mathematics and science. The really distinctive thing about the Christ's Hospital curriculum for new boys was that we all had to learn Ancient Greek. In many grammar schools throughout the country, new boys learned Latin, but Christ's Hospital was one of very few schools (perhaps the only one) where all new boys learned at least the rudiments of Greek.

I felt a sense of privilege in doing so. I liked the mysterious letters: α, β, γ, δ and so on, down to φ, χ, ψ, ω. I discovered that the Greek language had grammar, with words ending differently, depending, for example, on whether they were the subject or the object of a sentence, or whether they were the first, second, or third person, singular or plural, of a verb, and whether they were in the present, future, imperfect, perfect or pluperfect tense. The complications fascinated me, even if I found it difficult to disentangle all the various endings.

After a couple of years, when I was asked what I wanted to do in the future, I answered 'History' and was told that in that case I had better start learning Latin. So, I started Latin at the age of 12, in a class in which a substantial number of the boys were going on to win classics' or modern languages' scholarships to Oxford or Cambridge. After only two years, and at the age of 14, I took School Certificate Latin and failed it. Many boys going through a standard preparatory school and public school course would have started it at the age of seven or eight and taken it at School Certificate another seven or eight years later at 15 or 16. I did not know that at the time, and just thought that I was not very good at it.

Another large part of the day was spent on organised games, and I soon found myself learning to play rugby football, and again feeling privileged to do so. That rugby football was superior to soccer was impressed on us, and I enjoyed the rough and tumble of it. Because I was quite large for my age and not particularly skillful, I found myself playing in the middle of the scrum, and because I continued to enjoy and play it enthusiastically, by the beginning of my fourth year in the school – in the Great Erasmus; the form in which we took School Certificate – I was playing as a second row forward in the school under-14 team. (You had to be under 14 on 1st September, and I was not 14 until 1st November.)

I was less enthusiastic about time spent in the house (whether in the dayroom, the junior changing room, or the junior dormitory), where the life of a new boy was spent in an atmosphere in which relatively harsh, official discipline was combined with a continuing unofficial threat of brutality. Anyone who believes that the point of a boarding school education is to harden up the young would have been well satisfied. My own view, which developed clearly and consciously at an early stage, was that it was important to avoid being hardened, and essential to have a fixed determination not to give future generations the treatment we had had.

The discipline, such as it was, was enforced by house monitors. Minor misdemeanours (being the last boy on parade or having uncombed hair) were punished with 'quick changes' – change into games clothes, report, change back into uniform, and report again. And anything seen as more serious, such as 'insolence', was punished with a 'mile' – the same as quick changes, but with a one-mile run before changing back into uniform. Failure to do the punishments quickly enough resulted in further punishments, and some boys spent a large part of their spare time working off punishments. There were no official beatings by boys, as happened in many boarding schools at that time and for many years afterwards, so the punishments were no more than an irritating intrusion into one's spare time – but I resented them, nonetheless.

Far more unpleasant was the casual bullying by those boys in the middle age range, around 13 or 14, who made up for their lack of academic or sporting distinction by brutalising new boys. For no better reason than that a little boy was in their way as he walked past, they would pull his head down by the hair and 'foch' him several times, hitting with cupped hand on the back of the neck, keeping him still and aiming to get a loud sound as the hand hit the neck. Up in the dormitory, when no house monitors were present, a little boy might be made to stand with loosely-tied pyjama trousers, while older and larger boys tried to hit them down using the girdle, or belt, worn around the uniform blue coat. There was no particular villain; no Flashman who stood out from the rest. There was just a continuing atmosphere of insecurity and anarchy.

Since I was a stroppy little boy with a confident view of right and wrong, who would not keep his mouth shut and accept this sort of thing meekly, I more than once found myself held upside down with my head in the lavatory bowl as the chain was pulled to clean my mouth out. I was, I suppose, treated no worse than most others, and I had the advantage of having the companionship of a twin brother and of another boy, Barry Lendon, who was in the same year as us. But it must have been unspeakable for a ten-year-old who was alone and without friends. The occasional boy who left early, judged to be 'unsuited to a boarding environment', had usually been the victim of extended and excessive treatment of this sort.

One example I came across was when we had a reunion in 2002, fifty years after I left the school. The boy in question had left after only two years in the school, in the summer of 1944 – just before I arrived – after being badly bullied. He went to another school, left, got a job, joined the Gloucestershire Regiment for his National Service, was posted to Korea, captured by the Chinese at the battle of the Imjin in April 1951, and then spent three years in captivity in China, with even worse treatment than he had known at school, before being released in 1954 in the exchange of prisoners which followed on from the ceasefire in 1953. Why he came back to a reunion in the early 21st century, I could scarcely understand – perhaps to demonstrate that he had survived.

(Note: *Writing the succeeding chapter, which is mainly about his housemaster Eric Littlefield, aka Pongo, David Arnold describes in his own book schoolmasters who had fought in the war returning to CH and requiring high standards. It ends, 'Barnes A had been brutal and anarchical during the war. Some fairly tough assertion of authority was needed to turn it into a society in which boys were expected to treat each other at least decently, and preferably with some understanding and kindness, so that all could be free to engage in purposeful activity.' To this might be added the fact that such brutal, perverse behaviour was not exclusive to Barnes A but was endemic during these days and indeed until the headship of Clarence Seaman—ed.)*

My own solution to the unpleasantness of life in the house was to join anything which provided an excuse for being out of the house: the School Band, the Scouts, the Christian Union, the Debating Society, the Chess Club, and the Boxing Club. In our first term, John and I went up to the Music School and asked if we could join the band. He was given a clarinet; I was given a French Horn. The bandmaster gave us basic instruction on how to get a noise out of each instrument, on the appropriate fingering for the various notes, and on the relative lengths of breve, semi-breve, minim, crochet, quaver, and semi-quaver. From then on, we went up to the Music School regularly at the end of morning school at 12.15, and we gradually picked up more about how to play our instruments. In our last year at school, John was the band captain and I was the leading, if not especially good, horn player.

We also joined the school Scout troop, the 1st Christ's Hospital, and found ourselves in the Kingfisher patrol, whose patrol leader was a boy called Derek Baker. He taught me to tie reef knots and clove hitches, how to splice two pieces of rope together, and how to build a structure with wood and rope using square lashings and diagonal lashings. I got used to pitching a tent and digging a trench round it to keep out the rain. I learnt how to light a fire and cook in the open, and above all I enjoyed the luxury, afforded only to members of the Scout troop, of occasionally going off with another boy at a weekend in the summer with a hike tent on top of a rucksack, with an axe and cooking utensils slung below, wearing Scout uniform and carrying a stave, and being able to walk through the Sussex countryside, sleep out, and eat only what one could carry and cook oneself.

When Derek became the troop leader, I took over as the patrol leader of the Kingfisher patrol. When he left school, I took over as the troop leader. Derek, who had been a history specialist, known at Christ's Hospital as a History Grecian, left to do his National Service in the Royal Corps of Signals, went up to Oxford with a scholarship to Oriel College, became a schoolmaster and then a lecturer at Edinburgh

University, and in 1975 returned to Christ's Hospital as headmaster.

Another organisation which I joined, and which influenced me, was the Christian Union. It was entirely unofficial and operated within the context of an avowedly Christian school, in which everyone went to chapel every morning ,and everyone attended house prayers in the evenings. It had the merit of being run by senior boys like Jim Lewis, who proclaimed the importance of living in accordance with Christian principles in a society which often seemed only to pay lip-service to those principles, and in which many boys neglected them or acted in a manner entirely contrary to them.

On the other hand, the speakers at the Christian Union were usually young men from some such organisation as the Inter-Varsity Fellowship, with cheerful, abbreviated, and monosyllabic Christian names (Bill, Dick, Tom, and so on) who seemed to me, as I grew older, excessively sure that it was important to have a personal Pauline conversion, that intercessory prayer would result in divine intervention, and that if you gave your life to Jesus and encouraged others to do the same, all sorts of benefits would accrue to you both in this world and the next. It was the style and excessive self-confidence which bothered me, but in their own way they unintentionally encouraged me to think critically.

The Debating Society, meanwhile, consciously encouraged critical and structured thought. Whereas in the Christian Union it seemed that there was a clear line one was expected to accept, and any dissent was viewed with sorrow and suspicion, in the Debating Society the whole object of debating was to construct arguments and challenge the opinions of others. Two senior boys who were particularly good at it were Bryan Magee and Richard Cavendish, both in the same house as me and both History Grecians. And I remember with pleasure hearing Bryan speaking on the motion that 'this house shares with Caesar his preference for fat men'.

My ambition from a fairly early age was to become a History Grecian like them, and I also sought to emulate them in the Debating Society. It was unrealistic to expect to get anywhere near speaking as well in public as Bryan Magee, who went on to be President of the Oxford Union, a presenter of programmes about philosophy on television, and Labour Member of Parliament for Leyton. But I made a practice of attending and speaking regularly, and before I left school was elected a member of the Debating Society committee. I learnt enough to be able to run debating societies when I became a schoolteacher.

The Chess Club was an organisation which took me into other houses, something which was usually discouraged, and I enjoyed it enough to go on playing when I no longer had any particular need to escape from my own house. I continued to play spasmodically through much of my life, and taught my sons, who both became good enough chess players to beat me. Many years later, my younger son and I would sometimes play our way through the moves of the famous match played in a box at the Paris Opera House in 1858 between the world champion, Paul Morphy, and two talented amateurs, the Duke of Brunswick and Count Isouard.

Finally, I made my way to the Boxing Club, in an era in which boxing was a perfectly acceptable school sport. Barry Lendon was particularly good at it. He was a naturally talented boxer, upright and with a swift left jab and powerful right hook. When engaged in competitive boxing, we fought against other boys in the same weight range as ourselves (8 stone 7lbs to 9 stone, for example), and I remember being glad in our second year in the school – the Little Erasmus year – that although Barry was about my height, he was too light for me to have to fight him. Without him as an opponent, I won my weight. But he was growing, so the following year I had to fight him… and was soundly beaten. Fortunately, he went on growing, and the year after that he was too heavy for me to fight, and I was able to win my weight again.

By then, I was regularly fighting in school matches, and whereas I won more matches than I lost within Christ's Hospital, in matches against other schools I lost more often than I won. What is more, as I got heavier, being hit on the side of the jaw hurt a lot more than it had a couple of years earlier. I was never knocked out, nor did I ever knock anyone else out, but three one-and-a-half minute rounds, which sounds trivial by comparison with what professional fighters do, could be exhausting.

When I was 15, boxing at 10 stone to 10 stone 7lbs, I lost in the final of the West Sussex schoolboys' boxing championship, and that was my last fight. Barry carried on, getting bigger and stronger and more experienced. And two years later, by which time he was house captain and playing in both the 1st XV and the 1st XI, he also won the national heavyweight Amateur Boxing Association championship.

The School Band, the Scout Troop, the Christian Union, the Debating Society, the Chess Club, and the Boxing Club, all had their various influences on me. So did the CCF, which we had to join when we reached the age of 13, and in which we learnt about the Lee Enfield rifle and the Bren gun. We also practised foot drill, which had been an important tactical device in the 18th century and had somehow survived as part of basic military training a century-and-a-half later. We went on to learn more and more: setting a compass for a night march, and how to give orders for a platoon attack, for example. I was gradually promoted, and by my last year was one of the two senior boys in the CCF, Sergeant-Major in A Company, whose company commander was John Page, a housemaster whose war had been spent in Burma.

Playing the French Horn in the band led on to playing in the school orchestra, which had rather more interesting parts for the horn than did the band. Then when my voice broke, it led on to singing bass, first in the Big School Choir, which had fifty or sixty basses, next in the Chapel Choir, which had only about a dozen, then in the Madrigal Choir, which had only four, and finally even to singing the occasional solo. The band, the orchestra and singing, scouting and military training, Christianity – whether in chapel or the CU – debating, chess, boxing, and rugby football, with school work thrown in, and even learning to cope with life in the house, were all in their own ways helping to prepare me for the future.

In all, I had been at Christ's Hospital for eight years, from the age of ten until the age of 18. The first four were difficult; it often felt that it was a matter of surviving them. The next four were increasingly enjoyable, and I left with a genuine and lasting sense of gratitude for the benefits I had received there.

Keith Douglas

This second section provides an explanation of why the Old Blue poet, Keith Douglas, came to be significant to me. It begins with the fact that the Head of the History Department at Christ's Hospital when I was at school was the Honourable David Roberts, son of the first Baron Clwyd. He was known to the boys either as DSR or as 'Daddy' Roberts, probably because, unlike most of the masters, he was married and had three children. A remarkable teacher, he has a chapter to himself in my autobiography, and what follows here is an extract from it which relates to Keith Douglas, whom he had taught at CH in the 1930s.

The only poetry David Roberts ever gave me to read was by the former History Grecian, Keith Douglas, whose *Collected Poems* were published in 1951, the year before I left school. He was arguably the greatest English poet of WW2, and I have lived my life with the consciousness that it was the sacrifice of his young life, and that of so many other young men, that made it possible for me and others of my generation to live fulfilled lives – in freedom. I have also been conscious that, in terms of creativity, he had achieved more by the age of 24 than I by 84.

Keith Douglas had been born in 1920. At Christ's Hospital, we had been taught by several of the same masters, played in the same position in the 1st XV, won the same history prize, and afterwards went on to the same university. But a few weeks before I arrived at the school in 1944, at the age of ten, and four days after the Normandy landings, he climbed out of his tank and was killed by a shell splinter. He was 24. In 1952, I sat weeping in my study over his poetry.

Half a century after Keith Douglas was killed, I went to find his grave and found it in the small military cemetery at Tilly-sur-Seulles, north of Caen, plot no.1, row E, grave no.2. The inscription on the tombstone is *'These things' he loved. He died in their defence.* 'These things' is a reference to the passage which was always read in the Christ's Hospital chapel on Founder's Day. It is in the fourth chapter of the letter to the Philippians, where St Paul writes: 'Finally, brethren, whatsoever things are true, whatsoever things are honest, whatsoever things are just, whatsoever things are pure, whatsoever things are lovely, whatsoever things are of good report; if there be any virtue, and if there be any praise, think on these things.'

The biography of Keith Douglas by Desmond Graham, published in 1974, describes the large tempura picture of African soldiers at bayonet practice which Douglas painted in 1937, and which hung in his study during his last year at school. He left it with David and Peggy Roberts. And after Peggy died in 2010, having been a widow for more than half a century, their younger son, Pete, gave it to me. So, at one time I had a biography of Keith Douglas in my study; his *Selected Poems* in the kitchen, which then housed all my poetry books; his remarkable account of desert warfare, *From Alamein to Zem Zem*, in the sitting room; and the painting in the conservatory.

One of his poems which especially moved me was 'Aristocrats', written in the desert at Enfidaville in Tunisia in 1943, the year before he was killed:

The noble horse with courage in his eye,
clean in the bone, looks up at a shellburst:
away fly the images of the shires
but he puts the pipe back in his mouth.

Peter was unfortunately killed by an 88;
it took his leg away, he died in the ambulance.
I saw him crawling on the sand; he said
It's most unfair, they've shot my foot off.

How can I live among this gentle
obsolescent breed of heroes, and not weep?
Unicorns, almost,
for they are falling into two legends
in which their stupidity and chivalry
are celebrated. Each, fool and hero, will be an immortal.

The plains were their cricket pitch
and in the mountains the tremendous drop fences
brought down some of the runners. Here then
under the stones and earth they dispose themselves,
I think with their famous unconcern.
It is not gunfire I hear, but a hunting horn.

Keith Douglas's poetry has stayed with me for my whole life, and years later, in the autumn of 1999, when I was asked by Peter Southern, then headteacher of CH, to preach at the CH Remembrance Day service, I found myself turning yet again to Douglas.

Some 55 years earlier, on Remembrance Sunday 1944, just after 1st Airborne Division's attack at Arnhem had been defeated with heavy casualties, I had been sitting just inside chapel – in the bottom row, because I was in my first term in the school – as the Old Blues killed in both world wars were remembered. I explained that, and went on to ask why we were now engaged in an Act of Remembrance more than half a century after the Second World War and more than eighty years after the First, when none of us knew any of those who were killed. What or whom were we remembering? And why were we doing it in chapel?

I went on to suggest that remembrance is not quite the same thing as 'remembering', and pointed to the parallel with the Christian practice of engaging each Sunday in an act of remembrance of Jesus in the service of Holy Communion. Bread and wine serve as a memorial of the body and blood of Jesus. Past and present are mingled. The intention is for the past to be made effective in the present.

So it is with Remembrance Sunday. It is a deliberate affirmation about the past. For many, it has something to do with the idea that such things as heroism and the defence of freedom should be seen as part of our national identity. But it certainly should not involve a glorification of war, which, however much it may be necessary, remains a symbol of Man's corruption of his God-given potential for good. Still less should it be a celebration of victory.

It is, I suggested, first of all an occasion when we can hold up in remembrance those who lost their lives fighting, for example, in the Battle of Britain, the Battle of the Atlantic, in the Western Desert, in Burma or across the Lüneburg Heath, so that we might live in freedom. Secondly, remembering Jesus' command to his followers that they should love their enemies, we should spare some thought for our former enemies and their suffering. Thirdly, remembering the command to comfort widows and orphans in their distress, we should hold up before God in prayer the widows and orphans of war – of whatever nationality.

Of course, it was right to start by holding in remembrance our own dead, especially members of our own families or the 578 Old Blues who had been killed in the two World Wars. But if possible, we should then widen our sympathies, and that is precisely what Keith Douglas did in his poem '*Vergissmeinicht*', which in English means 'Forget-me-not'.

He wrote it – a veteran of desert warfare at the age of 23 – describing his thoughts when looking at the dead body of a German soldier at Homs in Tripolitania in the Western Desert.

The poem reaches out in sympathy to a dead enemy. And by referring to the photograph of the German girl who had written *Steffi, Vergissmeinicht* in a copybook gothic script, it leads on to think of those who mourn their loved ones. That German girl in the photograph could well have still been alive, in her seventies, and still remembering the dead, as were we. I finished the sermon with that poem:

Three weeks gone and the combatants gone,
returning over the nightmare ground
we found the place again, and found
the soldier sprawling in the sun.

The frowning barrel of his gun
overshadowing. As we came on
that day, he hit my tank with one
like the entry of a demon.

Look. Here in the gunpit spoil
the dishonoured picture of his girl
who has put: *Steffi. Vergissmeinicht*
in a copybook gothic script.

We see him almost with content
abased, and seeming to have paid
and mocked at by his own equipment
that's hard and good when he's decayed.

But she would weep to see today
how on his skin the swart flies move;
the dust upon the paper eye
and the burst stomach like a cave.

For here the lover and killer are mingled
who had one body and one heart.
And death who had the soldier singled
has done the lover mortal hurt.

Both 'Aristocrats' and *Vergissmeinicht* seemed to me worth learning by heart, and when I recite them to myself – as I still do, far more than half a century after first encountering them – I still find them moving.

Change in education

At the time I became a schoolmaster, in 1957, the public schools and grammar schools of England, which had developed over centuries, were both widely admired, in their different ways. Both charged fees, the boarding public schools about ten times as much as the day grammar schools. Christ's Hospital was remarkable in that it only accepted children whose parents could not afford to pay fees – though with some contribution towards the costs when they could afford it. In 1944, when I went there, only 2% of English children were receiving free secondary education, and it was in that year that an Education Act was passed which promised all children in the country free secondary education from 1947 onwards.

It was hailed as a great reform, but in the long run it was something of a disaster. Children were promised secondary education suited to their needs in grammar, technical, and 'modern' schools. But their parents were deprived of any choice over the type of school in which their children should be educated; too few grammar school places were provided; hardly any technical schools were built; and most 11-year-olds were humiliated by being treated as failures and directed to secondary modern schools, where they were given a curriculum unsuited either to their needs or their interests. The opportunity to integrate the public schools within a national system was missed, and provision by education authorities varied so much from one to another that there was nothing which could reasonably be described as a national system.

The grammar schools, most of which were no longer allowed to charge fees, had what was known as the 11+ selection procedure imposed on them. And that led to such dissatisfaction that it took only one generation to grow up for there to be a widespread demand for comprehensive schools, which in theory would provide high quality education for all. Strangely enough, the grammar schools – caught between the Scylla of Socialist suspicion and the Charybdis of Conservative contempt – were widely blamed for this, and in 1965 the Labour Secretary of State for Education, Anthony Crosland, issued Circular 10/65, asking local authorities to submit plans for comprehensive reorganisation. He told his wife, 'If it's the last thing I do, I'm going to destroy every f***ing grammar school in England.'

(Understandably, the editors of this volume wanted me to omit the last sentence, as likely to give offence to many readers. I declined. The facts of history are often unpleasant and have to be faced. They persisted, and eventually I agreed that the word should be printed as you see it.)

Circular 10/65 heralded the destruction of most of the country's grammar schools. Many were swamped under the large secondary modern element with which they were mixed, and because so little thought was given to the practicalities of the change, most comprehensive schools turned out to be too big, and with sixth forms which were too small. Problems proliferated, with widespread disorder in big city schools.

In 1975, another Labour government decided that the problem was that so many grammar schools had governing bodies which had been able to prevent them from being caught up in comprehensive reorganisation, and it found legislative and financial devices to put pressure on them to become comprehensives. It was a bad miscalculation. They almost all opted for independence, and a Labour government had unintentionally trebled the size of the independent sector and turned some of the academically most distinguished schools in England – such as Manchester Grammar School – into independent schools.

Back in the mid-1950s, when I was at Oxford, about half the undergraduates were from public schools, which were widely seen as socially superior, while most of the other half were from grammar schools, which were often academically superior. (Just a few of us were from neither. And in the case of Old Blues, we could say with pride that our school was a charitable institution.) But by the late 1970s, that perception had changed. Those teaching at public schools, and those who sent their children to them, were now increasingly inclined to speak of them as independent schools, and the many grammar schools which had been driven into independence were, of course, also independent schools. Between them, those schools were educating about 7% of each year's students, dominating Oxbridge entry, and getting about half of all university places.

Meanwhile, throughout the country, education officers were coming to realise that if children were not to be divided by ability, it was necessary to divide them by age, and the consequence was the development of sixth form colleges. There was no great sixth form college movement such as the comprehensive movement, but more and more were created as the best practical solution to the problems thrown up by the creation of comprehensive schools. And by the 1990s, there were 120 of them, educating roughly a quarter of all the country's A-level students.

Then, in 1992, a Conservative government made a mistake comparable in its foolishness to the Labour government's trebling of the size of the independent sector in 1976. When it created a new centralised education sector as a way of controlling and making more effective England's post-16 technical colleges, it included the sixth form colleges in that sector. One consequence was that no more sixth form colleges were ever founded, because if a local authority founded one, it would immediately be taken away from it. As the government reduced funding 'to take the fat out of the public sector', and as what was left was increasingly diverted to the technical colleges, another consequence was that a quarter of all sixth form colleges were unable to survive. Within a few years, there were only 90 instead of 120.

The way for a sixth form college to survive was to attract more students or reduce staffing, or both. Thus, during the time I was the principal of Collyer's, the student numbers increased from about 600 to 1,200, while the number of teaching staff remained at 60. That is, the student teacher ratio changed from 10:1 to 20:1. Meanwhile, nationally we reached a point where, using approximate figures, the annual funding per student in a sixth form college was £4,000; the funding per student for an 'academy' in an inner city which the government was trying to rescue from disaster, was £8,000; the fees charged by an independent day school were £16,000; and the fees charged by an independent boarding school were £32,000. All of them educated teenagers up to A-level.

Strangely enough, the best sixth form colleges were still producing more A-level passes and more high grades than were the leading independent schools, but they were doing it with large teaching groups and relatively few teachers, so that the government could make the savings required to cut taxes.

If the quarter century from the end of the Second World War to the late 1960s had been the Golden Age of the grammar school, then the 40 years after Labour gave its boost to the independent sector in 1976 was the Golden Age of the independent school, and it shows no sign of coming to an end. With a sense that something is wrong with English secondary education but with little idea of what to do about it, one government after another has thought up new sorts of schools as they tried to improve on what existed. After the

City Technology Colleges came Community Schools, Grant Maintained Schools, Specialist Language Schools, Trust Schools, and the rather grandly named University Technical Colleges. Faith Schools were applauded, and Free Schools were encouraged. Any new initiative, it seemed, might persuade the voter that something was being done. But they were all still comprehensive schools, and what had once seemed a great ideal was now more often viewed as a disaster. The latest practice is to call them 'Academies' and make them directly responsible to the Secretary of State rather than to their local education authority.

The independent schools were far less vulnerable to government interference, but had their own financial problems. Christ's Hospital, now clearly an independent school, was in such financial difficulty in the early 21st century, whether because of financial mismanagement or because it was a victim of circumstances (it was possible to take either of those views, or both), found it necessary to try to solve those problems by taking an increasing number of full fee-payers and fee-paying day pupils. By 2014, there were as many parents paying full fees as those who paid nothing, and instead of their children being housed, clothed, fed, and educated free (except for a means-tested contribution if their income increased), they were now being awarded bursaries as a percentage of the full boarding fee of over £30,000.

The scale on which those bursaries were given was vast. In 2014, when £60million was spent on bursaries by the 274 schools represented on the Headmasters' and Headmistresses' Conference (or HMC), a quarter of that total came from Christ's Hospital. It is impressive, but there is inevitably a danger that CH will gradually change into one more expensive public school, like so many charitable foundations before it.

Between 1861 and 1864, the Clarendon Commission, set up by Lord Palmerston when he was prime minister, looked into the affairs of nine leading schools, in order of foundation: Winchester, Eton, St Paul's, Shrewsbury, Westminster, Merchant Taylors', Rugby, Harrow, and Charterhouse. All had originally been charity schools, yet now they were charging fees to educate the sons of those members of the upper and middle classes who could afford to pay them. The Public Schools Act of 1868 ensured that they could go on doing so, and that they should not be a charge on the Crown, the Church, or the Government.

In the same year, another commission – this one led by Lord Taunton – reporting on the rest of secondary education in England, viewed Christ's Hospital with admiration and described it as 'a thing without parallel in this country, and *sui generis'* (i.e. unique), 'a grand relic of the medieval spirit – a monument of the profuse munificence of that spirit'.

For nearly 400 years after its foundation, Christ's Hospital was untouched by government interference – whether central or local. But in the changing world after the Second World War, decisions of both local and central government affected it. For many years, London boys and girls (and some from several other enlightened counties) who did particularly well in the scholarship examination for grammar schools (and later in the 11+), and who came from familes with a low income, were offered a place at Christ's Hospital. Many took it. They benefited from what CH provided, and the school's reputation benefited from their academic achievements. But the creation of the Inner London Education Authority in 1965, with its zeal for comprehensive education, deprived many of the next generation of Londoners of that opportunity. And thereafter the average level of academic ability of the school's intake was lower than when there had been a regular intake of bright, working-class London children.

When the Conservative government which took office in 1979 introduced an Assisted Places Scheme to help children escape from their local comprehensive to an independent school, Christ's Hospital took advantage of that. But the

Labour government which took office in 1997 abolished the scheme, and the hospital had to adjust to the loss of that income.

By the 21st century, the funding of maintained schools and colleges was being driven ever lower as politicians sought to cut taxes while at the same time finding money for such things such as health, defence, infrastructure, and pensions. And meanwhile, Christ's Hospital had its own financial problems. At the same time many of the leading independent schools were competing with each other to provide the most lavish facilities and the highest ratio of teachers to pupils. Some were even competing to have the highest fees, driving them up towards £40,000 a year, since that could be seen as an index of their excellence. If things continue much like that, it is possible that, while maintained schools and colleges will be struggling to survive as their funding is driven ever lower, the leading independent schools will be educating a small elite of attractive, intelligent, and talented children of the international super-rich, and sending them on to the best universities and to well-paid and influential jobs in finance, politics, law, and the BBC. Somehow, in that context, a unique institution such as Christ's Hospital has to find its place.

David Arnold, Horsham, July 2019

Note: Quotations from the poetry of Keith Douglas in this chapter are used by kind permission of Faber and Faber Ltd, taken from Keith Douglas, Complete Poems.

III

Thoughts, Memories and a Sermon for Remembrance Day

To go to Christ's Hospital from a small suburban village in Essex during the war, in 1944, was to enter into a broader world, culturally, educationally, and especially spiritually, than I had ever known. I took easily to worship in chapel and to 'holy prayer in duty made', loved singing, and eventually became leader of the chapel choir, which led to my becoming a cantor (choir man) at Cambridge. This turned out to be useful later when, as a cathedral dean, I had a choir to cope with. At some stage, I came to realise that I believed the words I was singing, at least enough to ask for baptism and confirmation. Shortly before the appointed day, I was confined to the sicker (sanatorium) and was baptised in a glass bowl there, together with my twin brother, David. Our housemaster, Eric Littlefield, stood godfather. I still cherish and use daily the silver napkin ring he gave me, inscribed with the date: 4th March, 1948.

Two days later, we were confirmed in chapel, not by the Bishop of Chichester, George Bell, but by his suffragan, the Bishop of Lewes. However, it was Bell who had the greater influence on me. I still remember the texts and the main points of the three sermons I heard him preach: 'Can these dry bones live?'; 'The foundations have been shaken, and what have the righteous done?'; and, in particular, 'I have called you friends, not slaves'. That is all I remember from my religious upbringing and, to be fair, one of the reasons is that Bishop Bell had a strange sing-song voice, and his sermons were gifts to mimics for months after delivery. One day I was walking along the Avenue and a thought came, unbidden, into my mind, 'When I am an old man, I want to be like Bishop Bell.' A strange idea indeed for a 16-year old. Even so, I later found that I had adopted his agenda: the beauty of holiness, cathedrals and the arts and, above all, discipleship, the ministry of reconciliation, and the ecumenical movement.

Confirmation training and religious education were lamentable, but the great advantage was that I realised how little I knew and that at some stage I would have to study theology properly. That sense of not really understanding has stayed with me and has been a spur to lifelong learning.

It was a privilege to be house captain of Barnes A 1951–2. Headmaster Flecker convened the school monitors and said, 'Never forget that the best form of government is benevolent oligarchy, especially if you are one of the benevolent oligarchs.' I have, indeed, never forgotten these words, and they stood me in good stead for the 25 years in which I was a dean with cathedrals, to govern with the help of a Chapter. At CH I had five house monitors, including my brother. Together, we formed an oligarchy which was benevolent enough to manage without any punishments at all in our last term. My only regret from those years is that the quatercentenary was celebrated not then but in 1953.

I was due to go up to Cambridge to read modern languages (German and French), so it was natural that for National Service, I should opt for the Intelligence Corps, be selected for the Joint Services School for Linguists, and graduate to the fabled Joint Services Russian Course (see *Secret Classrooms* by Elliot & Shukman, London, 2002). Two of my contemporaries were Michael Frayn and Alan Bennett. Our commanding officer said that he was not sure what use we were to NATO, but that our cabaret was the best in the Western alliance. Alan Bennett was later to reminisce (*Untold Stories*, London, 2005, p 393):

'Many of the others on the course were disconcertingly clever, particularly, I remember, a group of boys from Christ's Hospital – boys whose schools had been a world as mine never was; and when they talked of their schooldays there was often in the background a master whose teaching had been memorable and about whom they told anecdotes, and whose sayings they remembered: teachers, I remember thinking bitterly, who had played a part in getting them the scholarships most of them had to Oxford and Cambridge.'

I took advantage of the flexibility of the Tripos system at Cambridge to study German, French, and Russian, and to deepen my devotion to European languages and literature. I was beginning to sense that at the heart of this civilisation was the Christian faith. At the same time, I was deeply troubled by the horror – first of the Second World War, and then of the Cold War – for which I had been trained. How could the most cultured, best educated, and most deeply Christian nations of the world have done and be doing this to each other and still be exporting conflict to the rest of that world? And, like most late adolescents, I was looking for a meaningful life and for the opportunity to do something worthwhile with the splendid education I had been given at CH, in the Army, and at Cambridge.

The 1950s were a strange decade – wonderful in which to be alive and young, as Europe recovered from its self-inflicted wounds, but also haunted by the mushroom-shaped shadow of the atom bomb, by East-West tensions, and by the fear of another war of mutual, assured destruction (or MAD for short). This nervous expectation of the end, not just of our individual lives but also of the whole inhabited world or *oikumene*, is difficult to recapture. But it is best evoked by the theological word 'apocalyptic', which was one of the aspects of early Christianity at a time when much of the New Testament was being written. So, it was a good time to be studying theology, too.

During the long vacation in 1956, I attended a World Council of Churches' ecumenical work-camp in East Berlin – the first to be held behind the Iron Curtain. We worked with our bare hands on the rebuilding of Berlin, which still lay in the ruins to which it had been reduced in 1945, and we transformed a bombed site into a children's playground – a symbolic achievement later trashed by members of the Communist youth organisation. Towards the end of the camp, I was invited to administer the chalice at a Lutheran service of Holy Communion in St Peter's Church, roofless by courtesy of the Royal Air Force. I found myself in divided Berlin, at the heart of what had once been an evil empire, administering the cup of salvation in a ruined church to new friends and old enemies, and saying, 'Das Blut unseres Herrn Jesu Christi fuer Dich gegossen.' ('The blood of our Lord Jesus Christ shed for thee.') Suddenly, in the simple liturgical words of this simple liturgical act, the goal – though not yet the meaning – of my life was revealed to me; and I knew, not by speculation or rational thought but by experience, that this was the most important thing in the world for me, and that I had to give myself to the ministry of reconciliation, which, St Paul says, is entrusted to us, ordinary men and women, as ordinary as broken bread and poured-out wine, and to the quest for Christian unity. Now, as a retired priest at Canterbury Cathedral, I often administer the chalice on Sundays, and I always recall that moment of vocation.

Back in Cambridge, I was wisely advised to finish the modern languages Tripos before studying Theology and training for the ministry at Westcott House. I served my curacy in Sheffield and became a research fellow at Sheffield University, which was a useful preparation for being the first full-time Anglican chaplain at Southampton University during the heady days of the 1960s. I kept up my languages by working as an interpreter for the World Council of Churches and the Conference of European Churches – another fabulous chance for post-graduate, mind-stretching learning and, again, useful preparation for my next post as secretary of the board for mission and unity (in effect, ecumenical secretary) of the General Synod. Then, as dean first of Rochester (1987–89) and then of Durham (1989–2002), I was fortunate enough to participate in the new 'golden age of English cathedrals'. At the same time, I was privileged to assist in achieving communion between the Church of England and the Nordic and Baltic Lutheran Churches and increased fellowship with the German Protestant Churches. (I told my children that I had played for England against Germany at ecclesiology, seven-a-side.) I was fortunate enough not only to have played a part in sustaining the churches of Central and Eastern Europe during the period of Marxist-Leninist hegemony, but also to have participated in the life of the Conference of European Churches which held the churches of our continent together, despite all that man could do to keep them apart. Its languages were English, French, German, and Russian; it was only when I was elected its President (1992–97) that I understood the meaning of my life and of those long years learning vocabulary lists and construing irregular verbs. Life must be lived forwards, but it can only be understood backwards; and much of the best of mine goes back to Christ's Hospital.

When I was invited to preach in the school's chapel in 2004 for the ninetieth anniversary of the First World War, I took the opportunity to combine a visual memory from my time at CH with some of what I had learned since. And I chose as my text:

'Fear not; I am the first and the last, and the living one. I died and behold I am alive for evermore; and I have the keys of Death and Hades.' (Revelation 1:17f, RSV)

What follows is what I said then and would still say today.

In all the years I was in Barnes A, the pictures in the day-room never changed, so I had ample opportunity to study and admire 'The Surrender of Breda' by Velazquez (1634–5).

It shows the Dutch elders handing over the keys of the city to their Spanish conqueror, Spinola, in a famous episode in the Thirty Years' War. At the time, I was most impressed by the bristling pikes of the victorious infantrymen; only later did I come to appreciate the dignity of the vanquished and the magnanimity of the victors. Velazquez' masterpiece is rightly regarded as an early example of the hope of reconciliation after conflict. Still, the focus of the composition is on the keys as a sign of power and on their significance for victory and defeat.

The Christian faith is not that Jesus avoided death or that He escaped from the place of the dead. It is that He defeated them on the Cross. He took them on, armed only with faith in His Father, and defeated them. Having killed Him once in vain, they now have no more dominion over Him. He has dominion over them, as Spinola had over Breda. That is what is meant by saying that He has the keys of death and hell (which is what 'Hades' means). Holding the keys, Christ unlocks the door of death outwards, as well as in. So, when we die, we go not into a prison from which He has escaped, but to a country which He has conquered. We may comfort one another with these words; and we dare to do so, because in Jesus Christ God Himself knows what the fallen have gone through better than we do ourselves, for He has gone through hell before us, He has died and is alive again, and He has come back to tell us not to be afraid, because He has triumphed over death and hell. They do not have the last word any more than they had the first word; it was God who did, when He created Heaven and earth and men and women in His own image. And now He says to us, through the Risen Christ: 'Do not be afraid. I am the first and the last, the living one. I was dead, and see, I am alive for ever, and I have the keys of death and hell.'

Who is this Jesus who speaks so confidently? Not the spokesman of any one nation or people, but the one man who, because He speaks for God, speaks for all, for our common humanity, and for victory over death and hell.

I stress that now because this year,* 90 years after the outbreak of the Great War (1914–18), we remind ourselves that it was fought to be the 'war to end all wars'. But it only led to the Second World War; and the years 1914–1945 may be regarded as another Thirty Years War, with a long half-time break for developing yet more fearsome weapons, more terrible ideologies, and variations on 'man's inhumanity to man'. We cannot end wars by waging more wars, as God made clear when He forbade Adam and Eve to eat the fruit of the tree of the knowledge of good and evil. Humankind cannot bring good out of evil; when it tries to do so, it only produces more evil, and cuts itself off from the tree of life. Only God can bring good out of evil, as He did in Christ upon the cross, when He reconciled the world to Himself, and turned the tree of death into a new tree of life. John Donne, Dean of St Paul's and poet, said that in heaven there are 'no foes, no friends; but an equal communion and identity'; and we pray that that should be the case 'on earth as it is in Heaven'.

Still, we also pray that, just as they were the first world wars in history, so they may be the last in which the home front was also the front line, in which there was no real distinction between combatant and non-combatant – in itself, an appalling return to barbarism. As a boy in Woodford, between the Hurricanes of Hornchurch and the Spitfires of North Weald, I watched the Battle of Britain overhead and saw London burning, with the dome of St Paul's riding out over the billowing smoke and flames like a galleon in a storm. And for all its terrible beauty, I never want to see anything like that again, any more than I would have wanted to see Lübeck devoured by fire on Palm Sunday 1942, or Rotterdam, Coventry, and Dresden, or Hiroshima on the Feast of the Transfiguration in 1945. I mention this random selection of targets now because the time has come to stress the common humanity of those involved rather than what seemed to be more important at the time – the fact that we were on different sides; for our hope is that being enemies is temporary, while being human is permanent.

Three little stories, anecdotes, in fact, have helped me precisely with this point. The first dates from the 1950s when I was a student and, having done National Service, also an officer on the reserve. I was studying in France and visiting another Old Blue in Caen – scene of the most intense urban fighting in the battle for Normandy in 1944, where the armies on both sides and the civilian population had all suffered together. My friend's landlady started reminiscing about those terrible days, telling us of the two German soldiers, lads of about our age, who had died in her arms. She said of one of them, '*Il criait toujours "Mutti, Mutti".*' ('He kept on crying out for his mother.') She continued, '*Et moi, j'étais la seule maman qu'il avait.*' ('And I was the only mother he had.') Now, we had all been brought up with a clear, black-and-white view of the French then, which comes out in the old television series, *'Allo, 'Allo*. There was the Resistance, which was good, and there were collaborators, who were bad. For a while I couldn't speak, because I was prey to conflicting emotions. I felt my heart harden against this woman for harbouring the enemy; but hardness of heart, or porosis (as both St Paul in the New Testament and our doctors today tell us) kills unless it is cured. An angel came to my aid, and I understood that she was right and I was wrong. As St Paul again said, 'When your enemies are hungry, feed them; if they are thirsty, give them something to drink' (Rom 12, 20); and he might have added, 'if they are bleeding to death, hold their hands and cradle their heads'.

My second story concerns a German friend whom I met as a result of a visit to Munich in 1951, when I was a modern languages Grecian. Towards the end of the war, he had been enlisted with his classmates as a boy soldier in the forlorn defence of the Fatherland. In their first encounter with the Red Army, they were taken prisoner, and he spent seven years in a camp near Leningrad. He later devoted his life to training teachers in a spirit of peace and reconciliation, with frequent visits to the Soviet Union. One day, he went looking for the site of the camp where so many of his comrades had perished. There had been a lot of redevelopment; the street plan was changed, and he was lost. Then he saw an elderly woman coming towards him – a survivor from the generation which had been through the 900-day siege of Leningrad (one of the great epics of the war, with two million victims), doubtless a woman who, like all her generation, had lost father, brothers, husband, sons, among the 20 million Russian dead. So, he hesitated to ask the way, fearing anger and reproach and insult. But he plucked up courage and said who he was and what he was looking for. The woman stood still in front of him, and there on the street in the atheist Soviet Union, she made the sign of the cross over him and said, '*Slava Bogu, viy perezhili.*' ('Thank God, you survived.') – her motherly heart and Orthodox faith triumphing over national hatred.

My final story takes us back to 1969, when I visited the site of the concentration camp at Salaspils in Latvia, where the prisoners were worked to death, cutting peat in all weathers. There was none of the usual strident propaganda for the peace policies of the Soviet Union – just simple factual labels: this is where the daily roll-call took place; here stood the gallows; here the whipping block; this is where children were shot, and so on. A large sign over the exit gate had four words in Russian: '*Eto nye dolzhno povtoryatsya.*' ('This mustn't happen again.')

That is all that was needed and needs to be said. It mustn't happen again. That is what the fallen fought for, even if they did not know it at the time. May they rest in peace. Amen.

The Very Rev'd John Arnold OBE MA DD DD (Hon), Dean Emeritus of Durham: b1933; 1944–52 CH; 1952–54 Intelligence Corps; 1954–60 Sidney Sussex College (Cambridge); 1960 Curate, Millhouses; 1963 Chaplain, Southampton University; 1972 Secretary, Board for Mission and Unity; 1978 Dean of Rochester; 1989–2002 Dean of Durham; 1994–7 President of the Conference of European Churches.

IV

Science and Engineering

Introduction

Now therefore be wise, ye kings. Be instructed ye judges of the Earth. Psalm 2, v 10.

Although no Old Blues have so far been crowned kings and few have become judges, many are acknowledged to be 'wise' and 'instructed'. For this chapter, I was invited to give personal experiences of my schooldays and to speculate on the future of Science at Christ's Hospital, and elsewhere. This future-gazing was to be for the years up to 2052, the quincentenary of CH's foundation. Such prophecy was in addition to providing reflections on earlier CH Science. I declined to speculate, claiming ignorance. So, in this chapter, I confine myself to reviewing a period ending around 1960. Old Blue Professor Edmund Blunden writes in his poem 'Unteachable':

To some, thoughts flying into futurity's cloud;
To some, pale provings mocking time and space;
To some, the puzzling out to-day's hoarse crowd;
To each his own: I run a backward race.

This chapter will be a 'backward race', treating some causes of great pride in the history of CH's scientific teaching with a review of a selection of Old Blue scientists, engineers, and medical scholars. There are many other Old Blues whose scholarly achievements justify attention; doubtless future volumes in this *Christ's Hospital: Tradition with Vision* series will address this gap.

The author and Christ's Hospital

I entered CH in 1948, a ten-year-old West Gift's scholar from a provincial English town (Reading, Berkshire). Walking to the dining hall with my mother from the station on my first day at CH, initial impressions of Housey were the immensity of the school, with its many large sports fields and buildings. I had never previously seen such grandiose facilities in any educational establishment. My mother had attempted to prepare me for my new school, and found only one relevant book in the local public library. This was *Christ's Hospital from a Boy's Point of View, 1864–1870* by the Reverend W La Touche, a book hopelessly out of date when we read it in 1948. So, upon arriving at CH, after my short lifetime experiencing deprivation due to WW2 and the early post-war years, I found CH as modern and 'with it' as could be imagined by a ten-year-old then. By the time I left, it was a place that filled almost my whole world, from intellectual activity to politics and personal relationships. I imagined the next part of my life, as a university student, would simply be a modified CH. I was very wrong. Yet CH strove to allow pupils to seek understanding of all sorts. For me, this was Housey's most enduring benefit; but it was an unconscious benefit, for then I knew of little else apart from Housey life.

After university studies, and newly married, I left the UK for New York City as a nuclear physicist; in 1963, the USA was the Mecca of this field. My ambition then (never realised) was to stay there for a year or two and, with post-doctoral experience, to obtain an academic post in the UK in physics. My experience at Columbia University's physics department was stupendous. At that time, that department included three active Nobel prize-winners and five other staff members with whom I sometimes interacted and who all received Nobel prizes later. The five included my boss (though his prize-winning work had nothing to do with our joint research). Still in New York eight-and-a-half years and three children later, it was time to go home. I could not find a suitable post, but something reasonable was available in Cape Town. It seemed as if it might be an interesting experience for a short time. So, off we all went for a year or two, until the post I dreamed of at home should turn up. But then something totally unforeseen kept me in Cape Town for the next seven years. At the age of 35, I was able to start a degree in medicine, something I had wanted to do for many years. That was followed by internship.

When I qualified, I felt that I owed the country something and so stayed on, working always in the public service. This added great value to my life, both providing intellectual satisfaction and also permitting more service to others. Being an Old Blue in Cape Town also added much pleasure to my life here. There are about a dozen Old Blues in Cape Town, and most meet regularly, typically twice yearly. We all get on immensely well, even though our lives and ages are as different as can be imagined.

Some individuals at CH influenced me greatly, notably William Armistead, a brilliant and inspiring teacher of mathematics, and Eric Littlefield, the senior housemaster who, in spite of his failings, was the father figure I needed, although very remote and stern. Housey certainly provides a magnificent education; a socially supportive structure with an ethos extraordinarily appropriate for our troubled times. But growing up as an only child with a single parent, I believe that a happy home life with siblings (all, if available) offers advantages unobtainable elsewhere.

Louis Harold Gray, FRS (1905–65)

Louis Harold Gray, known as 'Hal', was one of the most distinguished scientists ever educated at Housey. Yet few have heard of him for reasons that I shall explain. His career well indicates the nature of the scientific education then provided by CH and more importantly its consequences, and his adult life reflects its ethos.

Hal is recognised as a founding father of radiobiology – a little known, young, yet most important branch of biological science. Radiobiology is concerned with the consequences of the interaction of certain radiations with any living matter. Some of its most important practical applications ensure the effective and safe applications of X-rays. So, every reader who has had an X-ray examination has directly benefited from Hal's work. But Hal contributed much more to the world. Radiotherapy, an efficient treatment of many cancers, was greatly improved by Hal's work. The understanding of how cells work (every living being is composed of large numbers of cells and their malfunction is at the root of very many illnesses) was increased by Hal's work, and he made many other contributions to scientific knowledge. Yet most are unaware of his main field of study – in part because he was an exceedingly modest and self-effacing man. All this contributes to Hal's work being unappreciated by the general public and by most scientists, because they are unfamiliar with radiobiology. However, he has been recognised by an honour considered by some to be more prestigious than a Nobel Prize, of which about 600 have been awarded for the sciences and medicine. In contrast, only about 30 scientists' names are used for internationally accepted names of units (including the Newton, Pascal, Watt, Ampère, Joule, and Volt). The Gray is the international unit for absorbed radiation dose. What an honour for an Old Blue!

When Hal was at Housey, which he entered in 1918 as a London County Council scholar, its science teaching was pre-eminent in British schools. This was mainly due to two persons: a governor, Professor Henry E Armstrong; and Mr Charles E Browne, who was the head of CH science teaching, 1899–1926. The teaching method they devised and practised, called the heuristic method, was the secret of

CH's success in the teaching of science, and for a couple of decades it was taught solely at Housey. This method takes its name from the Greek word, *heurisko*, meaning 'I discover'. This encouraged pupils to discover for themselves the science they had to learn, guided by the teacher. Neither textbooks nor lectures were their sources of knowledge, but instead the boys' own findings.

Hal's heuristic science training at CH taught fewer facts (which were predominantly sought in answers to most university entrance examinations) than conventional school science instruction. But Hal's heuristic learning ensured he had a wider and deeper understanding of scientific principles than those educated elsewhere. Hal did not gain the most prestigious type of scholarship offered at Cambridge University, which he entered in 1924. However, his ability and deeper understanding of physical principles were quickly recognised by Trinity College, Cambridge, where he studied physics, and after a year there he was awarded one of the College's most prestigious scholarships.

Browne's scientific training of his pupils always went beyond teaching them what they had to learn for examinations. Hal had studied hardly any biology before his last year at CH. Browne knew this and, after Hal's university place was secured, he encouraged Hal to learn the biology neglected in his previous curriculum, by providing a book and other material. This was solely to increase his general appreciation of science in its various forms, for Browne always encouraged investigations beyond the immediate curriculum, when this was appropriate. At that stage (and for nearly a decade afterwards), Hal was mainly interested in nuclear physics – a subject to which he made important contributions, notably the Bragg-Gray principle. At that time (*ca* 1930), nuclear physics was believed to be a fascinating intellectual pursuit, without practical implications. Because of Hal's deeply felt humanitarian principles (as an adult he was a pacifist), he felt that if he continued with nuclear physics, he would not aid humanity; so he changed his field of study to serve humankind more directly. He would instead use his knowledge to improve cancer treatments. Hal achieved this and much more.

In the 20th century, and today, scientific progress is usually made by persons who became highly specialised in their subject. Although Hal's important nuclear physics discoveries needed such specialisation, his greatest contributions to knowledge, in radiobiology, required exactly the opposite path: far rarer and far more difficult to attain. Hal mastered appropriate parts of several very different sciences, including physics, chemistry, biochemistry, physiology, and anatomy. All these were essential to allow an understanding of the new science of radiobiology. His polymathic ability was likely to be unique in modern times. Another outstanding polymathic Old Blue Scientist, in a different field of study, is the oceanographer Timothy Parsons – please see this book's Chapter X. Hal's experiences while learning science at CH well illustrate the nature of the heuristic method's early days there. At that time, Housey was unique in teaching science in this way, as were its laboratories, designed by Armstrong for inclusion in the Horsham campus, built to order, and first used in 1902 when the school left its London site in Newgate Street. Later, very many other schools followed CH's successful pioneering efforts in science education. Before 1902, mathematics was taught at CH, and Oxbridge scholarships were won in this subject by mathematical Grecians. But before the move to Horsham, there was virtually no instruction in science at Housey, nor apparatus available for its teaching.

Browne did much more than simply organise the teaching of science (although he was a formidable teacher of chemistry). He attempted to expand his science Grecians' knowledge with experience of the humanities. They were invited to Browne's home on Sunday evenings for play-readings, in which Browne's wife and daughter participated. Its origin was probably the result of similar play-readings first introduced by his headmaster, Dr William H Fyfe, who had such sessions in his home for the Grecians to whom he taught classics. An emphasis on all the humanities subjects and music for all CH's pupils continued for over half a century at both Hertford and Horsham. Unsurprisingly, therefore, a science specialist won the Charles Lamb Medal Essay prize, commemorating the 19th-century Old Blue literary figure, on more than one occasion; although it was unusual in education at the time, all science students were taught to write well.

Hal's love of Housey was reflected in his descriptions of his school days to his children. But he went much further. His will bequeathed everything to his wife; however, if she predeceased him, the bulk of his estate was left to Housey.

Origins of the heuristic method

The heuristic method of teaching probably arose from Britain's falling behind in the European manufacturing and technology race of the 19th century. This race may have begun with the unexpected discovery by the Englishman William Perkin in 1856 of the first synthetic dye – an intense purple, based on the organic chemical aniline. Aniline dye was a great improvement on existing dyes, derived from natural substances. This first synthetic dye was easier to produce, cheaper, and more colour-fast than its predecessors. Teaching of science then, and particularly chemistry, was far more advanced and extensive in Germany than in Britain. Perkin patented his discovery, set up a factory to manufacture his dye, and made a fortune. In spite of Perkin's great success, before long the synthetic dye industry was controlled by the German chemical industry, to such an extent that British textile manufacturers had to pay royalties to German companies which had discovered many more synthetic dyes. German progress in devising dyestuffs, as well as fertilisers, pharmaceuticals, and photographic products, were at the core of the successes of dominant German industrial companies. These advances all resulted from superior German general chemical knowledge, education, and researches. The dyestuff industry is only one example of the way the UK had fallen behind Germany, France, and the USA, in terms of technical applications, for these other nations had many technical schools and Britain had none for most of the 19th century.

That Great Britain was trailing other nations in trade, due to its inferior science education, was evident at the Great Exhibition of 1851. As a result, it was recognised by a few that determined efforts were needed to improve British standards of technical education. Instruction in general science was also inadequate in Britain. This was in spite of Britons having made some most important scientific discoveries in the 19th century and the pre-eminence of British railways and steamships. So, for scientific and technical innovative achievements, Britain gained 10/10, but that was not enough. For British technical education, the grade was only 4/10. A need to modernise both science and industry's understanding of science was recognised. Worthies of the City of London Livery Companies were persuaded that better technical education was essential to reduce British industries' dependence on German companies and products. So, in 1876, they founded the City and Guilds Institute, which later extended its activities by establishing the Finsbury Technical College. This college offered evening classes in the sciences and technology for men who had full-time employment. It became most successful, and one of its chemistry lecturers was Armstrong, who later became a professor of chemistry at a precursor of Imperial College, University of London. Apart from promoting dedicated studies in technology and science at schools and technical colleges, Armstrong believed that all school pupils, including girls, should learn some science (then a most radical idea), even if their later careers were in other fields. Armstrong was also a most competent researcher. Finally, the British Government understood the need for greatly improved technical education, and passed the Technical Institutes Act in 1889.

A Charity Commission scheme emerging from the Endowed Schools Act of 1869 led to a Scheme of Administration that was enacted by CH in 1891. This recommended that the school leave London for the countryside; that science should be added to the curriculum; and that CH's governing body should include representatives of learned societies such as the Royal Society. These proposals were adopted by CH. Armstrong was appointed in 1896 as the Royal Society's representative governor for Christ's Hospital. Armstrong seized this opportunity, and the transfer of the school from London to Horsham in 1902, to ensure that science would become an important part of the new school's facilities and curriculum. Armstrong also insisted on the appointment of several competent science teachers, which was most unusual for any school in the late 19th century.

As a governor of Christ's Hospital (1896–1937), Armstrong persuaded his fellow governors to include spacious laboratories in the new school, which was built at Horsham and received its first pupils in 1902. When this was done, four science teachers were appointed initially, to teach physics and chemistry, aided by two laboratory assistants. One of the most effective was the head of the new science department, Mr Charles E. Browne. He had been a former pupil, protégé and later colleague of Armstrong. Their relationship and successes have been well described as Armstrong being an 'apostle with revolutionary ideas' and Browne 'his devoted disciple with the wit and zeal to put them into practice'. Before becoming Armstrong's colleague, Browne had taught a conventional course in chemistry at a college in Aberdeen. There, the college's funding depended on exam results. Browne said the teaching methods imposed on him were 'to cram [and] not to impart understanding'. Meanwhile, Armstrong had never taught children, but he had discovered what they lacked as a result of the inadequate teaching they experienced in childhood. So, after Browne was appointed to teach at CH, they complemented each other very well.

Armstrong also designed the revolutionary teaching facilities for science for CH. They included four large laboratories, each sized 60x30ft with associated teaching areas, all housed in a large and prominent building (today called 'The Old Science School'). It forms the eastern side of the main quadrangle of the new CH campus. In each laboratory, a class of up to about 25 boys could be accommodated. In other British schools at the turn of the century, there were virtually no full-time science teachers. The number of CH's science teachers was increased to seven in 1911, with biology taught at an advanced level, so that Grecians could add this subject to their curriculum. This was principally intended to prepare those who later wished to study medicine or to farm. Steadily the popularity of science studies increased during and after WW1. So, a second science laboratory building (the New Science School) was built and opened by the Prince of Wales in October 1930. It provided a laboratory for organic chemistry, a science lecture theatre, and two large laboratories for each of the following disciplines: biology, geography, practical mathematics (mechanics, etc.), and a science library. Armstrong was no scientific chauvinist, although a chemist by profession and training. He took all science as his province, and always insisted that general science studies should include elements of botany, zoology, and geology, in addition to physics and chemistry.

Both the art school and the manual school were also included in the new CH school for boys at Horsham, as a result of Armstrong's insistence. In each, practical skills and handicrafts were taught. Armstrong also found the heads of both the art school and the manual school and ensured they were appointed, for he intended they should use heuristic principles, whenever this was practical. In the manual school, the facilities included a wood workshop, a smithy, a foundry, a metalworking shop, bookbinding training, and a printshop.

Engineering Grecians were also taught there after 1916. Early in the 21st century, its emphasis and function were changed by the manual school being transformed into The Doyle School of Design and Technology.

The headmaster who presided over the move to Horsham and the establishment of its revolutionary science laboratories was the Reverend Dr William A Upcott, a classicist and appointed in 1902. After some hesitation, Upcott fully supported the science teaching innovations introduced by Armstrong through Browne and his colleagues. Upcott's successor (engaged in 1919) was Dr William H Fyfe. Although Fyfe was also a classicist, he was enthusiastic and supportive for science, describing his attitude to education in general as 'nourishment, but never force-feeding'. Dr Fyfe noted that whenever he 'entered a classroom to speak to a master, all the boys sprang to their feet... welcoming the interruption. [But] I could enter the manual school, even accompanied by visitors, without attracting any attention, because the boys were happily absorbed in their work; their brains were as absorbed as their hands. It was the same in the art school.'

The heuristic method at Christ's Hospital

The heuristic method of teaching science at CH, Horsham, was as revolutionary as the facilities; and both Armstrong and Browne were its strong and enthusiastic developers and proponents. As already described, the heuristic method proved far more than the acquisition of facts; it taught *thinking*. In Browne's words, he 'taught by asking questions and adopting the attitude of a co-enquirer, not an authority'. Theory was taught in general only after experiments were completed. However, there was some slight modification of the initial heuristic teaching after a few years' experience; for example, some demonstration experiments were added.

Browne's application of the heuristic method was well illustrated by the eminent engineer Sir Barnes Wallis, FRS,

FREng one of Browne's most distinguished pupils. Wallis reminisced that he 'had given a perfectly correct answer to some question. But Browne wrung from him the shameful confession that he had got it out of a book and punished him for not discovering, or at least testing it, for himself.' Barnes Wallis was a great enthusiast for both Browne and his teaching methods, saying that, 'Uncle Chas did not teach science, in the sense usually attached to the word, he used science to teach us to think and to reveal to us the powers that we ourselves possessed.' Browne confirms this, by maintaining that 'the teacher is to afford guidance and suggestions mainly by questions – no telling – and should adopt the attitude of a co-enquirer, not an authority.'

At Horsham, other subjects apart from science soon began to be taught in a somewhat similar heuristic fashion. Such innovations were almost entirely due to Armstrong, whose influence went far beyond science. This was especially true for geography (using maps, guides, steamship and railway advertisements, etc.), French (always using spoken French, so that young boys could speak intelligibly, even if not fluently), and history (where at least two textbooks were used with different views). At that time, there was no two-cultures dichotomy at CH. Armstrong and Browne always wished to integrate studies of English, history, and mathematics with science, when practical. They encouraged science teachers to pay attention to literary style and the accuracy of written English. Also, boys read aloud historical notes on the subject under consideration, with their master correcting pronunciation and elocution.

Some science was taught to all boys after 1908. The most able of them, who elected to specialise in the subject, prepared for university scholarships, especially for Oxford and Cambridge, or entry to medical schools. The first Grecians who specialised in science were taught in 1911, with an engineering Grecian class set up in 1916. Soon afterwards, Oxbridge science scholarships were being won regularly. Science teaching at CH was evidently successful, for in some years of the first few decades of the 20th century more scholarships were gained in the sciences than in any other subject.

Christ's Hospital science after Hal

The superiority of the heuristic method was recognised, and more and more schools adopted a version of it for their teaching of science. Westminster School, for example, is a well-respected, traditional public school; and at the time of writing, it is graded as the best school in the UK by some internet school rating sites. Interestingly, in 1924 that school wished to set up science laboratories. Its headmaster received the following advice at the headmasters' conference: 'Go to Christ's Hospital; it is the most efficient school in the country; its science is the best there is.'

At CH, Browne's successors as head of science, Mr DH Burleigh and then Dr Gordon Van Praagh, continued to use versions of the heuristic method. Dr Van Praagh was a prolific author, renowned educational theorist and, like Browne, a teacher of chemistry. He had been a pupil of Browne, who during his early retirement lectured at the University of London's Institute of Education. Inspired by Browne, Dr Van Praagh taught at CH from 1933–64, except for war service, and became head of science in 1946. His 1949 textbook *Chemistry by Discovery*, applying the heuristic method, was very successful, and in 2003 he published *A Fire to be Kindled: The Global Impact of Christ's Hospital on Science Education*.

Although most of those who know CH are aware of many virtues of the heuristic method of teaching science in a high school, only recently has most of the rest of the world become aware of the method's desirability. A very recent, most prestigious presentation (The 2019 Oppenheimer Lecture, delivered by the eminent Stanford University physicist, Professor Helen Quinn) extolled a 'new' approach to science teaching. This approach has been adopted in 40 States of the USA and in numerous other nations. Some of the lecture's highlights included the following statements.

- Today's teaching methods in schools involve too much declaiming, providing too many facts and insufficient understanding.
- Current emphasis of theoretical problem solving should be replaced by deeper understanding of principles.
- It is essential to know the context of science taught and some details, rather than facts and numbers. Computers can easily solve the sort of problems which tax today's science learners.
- All pupils should learn some science, to be scientifically literate in the modern world, in which very much scientific information is provided for everyone.
- The relevance of the science being taught to daily life must be explained.

The lecture's conclusion elaborates heuristics, or 'learning by discovery', saying, 'All this is the student finding out for self, not being taught.'

My experience of science teaching in the 1950s

I experienced a modified heuristic method of learning science at CH in the 1950s. It seemed a satisfactory method from an enthusiastic pupil's point of view, although my experience with chemistry did not encourage much independent thought. In fact, it seemed to me to be rather ridiculous to make such a fuss about the 'learning by discovery', which in chemistry applied only for the introductory parts of the syllabus. Dr Van Praagh wrote that, 'Some parts of the syllabus are much more heuristic than others. They fertilise the rest of the work. But their frequency decreases in higher forms.' Certainly, there are other crucially important factors in school teaching, apart from the heuristic method and the provision of information. In my opinion, far more important are the personality and ability of the teacher. Whatever the advantages of any method to teach a pupil how to think and to investigate, ultimately, information is purveyed and absorbed. Most of my experience of the heuristic method with chemistry did not succeed in teaching me how to think or investigate. It provided lists of items to be remembered. Unlike Latin and mathematics, there seemed to be no beauty in the structures comprising combinations of remembered items at that level. In fact, the reasons for there to be modifications to the pure heuristic method were recognised long before by Armstrong and Browne: the influence of examinations, whose importance was steadily increasing, and economic restraints; for in practice, classes must often be larger than those best suited to teaching by the heuristic method.

I was most fortunate to have been taught by Messrs Ronald Crosland (physics), William Armistead and Ivor McConnell (mathematics). They inspired, and a consequence was enthusiasm for the physical/mathematical sciences. My chemical studies seemed to rely more on rote learning, so I (perhaps mistakenly) dropped chemistry. In contrast, physics and mathematics always for me presented new problems. I recollect we were studying the helical spring and its force and extension, Hooke's Law, and simple stuff. When shaken up and down, the spring quivered like a Slinky toy. Someone asked Mr Crosland exactly how the spring vibrated, and he quickly worked out for us a description of simple harmonic motion – somewhat less simple stuff. This was all for a hypothetical weightless spring. So, then he was asked about a real spring, which certainly had a significant weight. There was one nearby which seemed to behave likewise. We therefore wondered if he could provide us with its theory. Mr Crosland swallowed hard, for theoretical investigation of such a real spring with significant mass was not part of the syllabus. Then he got to work, with a little participation from his audience. He solved it. I was greatly impressed.

Similarly, mathematics questions taken from Oxbridge entrance papers included some problems invented for that paper and never before seen by teachers and boys. Sometimes these original problems were so difficult that our teachers could not solve them immediately. On one occasion, such a problem had to be taken to CH's resident mathematical genius, Mr John E Bullard, also an Old Blue, who quickly provided the solution. Such a high standard of intellectual activity greatly impressed me. Perhaps with inspiration from intellectual 'beauty', it represented a needed enhancement of the heuristic method that had not been described by its founders. But whether these nuances are necessary or not, I certainly experienced a very high standard in CH science and mathematics teaching. Often the beauty of these subjects was also conveyed to the pupils. For example, a prime contender in my opinion for the accolade of the most beautiful scientific equation is Einstein's $E = mc^2$, which I first met at CH. I was most fortunate to have experienced all these varied facets of science at Housey.

Other Christ's Hospital scientists and scholars

Sir Barnes Wallis and the Second World War

Barnes Wallis is well known for his WW2 invention of the 'bouncing bomb', which destroyed the Mohne, Sorpe, and Eder dams in Germany's industrial Ruhr region. This most ingenious device involved a horizontal spinning cylinder that bounced along the surface of the lake formed by the dam, so avoiding anti-torpedo nets. The flat parabolic hops were necessary to allow the mighty bomb to descend in the water next to the dam wall and explode at precisely the depth which would achieve the desired effect. It is difficult to convey how totally novel and unconventional was this scientific and engineering feat. The words of Keith Douglas, OB, poet and artist, who so well portrayed the intensity of his experiences in the Tank Corps during WW2, might be considered at this moment. This is the opening verse of his poem 'How To Kill':

Under the parabola of a ball,
a child turning into a man,
I looked into the air too long.
The ball fell in my hand, it sang
in the closed fist: *Open Open*
Behold a gift designed to kill.

Douglas, a tank commander, was tragically killed at the age of 24, three days after taking part in the Normandy landings. He is believed by many to be the most renowned poet of WW2. Although Douglas did not live long enough to write many poems, his account of the entire North African campaign tank campaign, *Alamein to Zen Zen*, makes compelling reading.

Barnes Wallis's bombing success was popularised by the film *The Dam Busters,* shown at Housey within a few days of its release in 1955 through his good offices. His other contributions to aviation engineering were equally important, especially the first use of geodesic structures for the construction of airships and bomber wings and fuselages This crucial achievement ensured British airships and his 'geodesic' aeroplanes were far superior to all others of the day (especially in general strength and ability to fly after suffering anti-aircraft hits), but regrettably few are aware of this. In the public eye, the Zeppelins are almost synonymous with airships, but the geodesic principle was never used in any Zeppelin craft. Barnes Wallis was also noted for his work on swing-wing aircraft and supersonic flight. A British Government Royal Commission handsomely rewarded Sir Barnes for his wartime innovations. In turn, he donated this bounty to CH, so providing bursaries for boys and girls in need and associated with RAF personnel who had served with honour.

Christ's Hospital and its Fellows of the Royal Society

Sir Barnes was elected FRS in 1945 and later noted that there were five other living Old Blue Fellows. He organised a memorable dinner for them in December 1961 at the Athenaeum Club in London, and all six attended. Others present were the Headmaster Mr Clarence Seaman (appointed 1955 – a non-scientist again); the school doctor, Dr Thomas L Scott (both Old Blues); and the head of science at CH, Dr Gordon Van Praagh.

Barnes Wallis explained that he wanted to celebrate the fact that, to his knowledge, no other school had ever had so many FRS old pupils at one time. The OB FRS guests were Professors Kenneth J Franklin (physiology, University of London); Phillip Hall (mathematics, University of Cambridge); Douglas G Northcott (mathematics, University of Sheffield); Sir Frank E Smith (chemistry, Imperial Chemical Industries); and Dr 'Hal' Louis H Gray (radiobiologist, British Empire Cancer Campaign Radiobiology Laboratory). There have been other Old Blue FRSs before and after 1961. After that year, Professors Christopher Zeeman (mathematics, University of Oxford), Margaret Gowing (history of British nuclear science, University of Oxford), Keith Bowen (materials engineering, University of Warwick), and Dr Philip R Evans (protein crystallography, Medical Research Council) were so honoured. The latter two, our current FRSs, have used X-rays to investigate metals and proteins respectively.

But how varied are Old Blues' fields of study! They range from the complete heavens (Ida Busbridge, whose work is outlined below) and the vast oceans (Parsons), down to the submicroscopic, ultra-precision, nano-engineering of Bowen and to individual (sizeable) molecules (Evans). Bowen has investigated the functioning and structure of metals down to a scale of 10 trillionths of a metre, working in both academia and industry. Unusually, he has recently retired to devote himself to clarinet playing, both orchestral and chamber, and its teaching. He has also almost finished a PhD on aspects of the history, repertoire, and accoustics of his instrument. Evans, now retired, has much increased our knowledge of the functioning of cells, especially how different substances enter and leave these building blocks of life in all living entities (except bacteria). Zeeman, too, was a pioneer in applying mathematics to very varied fields, some rarely associated with that subject. His researches began with topology (dealing in part with surfaces, and understanding how a teacup is like a doughnut) and catastrophe theory; these are unusual but well recognised facets of mathematics. Not content with those fields, he went on to increase understanding of committee behaviour, anorexia, evolution, and even dramatic art using mathematical insight. Old Blues so often think outside existing boxes. In addition, the eclectic Zeeman was best known outside the mathematical world for his popularising of mathematics: no paltry feat.

Before the six simultaneous Old Blue FRSs of 1961, many other Blues had previously achieved that honour. Professor Joshua Barnes (classics, University of Cambridge), Drs James Jurin (medicine and physics, Guy's Hospital), Caesar Hawkins (surgery, St George's Hospital), and William D Lang (geology, British Museum) were created FRS respectively in 1710, 1717, 1856, and 1929. James Jurin had an unusual career. He studied mathematics at the University of Cambridge, then became, in succession, firstly a Fellow of Trinity College, then a headmaster, and thirdly a medical student, again at Cambridge. On obtaining his MD degree, eleven years after his BA, he practised medicine and became a very successful physician, having Britain's first prime minister, Robert Walpole, among his patients. However, equally important interests for him were mathematics, inoculation against smallpox, and physics. He published many books and wrote passionately defending Newton's theory of calculus. He knew Newton well. Both were associated with Trinity College, and when Newton was president of the Royal Society, Jurin was its secretary. His defence of Newton's calculus, directed mainly against Leibnitz, was serious and often satirical. In contrast, his arguments for inoculation were based on firm, statistical observations, comparing mortality of those inoculated with those who had contracted smallpox. Jurin's physics included studies of capillary action, resulting in 'Jurin's Law' (the inverse relation between the height of a liquid's rise in a capillary tube and the capillary's diameter – a principle that I studied at CH, but the name of this law has long been forgotten). Jurin also instituted international cooperation in meteorological studies.

Hawkins was sergeant-surgeon to Queen Victoria (i.e. chief surgeon in the royal household) and very skilled in his profession. For many years, he was the only London surgeon capable of performing oophorectomy (removal of ovaries, with or without their adjacent structures). He wrote widely on many topics including his speciality, and also on rabies, tumours, colonic strictures, and snake bite. For all these achievements, he was twice honoured with the presidency of the Royal College of Surgeons and FRS.

Eleven more Old Blue Fellows should not be omitted: William Burnside (Professor of Mathematics, 1852–1927); Sir Alfred George Greenhill (Professor of Mathematics, 1847–1927); Sir Henry James Sumner Maine (Professor of Law, 1821–1888); Thomas Fanshaw Middleton (Bishop of Calcutta, 1769–1822); Vice-Admiral Thomas Abel Brimage Spratt (surveyor and hydrographer, 1811–1888); William Augustus Guy (physician and statistician, 1810–1885); Edmund Alexander Parkes (Professor of Hygiene, the 'founder of modern hygiene', 1819–1876); John Reeves (naturalist and botanist, 1774–1856); Sydney Samuel Hough (astronomer, 1870–1923); Sir Edward Thornton (diplomat, 1766–1852); and Ernest James William Barrington (Professor of Zoology, 1909–1985).

There were, too, other FRSs closely associated with CH who were not Old Blues. One was William Wales (astronomer, British government and CH). At the end of his working life, he was a teacher of mathematics (1776–95) in the Royal Mathematical School at CH in London. Other FRSs much concerned with development of the RMS in its early years (funded principally by an Old Blue, Richard Aldworth, not by the British government) were Samuel Pepys, John Flamsteed (Astronomer-Royal), Robert Hooke (natural philosopher, but in modern parlance principally a physicist), Sir Isaac Newton, and Sir Christopher Wren, all of whom served as governors. Wren was a member of the Mathematical Committee as well as a governor.

Christ's Hospital and medicine

The contributions of Old Blues to medicine have been as varied as the subject itself, but with an emphasis on surgical innovations. The work of several (Jurin, Hawkins, and Gillon) is described elsewhere in this chapter, but others have proved equally ground-breaking. Baron Berkeley Moynihan (1865–1936) started his medical career in the army, ending as a Major-General in 1918 at the end of WW1. He then worked in Leeds, where he finally became professor of surgery. When he first introduced rubber gloves and white coats to be worn during surgical procedures, he was roundly ridiculed, until the great advantages of these simple antiseptic precautions were widely understood. His fame and knowledge of abdominal surgery was appreciated throughout the world, and surgeons from many countries came to work with him. He, too, was an Old Blue president of the Royal College of Surgeons.

Baron Russell Brock (1903–80) also held this presidency as a chest and heart surgeon. He pioneered several important life-saving procedures, concerning malformed heart and lungs (in the tetralogy of Fallot) and heart valves partially destroyed as a result of rheumatic fever infections, more commonly encountered in his days than now. His achievements were widely recognised and resulted in his being awarded many medals and five honorary doctorates.

Professor Norman Gutkelch's (1915–2016) pioneering surgery earned him the title of 'father of British paediatric neurosurgery', for he was the first person to hold any post in this field. His school career shows CH's understanding that career choices can change and appropriate funding could then be provided. After starting classical studies, Gutkelch wished to study medicine. So, in his words,

> 'I was promised that if I obtained a scholarship to Oxford or Cambridge (and remained unmarried!), Christ's Hospital would give me financial support to doctoral level. In due course, I won a scholarship in Classics to Balliol College, Oxford, with permission to study medicine.'

He practised in the north of England for many years, where shaking babies was a common practice, without any associated stigma, and parents would frankly admit this had been done. However, Gutkelch realised that such shaking could produce bleeding in a baby's brain; that blood might collect inside the brain's covering with very serious results. He called this the 'shaken baby syndrome' and was later horrified when the term was misused, resulting in imprisonment of parents whose baby might in fact have suffered from other medical problems. As a result, he spent the last few decades of his long life reviewing appropriate medical records, working to exonerate those who had been wrongly convicted of harming babies by shaking them.

Unfortunately, in the USA, where he lived after retirement, this happened far too often.

Architecture

Although some regard architecture as an aspect of engineering rather than a science, others consider it principally an art form. Professor Andrew Saint, Old Blue and architect, fully appreciates and writes perceptively on both extreme opinions. He has held chairs at the Universities of Cambridge and London, and his well-received books (written on his profession and its history, with 'verve and assurance') deal with these polar opposite conceptions of architecture. His literary discernment (so typical of many Old Blue scientists) is expressed in writings on architecture's fine art and 'anthropology', with reference to Charles Dickens' and others' appreciation of the subject. At the other boundary, Saint's perception of the too often unappreciated contributions of engineers to the most innovative architecture reveals to his fellow architects that they, together with engineers, are members of the same wide brotherhood. The highest accolade for British engineers is the Fellowship of the Royal Academy of Engineering (FREng); two Old Blues have attained this distinction: Barnes Wallis and Keith Bowen.

Old Blue educationalists

Many other Old Blues have excelled in both scientific and non-scientific fields, and there is too little space available here to recount most of these scientists' achievements which justify the telling. So, a selection is inevitable. One event of which CH can be most proud was when there were five Old Blue heads of colleges at Oxford University in 1996. This feat has also almost certainly never been equalled by any other school. These heads of houses were Drs John Davis (All Souls' College), Elizabeth Llewellyn-Smith (St Hilda's College), Alan

Ryan (New College), Christopher Zeeman (Hertford College), and Baroness Ruth Deech (St Anne's College). At the same time, another Old Blue, Sir John Daniel, was the Vice-Chancellor of the Open University, so responsible for far more students than the total of all those in the five Oxford Colleges just mentioned. Daniel's career continued in Canada and France. Both countries (and the UK, too) recognised his merits with comparable honours.

Other distinguished OBs who devoted themselves to science deserve consideration, although sufficient space for them all is unavailable in this volume. Such notice could illustrate interesting common characteristics showing CH's influences can be detected as a sort of *sui generis* in science, since the heuristic method in its pure form requires independent thought rather than rote learning. Perhaps this reality is reflected in so many distinguished Old Blue scientists seeking niche fields of study and rarely following the main highways of their disciplines. Radiobiology has already been mentioned and is an excellent illustration, though Hal was also much motivated by a desire to help humankind.

Housey and metallurgy

In the last few decades, four other Old Blues have been very distinguished scholars in another 'niche' subject, metallurgy, all four studying at Oxford. They are Sir John Daniel and Professors William Pearson, Keith Bowen, and David Taplin. Daniel's doctorate was from the University of Paris, and the latter three each obtained a DPhil (Oxon). All were taught and inspired to become metallurgists by Dr Van Praagh, and taught by the equally legendary Professor Wm Hume-Rothery FRS at Oxford, with William Pearson, an Engineering Grecian, the first of the four to become a metallurgist. This was after Pearson had been Senior Grecian and gaining a DFC, serving with distinction as a pilot with the RAF during WW2. Pearson's eminent career was then pursued in Canada after Oxford, and in 1967 he produced his identification system for alloys and intermetallic structure types. Today, over 50 years later, it remains in wide use. Professor Taplin's research career was also mainly pursued in Canada, including 32 years (1985–2017) as CEO/Treasurer of *The International Congress on Fracture* (ICF) – the premier world society in the discipline of Structural Integrity and Fracture Mechanics (Taplin now serving as ICF President Emeritus), especially organising international fracture conferences quadrennially at major research universities around the globe. There were at least three other Old Blue metallurgists who studied at Oxford through the inspiration of Van Praagh. One, St John Sandringham, then followed a totally non-metallurgical calling. After completing a BA in metallurgy at Oxford, he became a theatre manager in Derby, followed by work at the National Theatre and beyond.

Christ's Hospital's contributions to science in Australia

Although much emphasis has been given to science and engineering of the 20th century, when the influence of the heuristic method was most evident, there is an earlier example of a most important Old Blue niche scientist. This was William J Farrer (1845–1906), whose varied education included no formal training in agriculture. He won medals at CH and a scholarship at Cambridge, all for mathematics. After his degree, he started medical studies, which he never completed due to ill health. So, in 1870, he sought a better climate in Australia. There, he was first a private tutor, later qualifying as a surveyor; he worked for the government for 11 years. After marrying and buying a smallholding (suitable for wheat growing, but too small to provide a living), he noticed on his work-associated travels the near total failure of wheat growing. This was due to drought and the fungal disease wheat rust. Paradoxically, rust infection is worsened by humidity during the wheat's ripening period. It is likely Farrer had read Charles Darwin's book, *The Variation of Animals and Plants under Domestication*, for Farrer was distantly related to Darwin. Farrer proposed that selective breeding of wheat could overcome the severe problems that were preventing its successful commercial production in Australia. Experts ridiculed him. Undeterred, he started experimental cross-breeding on his smallholding, under difficult circumstances; for without proper tools, he had to use his wife's hairpins to transfer pollen. But after 12 years, he produced unique strains which overcame the two overwhelming problems mentioned above. Wheat growing then became a most profitable and much practised commercial venture in Australia.

Farrer was extensively honoured in his lifetime and afterwards. He is the only Old Blue whose portrait adorned both a banknote ($2) and a postage stamp. (Earnest Giles, an author and explorer, was similarly honoured, with his portrait on another Australian stamp.) Other Old Blues contributed much to Australia and deserve a mention. The first was a 'gentleman convict', John Grant, who arrived in 1804 bringing with him the continent's first harpsichord. (If the exploits of unworthy Old Blues are ever fully described, Grant will be joined by Sir Cyril Burt (1983–1971), an eminent psychologist, believed to have falsified data which he then published.) John S Roe was a member of the RMS and later a Royal Navy officer. For 40 years, he was the Surveyor General of Western Australia who laid out the cities of Perth and Freemantle, and probably knew Farrer. He is known as 'the father of inland exploration' and is commemorated by having a poison, an orchid, and various geographical sites named after him.

Two other former RMS Old Blues made their name in their adopted country 'Down Under'. They are Earnest Giles (1835–97), the first European to climb Ayers Rock/Uluru, and his second in command on several expeditions, William Tietkens (1845–1933). They used horses as pack animals and, after their loads were consumed, slaughtered the horses for food, smoking some of the meat as later provisions. Giles remarked that these victuals were disgusting, and he could only stomach them as the food had been so bad at school!

Another niche subject for Old Blues – medical ethics

Yet another former niche subject, which in the last few decades has been transformed into a much-discussed topic beloved of all types of media, is medical ethics. Two Old Blues have been pre-eminent in this field in very different ways: Professor Raanan Gillon, and Baroness Ruth Deech. Raanan Gillon became a medical doctor, but even as a student was concerned with medicine's ethical aspects, devoting himself to making a career in that field and along the way obtaining a degree in philosophy. (At CH, he most, most unusually had added A-level English to his scientific studies, a tribute to Housey's curricular flexibility in 1959.) For many years, he had a Chair at the University of London, edited the pre-eminent journal in his field, and wrote influential books and many articles. Gillon's influence on the broad field of medicine was recognised in mid-2019 by his election as President of the British Medical Association. Hertford Old Blue Ruth Deech, however, approached medical ethics along a different path – as a lawyer. But she has always been involved in education, mainly as Fellow and Principal of St Anne's College. After retiring from Oxford, she continued serving education in many ways, including an appointment as the first ombudsperson for students at all UK universities, a trustee of the Rhodes Trust for ten years, and then a founding trustee of the Mandela Rhodes Foundation. Deech also held a chair at Gresham's College, London. Other public offices she held included a governorship at the

BBC; and, most importantly of all, she chaired the UK Human Fertilisation and Embryology Authority for eight years. During this time, she oversaw the application of statutory and medical ethical standards to new developments in the treatment of infertility and the use of stem cells to develop treatments of serious diseases.

The evolution of Old Blues' tertiary science studies

Three overwhelming changes affected CH's science pupils after 1900. The first was in 1902 with the removal of the boys' school from Newgate Street in the City of London to Horsham, where it occupied a brand new, purpose-built campus, including large, novel, well equipped science laboratories with competent teaching and supporting staff who used the heuristic method. CH's move from London's Newgate Street to Horsham, and subsequently of the girls from Hertford to Horsham, are well documented elsewhere. The other revolutionary transformation affected all of Britain: it was the introduction, soon after WW2, of direct payment by local education authorities of all university tuition fees, together with an adequate maintenance grant. These payments were not loans; so any pupil who obtained a place in an institution of higher learning could then take up that place and be supported for the entire course, with no further financial obligations. Before this time, all CH science pupils were streamed; only the upper stream finally became Grecians. The criterion for this selection was a belief that they were capable of obtaining scholarships for university studies, most usually at Oxbridge. To enter Oxbridge then, it was essential to have studied either Latin, Greek or Hebrew; this requirement was abolished only in 1960.

One Old Blue, who later became Baron Michael Stewart, was for a time Secretary of Education in Harold Wilson's first government. Earlier, he had been Shadow Minister of

Education for four years. While a minister, he partially succeeded in improving state secondary education by following the assertion in the Labour Party's election manifesto to provide 'grammar school education for all'. Baron Stewart later was Foreign Secretary for almost four years, thus holding the highest political offices of any Old Blue. It is likely his aims as Education Secretary were inspired by his CH education, which resulted in a scholarship to Oxford University. When responsible for the nation's education, he worked to 'enable others [in state schools] to enjoy the same [educational] advantage'.

In contrast to those believed to have Grecian potential, pupils in the lower stream at Housey never followed classical studies; so, effectively, they could not become undergraduates at Oxbridge. Before the introduction of state financial support for tertiary education, CH pupils who had aspirations for a university education could only follow further studies if they gained scholarships. Their families' incomes were otherwise too low. Pupils thought unable to win scholarships were forced to leave school at age 16 or soon after, and were guided towards occupations not involving university studies.

Christ's Hospital is rightly proud of all those successful Old Blue scientists mentioned here. However, it can be suggested that some of them were short-changed by CH's strict rules, which decided the age at which boys had to leave school. Although Barnes Wallis did well in mathematics and some other subjects, he had never studied classics and was not believed to be capable of winning a university scholarship. So, he was forced to leave CH aged 16, and became an engineering apprentice. Perhaps CH should not have been so inflexible then. Mr Browne recognised his ability and appealed to the headmaster (Dr Upcott, a classicist) to allow Barnes Wallis to remain at Housey as its first science Grecian, and prepare for (non-Oxbridge) university studies. Dr Upcott refused. In those days, only classicist and mathematical pupils could become Grecians.

However, later, Dr Upcott relented; Grecians' subjects were extended to include science and engineering. The norm was that those who showed their academic talents early were placed in the school's upper stream, learned a classical language, became Grecians, and entered Oxbridge with scholarships. Hal Gray and Michael Stewart followed this path. But occasionally in the humanities, too, there was an inflexibility, somewhat similar to that which determined Barnes Wallis's early post-CH career. Keith Douglas passionately wished to study English at Oxford, and finally did so. However, at CH he could not be an English Grecian and had to specialise in history. That decision was made by the headmaster, Mr Henry Oswald Lael Flecker (appointed in 1930 - also a classicist). So, Keith Douglas had no choice and succeeded in history studies, gaining a scholarship at Oxford, and always acknowledging how much he owed to his history teacher, Mr David Roberts.

Even if a pupil were educated in the lower stream without any classical studies, efforts were made to ensure she or he continued with non-Oxbridge university studies, if this were thought appropriate. Such an example was Timothy Parsons. It seems highly likely, as he readily admits in his autobiography, that his placing in the lower stream was due to his atrocious spelling at every age. To the credit of CH, an early erroneous deduction that a pupil was unable to win a university scholarship could be corrected later – though, as for Barnes Wallis, this was sometimes not true. In subsequent years, the guidance for those who wished to continue with science studies became more flexible.

Housey women and science

Armstrong's desire for all to study some science had positive effects on teaching of Housey's girls in the 20th century. Resulting benefits include CH Hertford's laboratories being satisfactorily equipped. Also, Hertford's prospectus in the

1970s stated, 'The importance of chemistry in modern society, and therefore as a subject for study as part of a general education, cannot be over emphasised.' This illustrates Armstrong's continuing influence for CH's girls, as do the careers of two distinguished Hertford scientific alumnae.

Of the women OB scientists, the most prominent and successful was Professor Margaret Gowing, née Elliott (1921–96). After leaving CH, she studied history at the LSE, winning several prizes. Professor Margaret Gowing devoted important researches to yet another niche subject – the history of atomic energy in Britain during and after WW2. This especially concerned nuclear weapons development and its associated science. Her final post was as first incumbent of a chair at Oxford, in the history of science, which she took up in 1972. This appointment resulted from an unusual variety of previous activities, including 14 years working as a historian in the Cabinet Office and then becoming archivist of the UK Atomic Energy Authority, before entering academia with a readership at the University of Kent. She is the only woman to have been elected to Fellowships of both the British Academy and the Royal Society. Her public service also included trusteeships of the National Portrait Gallery, the Imperial War and Science Museums. Notably, her magisterial studies went far beyond recording details of scientific history. She enlarged the scope of the history of science, which until then had been studied mainly in parallel with the philosophy of science, by demonstrating that such history should favour 'social, economic and political perspectives, as against the examination of scientific practice', in the words of Roy MacLeod, a leading specialist on the history and sociology of science and knowledge. Robert Fox, Professor Gowing's successor at Oxford, well sums up aspects of her work, writing that she was a 'peerless chronicler and analyst of a crucial facet of the war effort and of Britain's subsequent struggles to maintain great power status, but also as a leading commentator on the relations between science and government'.

Another ground-breaking woman scientist produced by Housey was Dr Ida W Busbridge, a mathematician at the University of Oxford. Busbridge was a pioneering academic, being the first woman to be awarded a mathematical fellowship at Oxford (1946), to receive a DSc in mathematics at Oxford (1962), and to be the President of the Mathematical Association (1964). Her first degree was obtained at the University of London, where she was the best student in mathematics of her year (1929) in that large university. Her chosen research field then became integral equations and radiative transfer, which she applied to astronomy. For Dr Busbridge, service to others was the basis of her career. During WW2, she volunteered for an exceedingly heavy teaching load, being aware of the great lack of mathematics teachers, since a very large proportion of them were engaged in the war effort. She was also noted for her very great efforts to aid her tutorial pupils of both genders, in many matters: mathematical, personal, and other.

Science for all at Housey?

In spite of this chapter's paean of praise for the accomplishments of Old Blue scientists and engineers, some Old Blues feel they have not been served well by science studies at Housey. Those who specialised in the humanities were compelled by the CH curriculum (certainly in the years up to 1970) to stop all science study when boys and girls were aged about 14. One such Old Blue from that era, who later studied anthropology and history at Cambridge, has written, 'My school reports for my first two years, 1952–4, includes something called "physics". (I seem to remember a Bunsen burner and tadpoles.) … but after that nothing for the remaining six. I have always considered myself to be scientifically illiterate due to Housey's then focus on early specialisation.'

What Blues retain from Housey

Old Blues almost all have much affection for Housey and are most grateful for what they received there. This gratitude may have two origins: the ethos of the school, and the attention these scientists paid to the Leaving Charge in the poignant leaving service. Blues about to leave Housey are all enjoined, '*never to forget the great benefits that you have received in this place and… to do all that you can to enable others to enjoy the same advantage.*'

An education at Christ's Hospital has provided Blues with far more than academic knowledge.

Further reading

1. *The Christ's Hospital Book*, by 'A Committee of Old Blues,' Hamish Hamilton, London, 1953
2. *The Sea and the Sky: The History of the Royal Mathematical School of Christ's Hospital*, Clifford Jones, CH Heritage Series, Horsham, 2016
3. *Henry Edward Armstrong: Educational Work,* Charles E. Browne, Christ's Hospital, Horsham, 1968
4. *Charles E. Browne: An appreciation of his work for the Reform of Education at Christ's Hospital,* E. H. Rudd, Christ's Hospital, Horsham, 1968
5. *Sir Barnes Wallis and the RAF Foundationers' Trust, 1951–2003,* David Miller, Christ's Hospital Club, Horsham, 2003
6. *Louis Harold Gray, FRS: A Founding Father of Radiobiology,* S Wynchank, Springer Int Press, Berlin, London & New York, 2017
7. *Keith Douglas: Genius Overlooked,* Morgan Merrington, Cecil Woolf, London, 2016
8. *The Sea's Enthrall,* Timothy R Parsons, Trafford Publishing, Vancouver, Canada, 2004

9. *Margaret Gowing: An Appreciation,* Lord Bullock, in *Science, Politics and the Public Good; Essays in Honour of Margaret Gowing*, Ed Nicolaas A Rupke, Macmillan, London, 1988
10. *Science, Engineering and Art as well: Why it is hard to be a good teacher of science at any level,* The 2019 Oppenheimer Lecture, HR Quinn, March 2019. https://www.youtube.com/watch?v=eAj13hqb0Hs
11. *Response to challenge: William Farrer and the Making of Wheats,* The Farrer Memorial Oration 1970, LT Evans, J Austr Inst Agric Sci, pp 3–13, 1980
12. *Strength, Fracture & Complexity*, Proceeding of a *Festschrift* in Honour of Professor David Taplin, Ashok Saxena, 2018 Volume 11, pp 73–278
13. *Wikipedia articles* (as of August 2019) whose titles are those of persons named in this chapter.

Acknowledgements

I am greatly indebted to Roger Wickins for much valuable information concerning Australian Old Blues, resulting from his extensive researches.

Dr Sinclair Wynchank, MA, DPhil, CPhys, CEng, MB ChB, MD, FInstP

Born 1938; 1948–57 CH; 1957–63, Christ Church, University of Oxford; 1964–69, Columbia University; 1969–72, City University of New York; 1972–81, University of Cape Town (UCT); 1981–83, University of Bordeaux; 1983–2013, UCT & Medical Research Council; 1998–2004, Secretary-General, African Association of Nuclear Medicine.

Note: *The editors are grateful to the Estate of Edmund Blunden, and David Higham Associates, for kind permission to use lines from the poem* 'Unteachable' *by Old Blue Edmund Blunden; also to Faber & Faber Ltd for the use of lines from* 'How To Kill' *by Old Blue Keith Douglas.*

V

The World in a Grain of Sand

Introduction

To see a World in a grain of sand
And a Heaven in a wild flower,
Hold Infinity in the palm of your hand,
And Eternity in an hour.

Opening of 'Auguries of Innocence' by William Blake, from *Selected Poems: William Blake* (Penguin, London 1996 reprint), page 171, this poem originally written between 1801 and 1803.

We shall not cease from exploration
And the end of all our exploring
Will be to arrive where we started
And know the place for the first time.
Through the unknown, remembered gate
When the last of earth left to discover
Is that which was the beginning;
At the source of the longest river
The voice of the hidden waterfall
And the children in the apple-tree...

(Extract from T. S. Eliot's 'Little Gidding', *The Four Quartets. Collected Poems 1909–1962* (London: Faber & Faber, 1963), p 222, used with permission.)

When I was Professor of Engineering at Trinity College Dublin, these eternal poems by Blake and Eliot opened my undergraduate Materials and Microscopy lectures – exploring the changeless unity between poetry and science. This chapter focuses on what has changed at Christ's Hospital, especially since the quatercentenary in 1952; and what is changing and might change at Christ's Hospital as the quincentenary approaches in 2052.

What has changed since 1952?

This opening question is very ambitious, but it is helpful to make a stab at referencing the sweeping changes since 1952. Consider, for example, Francis Crick and others unraveling the origins of life through the decoding of DNA in Cambridge in 1953, and the subsequent 21st century genome projects; physicists and cosmologists such as Stephen Hawking advancing and popularising our understanding of the origins of the universe, space and time – and of the origins and structure of matter by such as Peter Higgs; Tim Berners-Lee bringing us the internet in 1989, jointly winning the inaugural engineering 'Nobel Prize' – the Queen Elizabeth II Prize of the Royal Academy of Engineering in 2015; the modelling and predicting of anthropogenic climate change by scientists such as Tom Wigley; Katie Bouman and her team at CalTech imaging a black hole in 2019; in cancer cures, satellite technology, radiobiology, new materials, the digital revolution, quantum chromodynamics, laser physics, microbiology, artificial intelligence… the list goes on.

Meanwhile, there have been great shifts in the social and political fabric of global society: the end of the Cold War; the break-up of the Soviet Union; the rise of China; Sputnik I in 1957, the Apollo 11 moon landing in 1969 and the great adventure of space exploration; the end of Apartheid in South Africa and the presidency of Nelson Mandela; the Martin Luther King-led civil rights movement resulting eventually in an Afro-American US president; the emancipation of women through those such as Ruth Bader Ginsburg, evidenced by the

UK's having now had two women prime ministers, both from modest beginnings and state grammar-school educated in the sciences (chemistry/geography) rather than at public schools in classics/philosophy – and at Oxford (extraordinarily, ten of the thirteen prime ministers since WWII were educated at Oxford – some 50% at independent/public schools).

And what has changed in education since 1952?

For many years, the seven original 'public' schools (Eton, Harrow, Winchester, Charterhouse, Shrewsbury, Rugby, Westminster – defined by *The Public Schools Act* of 1868) have drawn their pupils from the aristocracy and upper-middle classes. However, in 1950, Christ's Hospital stood with the best of these public (private) 'independent' schools in Oxbridge entrance, science, philosophy, rugby, cricket, and debating, as indeed had CH for centuries. In 1950, Christ's Hospital was particularly strong in science and engineering as a result of the innovations in heuristic teaching by discovery created in the 19th century by Henry Armstrong and extensively practised at Horsham since 1902 – and through the social and educational legacy of Barnes Wallis. Independent schools are generally notorious for their untoward emphasis on a classical (Greek/Latin) education and neglecting education in science and engineering, so that CH was unusual in this regard.

These seven ancient public schools generally had similar charitable origins to those of Christ's Hospital. Eton (where George Orwell was a pupil) was founded in 1441 by Henry VI, after the hundred years war with France, as a charity school to provide free education to 70 poor boys who would then go on to King's College, Cambridge – also founded by Henry VI – integrating school education innovatively with university education in a joint 15th-century foundation. An *amicabilis concordia* between Eton College, Winchester College, King's College, Cambridge, and New College, Oxford, was signed on July 1, 1444.

Eton announced plans in 2014 to increase the number of pupils receiving financial assistance from the school's endowments – presently standing at around 25% – with ongoing since 1441 the charter commitment to there being 70 pupils educated free of charge, and with the intention that the number of pupils receiving charitable assistance from the foundation will continue to increase. Eton also co-sponsors a state sixth-form college founded in 2012 (London Academy of Excellence) – and, as well, Eton sponsors a new purpose-built (2014) co-educational state boarding and day school (Holyport College) in Berkshire that provides free education for around 500 pupils.

The oldest independent schools in the UK are probably King's School Canterbury (said to be the oldest charity in the UK, with Somerset Maughan as an alumnus) founded in 597 by St Augustine, and St Peter's York (with Guy Fawkes an alumnus) which was founded by St Paulinus in 627 as first Master. St John of Beverley became Master in 705, and a renowned library was established at the school around this time by Egbert, the Archbishop of York. The pupils studied Latin, grammar, rhetoric, time-reckoning, logic, astronomy, geometry, arithmetic, and natural history, as part of a varied classical curriculum. St Peter's presents itself today as 'a school like no other' – as does CH – providing day and boarding education for around 560 boys and girls aged 13–18 years, with scholarships for poorer children covering up to 100% of fees.

Winchester College, one of the oldest public schools, was founded in 1382 by William Wykeham, Chancellor to Edward III. The first 70 poor scholars entered the school in 1394. In 1540, Henry VIII ordered the dissolution of the monasteries in England, including that of the powerful abbots of Westminster; however, Henry VIII ensured the associated school's survival by royal charter. Thus, the Royal College of St. Peter (Westminster) carried on with 40 'King's Scholars' financed from the royal purse. Westminster School (where

Christopher Wren was a pupil), with early origins in the 11th century, generally now dates its (re-)foundation to 1560 by Elizabeth I.

Following a petition from the townspeople of Shrewsbury for a free grammar school, Shrewsbury School (where Charles Darwin was a pupil) was founded by charter in 1552 of Edward VI. Harrow (where Winston Churchill was a pupil) and Rugby (where Lewis Carroll was a pupil) were also both founded as free grammar schools in the reign of Elizabeth I. Charterhouse (where Robert Graves was a pupil) was founded as a charity school in a former Carthusian monastery in London in 1611, in the reign of James I; then, in 1872 during the reign of Queen Victoria, Charterhouse (viewed by some as a sister school to CH) moved to Surrey and is now co-educational, with a proportion of pupils still admitted on merit, irrespective of means. Dulwich was founded in 1619 by Edward Alleyn with the purpose of educating 12 poor scholars as the foundation of 'God's Gift'.

It seems appropriate to note that Isaac Newton attended King's Free Grammar School, Grantham, with origins back to 1328 in the reign of Edward III – re-established in 1528 in the reign of Henry VIII; that William Shakespeare attended King Edward VI Free Grammar School, Stratford-upon-Avon, with origins of the school back to 1295 in the reign of Edward I – re-established by Royal Charter in 1553 by Edward VI.

As David Arnold discusses in some detail in Chapter II, since the 1950s there have been many changes in UK secondary education with the closing of many of the ancient state grammar schools. The loss of high-performing state grammar schools – in moves towards a more equal, comprehensive education system – diminished the top quality of state secondary education. The first Secretary of State for Education and Science 1964–5, responsible for leading the reform of secondary education and the conversion of the Colleges of Advanced Technology, CATs, to universities (such as Birmingham CAT to Aston University in 1966), was the Old Blue, Michael Stewart, MP, later Baron Stewart of Fulham. From my own perspective, Michael Stewart should have turned the CATs into premier technological institutes, as in India and the famed Indian Institutes of Technology (IITs); as in the USA like MIT and Georgia Tech; and as in Singapore. And, instead of integrating just the diverse state secondary schools into comprehensives, Michael Stewart should have also integrated the whole divisive calabash of public, independent, grammar, technical, and secondary modern schools. The socially reforming Attlee-Wilson governments, in which Michael Stewart played such an influential role, didn't in their zeal get everything right by a long chalk.

Recently, the introduction and evolution of state sixth-form colleges, especially for disadvantaged children in London (Brampton Manor Academy and Harris Westminster), is enhancing the overall performance of the state sector promisingly. Brampton Manor Academy was founded in 2011, with the sixth-form centre opening in East London in 2012. Harris Westminster Sixth Form (known as HWSF) is a selective mixed sixth-form college founded in 2013 in central London, established in association with Westminster School with the goal of increasing the rate of entry to top universities among students from areas of socio-economic deprivation.

The number of pupil places gained each year by secondary schools to Oxbridge is probably now an outmoded yardstick. However, in 2018 the number of Oxbridge offers accomplished by the five top UK schools by this measure of performance are: Eton (independent) 68; Brampton Manor Academy (State) 41; Harris Westminster (State) 37; Dulwich (independent) 26; Charterhouse (independent) 24. This is in the context that at Harris Westminster a third of the pupils qualify for pupil premium state support

Remarkably, the university sector in the UK has developed extraordinarily well since Christ's Hospital's quatercentenary, with only twenty universities in 1952 as against 136 much bigger, better universities in 2019. Nowadays, almost all Blues attend university on leaving Christ's Hospital (more than 95%), whereas the proportion of Blues who went on to university on leaving in 1952 was fewer than 20%. The overall quality of the UK university sector has improved significantly since the quatercentenary, based on the evidence of world rankings and scholarship/research metrics.

Nanyang Technological University (NTU), Singapore, has led new creative research in education in science, technology, engineering, entrepreneurship, materials & mathematics (STEEMM). NTU (where I was a Professor of Sustainable Manufacturing 1997–1999) was ranked during 2012–2016 as the top university in the world for research citations in artificial intelligence; NTU has embraced digital technologies for better learning and living as part of its Smart Campus vision. NTU has partnerships with many of the world's leading technology companies in areas of societal importance and impact that include artificial intelligence, data science, robotics, smart transportation, computing, personalised medicine, healthcare, and clean energy. These developments have run alongside the evolution of the Silicon Valley giants on the North American Pacific Coast (Apple, Google, Dreamworks, Intel, Microsoft, Facebook, Amazon, Tesla, Oracle, Electronic Arts, Salesforce, Disney – for example) around Los Angeles, San Francisco, Seattle, and Vancouver, and in ever-burgeoning Singapore.

Today, Blues are no longer hot-housed for Oxbridge as in 1952 at the quatercentenary. Nowadays, instead, Blues proceed to the full range of the 136 UK universities directly after A-levels – or the International Baccalaureate – as well as to many top overseas universities. Christ's Hospital has become a co-educational, multicultural, international school, and there are Blues today who are members of all the main belief systems – housed and taught within an Anglican foundation and heritage.

Christ's Hospital has changed in many ways since 1952, including constitutionally (structurally/administratively) – in, for example, unifying the school itself with the separate Charitable Foundation under a streamlined Council, and substantially amending the admissions/discharge policies. The school is now 50/50 co-educational on one site, with a much greater diversity of Blues in 2019, as well as a new, reforming headteacher and a new Old Blue Treasurer/Chair of Council committed to the original mission and charitable ethos, alert to and engaged with the Old Blue community, ready to harness and adapt to the foreshadowed, extraordinary technological and sociological challenges ahead. Are the recent constitutional developments working? And what future progressive changes might be envisaged for the renaissance of the charitable mission for the common good in the context of the Royal Charter?

Is there now a potential convergence/integration in public/private support of world-class school education in the UK? And might this enhance social mobility, diversity, fairness and equality of opportunity for the common good, with CH as a new model for all independent schools – as once suggested by Percy Lyon, a former headmaster of Rugby School?

A Christ's Hospital Royal School of Engineering?

In 1986, when I was Professor of Engineering at Trinity College Dublin, I applied for the headship of Christ's Hospital, entering discussions with the then Clerk, Old Blue Michael Pearey. I had plans at that time to build on the ideas of Armstrong and Wallis and establish Christ's Hospital as a world-class school in engineering and entrepreneurship. These ideas have even greater currency today, and it is hoped that this book may at a more auspicious time help in some small way towards this vision. As it happened in 1986, however, Richard Poulton won the appointment, proving to be an excellent headteacher, one presiding over the momentous, ground-breaking merger of the Hertford and Horsham schools and full 50/50 male/female balance within Christ's Hospital. Is it, though, now time in 2020 to create a new 21st century collaboration with the Royal Academy of Engineering and the Royal Society, establishing a Royal School of Engineering building on the inspiration of Barnes Wallis and the 1673 Royal School of Mathematics celebrated in the great painting by Antonio Verrio?

How, then, should Christ's Hospital accurately measure and then improve its contribution in the context of the *sui generis* mission and charitable ethos?

Universities partly measure their performance by how many Nobel Laureates they produce (Harvard 158; Cambridge 118; Oxford 69; Berlin 55; Paris 50; UC London 33; Manchester 25). Certainly, the performance of alumni in their later careers is a widely embraced measure of success. Universities also tend to specialise and find competitive niches so that a new university might aim to become world-leading in a particular realm (Bournemouth in Computer Animation and Special Effects; Plymouth in Marine Sciences; Falmouth in Graphic Design). What performance outcomes might be the specialty of Christ's Hospital? Should Christ's Hospital specialise to enhance the fulfilment of its mission? From 1673, Charles II successfully established within CH the Royal Mathematical School specialising in mathematics, navigational science, and engineering. From 1902, CH specialised in science and engineering successfully through the heuristics approach of Henry Armstrong. Christ's Hospital must look to its past accomplishments and create a new, imaginative strategy within the framework of its charitable mission. Possibly for a new Royal Science, Technology, Engineering, Entrepreneurship, Materials & Mathematics School (STEEMM)?

Christ's Hospital: Tradition with Vision seeks to delve into some of the great questions for humanity for the 21st century, in the context of the fourth technological revolution. Arguably the greatest engineering feat of the 20th century was initiated by USA President John Kennedy through NASA's 1969 landing of Neil Armstrong on the moon – such that humanity could fully, visually, grasp that we live on a rare speck of a blue ocean-encompassed four-billion-year-old planet in a vast, expanding fourteen-billion-year-old universe. The greatest technological feat of the 21st century could be to effectively combat anthropogenic climate change. Could all the feats of humanity pale before this feat?

Antonio Verrio's great painting celebrating this foundation has watched over Blues for three centuries in the dining halls of London and Horsham. This iconic painting still challenges us to look forward to developments yet to come, but to remain firmly rooted, too, in the ethos and charitable vision of those that have inspired the school's past.

David Taplin, Autumn 2019, Vancouver, BC

VI

Tradition with Vision

A sequence of poems written
in celebration of Christ's Hospital

Lizzie Ballagher

lizzieballagherpoetry@gmail.com

CONTENTS

A Few Words on Words

My astonishment when first invited to write this sequence of poems was only equalled by the doubts that followed: how to write such a collection? How approach the task? Yet the thought of writing about Christ's Hospital was intriguing; and in no time I'd recalled a moment from the Hertford art school that seemed symbolic of others; hence the poem that follows – one of the few written in my own voice.

I started with the idea that I might call the collection *Voices from the Lime Trees*: those bright trees with heart-shaped leaves have reminded me all my life both of the square at Hertford and, at least until the late 1980s, of the avenue at Horsham. Not all the voices were from those lime trees, however, which in any case were felled by the great storm of 1987. I needed to think again.

Gradually, once I had formally appealed for Old Blues' and Blues' stories to inspire me, they flooded in – the hopeful, the worried, the cheerful, the funny, the indignant, the affectionate, the cheeky, the sporty, the nostalgic...so many different voices and experiences. As well, I turned to the CH Museum and the London City Museum for more ideas, more stories. That's when a tide of history spanning nearly 500 years rose up to meet me.

These poems have been written with the simple hope that they will inspire, entertain, and amuse you; that you will enjoy them; and that they will be a fitting acknowledgement and celebration of a unique and ancient school.

Lizzie Ballagher
Summer 2019
https://www.lizzieballagherpoetry.wordpress.com/

Beginnings and Endings: at the Hertford Art School, *1964*

threads tangled
ravelled in twists and Gordian knots
unfollowable
unworkable
            when wool's line snags
            when soft twine snaps

so tell me
    how   to find   the beginning or the end
                        that single strand—
                        just one I can tease out—

    how   to pin it down
                        go back and trace
                        unlace the rhyme
                        and so to separate, undo

    how   to find   the grace:
                        the fibre I can follow through
                                untangling the gold and blue
    to try to make some sense
    of what I trust is true:

a thread unbroken in four centuries
                                        and more
but slowly, slowly running out, to be unspooled

and when all's untied, unknotted
I may then roll it in a ball—

to weave the lines of poetry
even with a ramshackle shuttle
on an ageing loom

the way Miss Keppel-Barrett taught me

Learning

&

Loving-kindness

Devon Boy: The Reader, ***1780***

As a boy, Coleridge was famed for being what others called helluo librorum*: a voracious reader.*

In Crediton my aunt,
beloved̀ of my father, and by me,
kept shop.

It was a place of refuge.
Light gleamed on gilt-edged books
in her shining window,

and when I could I snatched them up
crept to a corner
and lost myself

in their stories of woe and wonder:
Arabian Nights, fairy tales, *Robinson Crusoe*—
whatever I could lay my hands on

I devoured
and like a traveller on tropic shores
I basked, basked in their delicious sunshine.

London Boy: Coleridge The Swimmer, *1785*

We learned Greek legends:
    love   that branded men
            that seared the souls of women in Greek stories.

They opened up wide worlds to us
    in harsh and sometimes hungry schooldays
        gave food   for hope
                     for lives of love so far unlived.

And so it was I dreamed myself
    in love with Aphrodite's virgin priestess, Hero;
        I, like Leander, used to swim the Hellespont each night

on Cheapside or the Strand,
        bravely breasting time and tides
            to win my dreams, my love.

There, bathed in my imagination, swimming my way
                                        along the street
    I was arrested by a gentleman
        who vowed I'd tried to pick his pocket.

I told him truly, 'Nay, sir, that I never would!
    I am Leander,
        swimming for my Hero.'

He stood amazed. 'My heart is touched,' he said.
    'Poor boy! I see you are a bluecoat child.
        But are you not a mathemat?'

I humbly shook my head in shame. 'Numbers, sir,
    are not within my grasp, unless they be
        to count the metre of fair poetry.'

He laughed, gave me a metal token.
'Here, this will give you leave
to enter King Street Library every day on Cheapside.

'Two volumes daily you may borrow,
so you may multiply your learning.'
Surely he was a man of wit and wisdom!

So from that time I skulked from school
each day to read and learn
and swim the rolling seas of literature.

Coleridge in the Limes, *1797*

In June 1797 Charles Lamb arrived to stay at the Coleridges' home in Somerset at the same time as William and Dorothy Wordsworth. Temporarily unable to walk, Coleridge spent time sitting under a bower of lime trees grieving the fact that he could not join his friends on their walks.

'Well, they are gone, and here I must remain,
This lime-tree bower my prison!'

Midsummer, and the light is green
with growing overhead, even
at twilight, green with glowing.
But I who longed to walk with Lamb, my long-time playfellow,
with Wordsworth and with Dorothy,
am sorrowful, alone,
imprisoned in these lime trees
by my injuries:
denied the joy
of walking with my friends.

Luminous the light:
it pierces eye and heart,
yet joy assails me now,
seeing in my mind's eye, too,
the sunset filtered by these linden leaves,
the dappled shadows overhead.

Imagination, my dearest love, comes swiftly out
to sit with me. She blesses me, reminds me
like a gentle nurse
that Nature is my consolation.

Even as I think
in solitude of Lamb, of Wordsworth, of Dorothy
who walk the hills without me,
a plain old rook winging home to roost
is suddenly a holy messenger
of peace, contentment, comfort, hope.

© Lizzie Ballagher

Literary Labours: Deputy Grecian Leigh Hunt Sweats over His Studies, *1798*

Homer is a horror for me
and Milton's *Paradise Lost* a book I'd rather clang shut
like the gates of paradise when the devil made his mark
and an iron-willed sternness brooded over all
in seeming spitefulness...

Cicero, Demosthenes: although I bear the label 'Grecian'—
working hard at wisdoms of the Greeks and Romans—
I do not find the lessons coming easily to me.

Essays I'm asked to write to make some moral case
baffle me entirely! The master duly screws them in a ball
and hurls them to the others boys, out
across the room for their amusement—and my shame.

But English poetry—ah, a world I swim in
as a friend would frolic
in the seas around our islands.
Yes, I am in love with Gray,
with Spenser and with Collins: the wonder,
sweetness of our native poetry.

And after school, have I a silver sixpence in my pocket,
I'll make my way to Paternoster Row
and there procure not sixpenn'th of sweetmeats
as many of my fellows rather would consume,
but a sixpenny number of the English poets—
Edmund Spenser, Thomas Gray—works I then devour:
more savoury to my taste than crumpets buttered
to be eaten under Verrio on a day of special feasting:

Yes, I pluck their verses
like ripe plums.

James Henry Leigh Hunt (1784–1859), after whom the boarding house is named, was at the school 1791–1799, from the age of seven. One of a rather large family born to an American émigré who then served as a parish priest in Middlesex, Leigh Hunt grew up to be a poet, literary and political critic, friend of many other poets (Byron, Shelley, Keats), satirist and—for a two years because of a critical piece he'd written about the then Prince Regent—a prisoner in gaol. While he served time he was visited by a parade of other literary giants, including fellow Old Blue Charles Lamb.

The Wests' Gift Child, *1957*

Lime trees stand sentinel:
lined lovely in a leafy row
down Derby Road, where leaf
leads to loam beneath
in days, not weeks.

Pens sheafed in my pocket,
clenched in hot fingers;
notebook leafed in my satchel,
I walk between the trees,
or ride my bike and dream.

As yet I've read scant poetry
but doggerel and nursery rhymes;
have heard no tales of bluecoat children:
just scribbled lines on empty pages
and chewed my pens...

before I dawdle home
with blue ink on my mouth,
green ink staining face and hands
and no words yet upon my watching tongue
or listening eyes.

Early Riser, Hertford, *1967*

The early riser leaves the dormitory in darkness, tip-
toes on polished parquet
while others still lie sleeping.

No need of an alarm clock
bleating under the pillow
when exams begin today:

she's been awake since 4am
counting sheep out on the marshes of her Romney home,
winding herself in tangled fleeces of doubt, anxiety...

She feels her mind has drifted back to Kent:
all she has learned is muddled in her head
as balls of wool in the art school.

Now, closing the wardrobe room door
she finds a place
above the drawers of pinafores,

beside the sash,
where light comes in
with ever-growing certainty.

So she spreads her history notes
across her folded knees and waits
for the steady warmth of the close room

to seep in through her skin
till she can breathe more evenly;
rereads, reminds, recites, reviews...

whispering the dates, the details and debates, softly,
so as not to wake the ward-mistress
                    or monitresses on the floor above.

Deep folds of curtains brush her skin.
Comforted, she wraps herself in billowing yards of broadcloth
and gazes out at lime trees: pretends
she's in their branches, rock-a-byed,
where sap is rising like her own,
where leaves are newly minted—
a gorgeous green that will outlast exams:

a comfort to be lullayed by old lime trees.
And thus, unwillingly, she falls asleep, at last.

© Lizzie Ballagher

The Great Storm, Horsham, *1987*

This night a gale blows in
        that isn't meant to be a hurricane (or so they say).
            The wind comes up:
                not like some mischievous child

                    but like a blunderbuss

                    and tosses trees in rage as savage
                as though giants stalked the hills, the downs,
            plucking them up for jealousy because they are
        too beautiful for some malicious heart to countenance—

                    yellow leaves still clinging on black bark.

Thick branches crack.
                Great boles heave up
            and down they rain.
            and up they stack

while   the wild wind shrieks
        the ground quakes
                with thunder   thunder
                            all those lime trees rent asunder:

and the long avenue
        of limes is cast
                down
                    on ground

that once had held them fast.

Limes: They Are No Longer, *2019*

Limes: they are no longer growing there
the long length of the Avenue, the Square—
as far as I know
replaced by whitebeam.

They will not grow as tall as limes;
they will not, falling,
shake the earth.

I'm told that whitebeam made
the tightest cogs,
the finest craftsmanship
before mankind had made cold iron,
before a joint was ever hinged
with shivering metal.

Limes: they are no longer growing there
the long slow length of the avenue, the square:
much mourned but now—
as far as I know—
replaced by whitebeam.

The Tenth of Ten:
William Wales, Master of the Royal Mathematical School, Reflects Despairingly on One of His Pupils, *1788*

William Wales, formerly the navigator for captain Cook's expeditions, became Master of the Royal Mathematical School in 1775. A decade later, Coleridge was not deemed a suitable candidate for a naval apprenticeship and did not aspire to be a mathemat. Nevertheless, it was William Wales' awkward duty, before Coleridge could take up a place at Cambridge University, to ensure that his mathematical abilities were almost as sharp as his literary skills.

When winter evenings dark are drawing close
and boys come trudging in from sport without—
dull-eyed—for lessons in astronomy and navigation
or other mathematical calculation—
I watch their faces for a spark or sign of wit.

Among these sits a dark-haired boy,
the tenth of ten (surely that should signify?)
fresh of face, lively, with direct and piercing gaze,
who lifts his head at lessons' end
when I tell those stories of my sailing years:
tales of sunlit seas—or of Captain Cook
and voyages on the Resolution to Antarctica.

By then the other boys are weary of their tutelage—
waterlogged, perhaps; at sea, riding low in the water—
but Samuel Coleridge fixes eyes on mine,
especially when I tell of days
becalmed in deepest Doldrums
when with Hadley's clever quadrant
we used to plot and calculate our course
although perforce we drifted...till the wind had shifted,
filling sails—so we made headway once again.

Here, only careful measurement,
keen mathematical observation,
saved us all from shipwreck, ruination.

This week, I found the Coleridge child
shunning tasks I had set before him:
scribbling, muttering aloud,
dreaming at the ceiling.
I knew not what to make of him.

I overheard him say of me
to one of his schoolfellows,
in playfulness and glee,
'Our master Wales is, indeed,
a crabby ancient mariner!'

Newly made a Grecian,
perhaps he thinks he has the judgment of a god.
The sorry truth is that mathematics flies
as straight across his brain
as latitude upon a chart,
or arrows that we used to shoot at birds
when we were starved for food at sea—
oh, how shall I ready
this unruly boy for Cambridge?

And yet he is the tenth of ten,
the boy with this direct and piercing gaze.
Sure, that must signify.

Verrio's Views: Mathematicians, Mariners & Mapmakers, *1673 (as viewed from 2020)*

In an epic oil painting executed over years, Antonio Verrio was commissioned to commemorate the 1673 founding of the Royal Mathematical School.

Eat your heart out, Spielberg, Lucas,
Hitchcock, David Lean—yes,
even that other Italian, Federico Fellini...

Antonio Verrio! Now here's a man of years ago
who knows a thing or two about a spectacle:
the grandeur of the Versailles court,
the Stuart splendour in Whitehall—
those shadowed portraits of the good and great,
the sweeping drapes and sculpted arches,
fluted columns, falls of damask...

for here's a man of centuries ago
whose brush on canvas opens up
new truths about uncertain maps:
of agèd landscapes newly classified,
of scrolls re-understood
and errant charts remade
by confident young hands...

who soon would sail away as bold apprentices,
returning after seven years as seasoned mariners;
who then might draw with mathematical precision
a new world order: serving as
cartographers and captains, navigators—
all to bring back honour to war-weary England
in febrile days and fears of Dutch invasion.

Here Verrio unveils new history, a new geography—
securing hope for men at sea
and mapmakers in this shifting, chancing sphere.
Now harsh shoals and tides no more prevail
—as in past days—on ship or keel or sail;
the Admiralty will float new vessels without fear;
masters, through mathematics, of the seas at last.

© Lizzie Ballagher

Verrio's Views: The Hands That Steer by Stars, *1673*

A year from now
and I should be at sea—
out of these yellows
and exchanging for the ancient bluecoat
I have worn for five long years
a sailor's stripes and bright-blue swagger;
a sailor's silver buttons.

Then away, away to see a world
that I have only known till now through psalms
we sing in church; or drawings of my masters—
their tales of marvels: raging seas
and waterspouts and whales;
porpoises leaping through the waves,
and vengeful, fearsome sea-beasts.

My masters bade me carry to the king
the latest drawing I had done.
Impatiently, I wait my turn, ogling
the monarch on his throne;
fidgeting, I kneel with all the other lads.
Nearby, the youngest boys
grow more than restless, fall to chattering
until our masters issue stern rebuke
and one by one
we do present ourselves unto his majesty.

A stately man in red—perhaps
the Lord Mayor of London—
beckons me forward at the last
to bow before the king.

Close to his majesty's slippered feet,
a sleeping hound sighs, winks an eye at me;
but I am fast transfixed
to see a man in so much silk and lace.
He murmurs words of commendation...
then he looks away.

My head swims as I turn back from the dais.
I am at sea already,
fevered with thoughts of times to come
that now I only dream of.

Verrio's Views: The Hands That Rock the Cradles, *1673*

They think we have no words to offer,
    so we're waiting on our knees.
Behind me, I hear an older girl plead
    to be given leave to stand,
    to rest from kneeling.
We do not even have such drawings
    as the boys have brought
    to show his majesty.
For we are lowly, low:
    of little account or reckoning
    in their mariners' calculations.
Yet think ye on this:
    without our mothers there would be no brothers
    to grace the halls of Christ, his Hospital.
Without their sisters
    there would be no wives
    for captains, seamen, star-men, map-men...
    and no one to darn their bluecoats, yellows.
No one to curtsey in the cloisters
    when they swagger past
    puffed up with their achievements.

I've heard my grand-dame say
    that any hand
    that rocks a cradle
    rules the world.
One day, like most of womankind,
    I'll rock my child in gentle cradle
    even as a boat rocks back
    and forth upon the swell.
But for today I'll watch and learn
    what little that I can
    of maps and mathematics,
    of naval captains, kings.

It is a world I never thought
to hear of save in broadsides
bawled on Cheapside, or in tales
we read before we fall asleep;
never dreamed of: not even to look upon a king
who helps to make more possible
the numbering, charting of the stars;
the sailing of the tall-ships
into sunset's storybooks.

Samuel Pepys contemplates the royal meeting he will attend the following day: *24 January 1675**

And so to bed...
though not to sleep:
perchance to dream of fleets
of seamen, navigators
with telescopes raised,
stars in their eyes,
and solid oaken decks beneath their feet—
the admirals of future days,
mapmakers of uncharted ways...

Full two years have gone below the keel.
In *Anno Domini* sixteen and seventy-three
His Majesty signed Letters Patent
that would grant to forty poor boys every year—
those who wear the ancient bluecoat—
tuition in grammar, mathematics,
(in the main, geometry);
navigation and astronomy:
as well as all the tools
pertaining to those trades...

Still the Admiralty has need
of more, yet more.
I fret to think of this each day;
my poor head aches
with all the trouble of it:
more than ever when the word comes in
of yet another vessel lost at sea
with all good hands,
with all her charge.

Tomorrow I shall go once more
to see the king,
to urge upon him once again
that he may grant a second royal charter.
The sum I have in mind is nigh on
four times a hundred pounds:
so boys may be apprenticed
to ships' masters who have need of them;
so boys may with the Astronomer Royal
study at Greenwich: there to learn
the art and science of steering by the stars.

So now I set my sail to drift away—
cast off—in sleepy hopes of better times
for those who sail upon the seas.

** Samuel Pepys, diarist from 1660 to 1669, Secretary of the Admiralty in the reign of Charles II, and governor of Christ's Hospital (who was later honoured with freedom of the City of London for his 'great zeal and concern for the interest of Christ's Hospital'), worked with others to negotiate a crucial royal charter in January 1675 (January 1676 by the modern calendar). As a result of work he did with other benefactors such as Jonas Moore, Robert Clayton, and James Duke of York, the second Royal Mathematical School Royal Charter was signed into existence on 24 January 1675/6 with an award of £370.10s (more than £50,000 in modern currency) payable annually to support the mathemats, or King's Boys, in apprenticeships to masters of merchant ships after they left Christ's Hospital.*

Although, now a widower, he was no longer keeping a diary by 1675 or 76, I have imagined for the sake of this poem that he must still have spent late evenings turning matters over in his mind as he had done while his eyes were good enough for him to maintain the diary.

Charles Frodsham: Chronometrist, *1834*

Elizabeth Mill, fiancée to Old Blue Charles Frodsham, writes to him just before their marriage.

Your eyes: they bore as straight into mine
as the barrel arbor
on the mainspring,

as straight as lines
on navigation maps
you studied when at school.

You have the jaw-line of a man who knows
to where his ship is sailing,
whose eyes look out on clear horizons
Greenwich had not dreamed about e'er now—
not even with the ingenious timekeepers
John Harrison used to make.

You told me how your father knew
(and now you know it well yourself)
there was a hunger for precision far at sea:

a desperation to save the loss of lives,
to stop the foundering of ships
on broken shores and hidden shoals.

Apprenticed at fourteen, mere boy
but visionary long before your eyes met mine,
shedding your bluecoat for the very last time,
you stepped into the workshops of timekeeping:
the measured clicks of ratchet wheels,
the polished run of pinions.

Ten years and you have learned your trade,
won prizes for your clocks: most accurate
of all the ones they tested in the Premium Trials.

Now, in the morn, dear man, I'll be your bride.
That morning cannot come too soon.
Before the altar I shall stand with pride
to be the woman at your side
through all the time—the timekeeping—
God grants us to abide.

© Lizzie Ballagher

In 1834, newly married, Charles Frodsham set up his business—which still runs to this day—as a principal maker of chronometers and timepieces. Even as early as 1830 when he was only 20, his designs for marine chronometers were winning accolades for their precision; far more than watches worn for simple vanity or mantelpiece clocks displayed for beauty, his instruments saved the lives of men at sea and the cargoes they carried.

Later in life, Frodsham won a first-class medal at the Great Exhibition of 1851; he became Superintendent and Keeper of HM Queen Victoria's clocks at Buckingham Palace and in 1855 and 1862 served as Master of the Worshipful Company of Clockmakers. His marine chronometers became the gold standard for navigational instruments, the Admiralty buying dozens for ships in the Royal Navy. Not only was he a prolific craftsman, but also a prolific writer about the use of chronometers for calculating longitude at sea.

When Lights Were Lit, Horsham, *1959*

Your wandering glass eye
captured everyone's imagination,
distracted us in chemistry at Horsham,
might well have deflected us, too,
from scientific progress...
but there was more, much more to you
than teenaged boys could realise.

Two days, two lessons beam out, gleam out
like limestone hot and glowing into limelight
in the science school:

the first when you unfurled the canvas drop-display
that revealed the periodic table
in all its glory, logic and integrity:
pieces of a scattered puzzle
assembled now before our eyes,
connections made,
disparate facts we'd learned
now suddenly falling into place
in order we could comprehend...

the second when you held a square of copper in a flame
and urged us to enquire minutely of each other
why it had turned
from russet brown to sooty black.
One after another we tested every theory,
each confident that his conclusion was scientific,
his the only possible logic.

Not so.
Our hypotheses fell empty as cheap playing cards
into a discard pile, one by one unworkable
until we dropped the blackened metal
into sulphuric acid; saw the black dissolve, radiate
into a copper sulphate's burning blue...
more mysteries!

We were fourteen and we knew it all
or so—at the start—we had thought.
What could a man with a glass eye
have to offer us, the clear-eyed ones
who had our lives mapped out before us?

You showed us otherwise:
to test, observe, deduce, discover:
never to extrapolate
what was not found in data;
to bring a hungry curiosity to the lab:
handle, weigh, assess,
record in unambiguous notes;
use hands as well as ears and eyes
to measure reactions, apply equations
that explained what we had found.

As if bright shafts of light had pierced
our ignorance and our arrogance
we came to grasp
that we were seeing, still,
only through a darkened glass—

while you were the one with the insight:
seeing plainly, face to face.

One of Christ's Hospital's chemistry teachers from 1939 to 1970, Paul Beaven influenced generations of pupils. His lessons were among many at the school that perhaps helped make sense of St Paul's words, oft-recited in chapel: 'When I was a child, I spake as a child, I thought as a child; but when I became a man, I put away childish things. For now we see through a glass, darkly; but then face to face.' (I Cor 13: 11–12, KJV)

Science in the Sixties, Hertford

We knew her then as 'Chemi T'
and worked to match her mischief
in her curiouser and curiouser laboratory.

We learned to wash lab glassware
within an inch of its life, to hold a pipette,
a burette with perfect precision,

          to work with polished and practical skill
as well as to appreciate the fascinations
of Christmas Lectures at the Royal Institution.

Those destined to be doctors, teachers, dentists
did not take kindly to our bad behaviour
on the chemi lab's back benches.

What then were the disapproving ones
to make of it when our teacher
took some part in all the fun?

We loved the purple smoke
she conjured up for us
in the closed fume cupboard, stoked

          if the lessons lagged
in the minutiae of the syllabus,
or when we got bogged down

          in the cryptic syllables and symbols
of the crucial periodic table...
and all of us had grown too bored!

She kept a catapult at the front of class:
of rubber bands and broken chalk,
and when we had annoyed her past endurance

            she pinged out chalk across the room
and hauled the lesson back to order
through the merriment that ensued.

How some of us ever did become
teachers, pathologists, doctors, hydrologists...
we're not entirely sure..yet here we are!

Miss Mary (Chemistry) Thompson had the distinction among Hertford staff in the sixties of being Irish. Held in affection by many pupils, she somehow made her subject fun even for those who found it difficult. Originally trained as an industrial chemist, she brought to her teaching years of experience and an eminently practical approach. Hertford Old Blues have commented both on the fun of chemistry lessons and on the excellent foundation she gave them for working in a range of scientific arenas.

Sporting Calculations, *2008*

I did not know it
when I was a kid knocking about
in the waste-grounds of the Isle of Dogs,
bouncing balls against brick walls
or through tall playground hoops—

but all that play,
haphazard at the time,
was turning me slowly,
slowly into a scientist.

At Horsham I later learned
the netball courts by heart;
to gauge the exact trajectory
of bounce and drop and rise
depending on the speed and strength of wind.

And on the hockey fields
to know the ratios between
the day's rainfall and the ball's curve,
its angle when it left my stick;
the application of a simple physics formula
work equals force times distance—
thus the effort I must put in
to make the ball travel
far enough when I slogged it
down the Astroturf:
calculations made unhindered
even when our hands were frozen
to our hockey sticks on wintry days.

We learned to do mathematics
not just in a lab or classroom
but in the applied maths of fast-moving teams:
the energy we'd need to generate,
the combustion we'd create.

We learned to figure the odds
of beating our opponents in the equation
of a level playing field:
raising the stakes, adding all our values
to make a whole larger than the sum of parts.

And if we won, all panting out our CO_2 in chorus,
we'd argue out the first law of thermodynamics
and how it might have played out through our game.

Prayer of Edward VI
Bishop Ridley's Spital Sermon Rouses Edward, *1552*

Whatever they may say to me about the might of earthly kings,
I know my weakness now:
I sat upon the throne of England
at the age of nine
without a sense of how I was to bear myself,
of whom I was to trust.
I fought against the smallpox. Did prevail.
So now I am content to throw myself
on your sweet mercy, Jesus, Lord.

In London town with all its pomp and pageantry
five years into my reign
I feel ashamed
when I see beggars,
paupers, all the destitute and helpless
wasting on the streets Mayor Dick Whittington
believed were paved with gold.

For sure no gold gilds streets
or alleys deep in London town
unless it be the mayor and corporation's gold—
or the gold within my palaces.

And Bishop Nicholas seems to know my wealth.
I vow he preaches to my soul,
driving the sword of truth into my heart;
exhorts me in the name of Christ
to feed the hungry,
proffer water to the thirsty,
house and shelter all the homeless ones,
clothe the children—ragged, rank with soil—
visit those imprisoned—
in other words show mercy

as I hope to know your mercy, Lord
when 'tis Your throne I stand before—
not my poor seat.

My heart is touched.
I will go seek the mayor,
implore the bishop so to guide my steps
that waifs and strays may all be sheltered, clad,
taught, and fed their daily bread.

Amen! I cry your merciful redemption, Christ, my God.

Bonnie Jean Burns Writes a Letter, *1802*

My husband whom I loved too well
                                        is gone:
        no longer excise man,
        no longer man of letters
            whom the world may celebrate
            in better times and better days,
            in better ways than it does today.

No longer shall we live
        by his wild wits,
        his derring-do with smuggling men,
        his drunken bouts and dalliances with other women;
no longer shall we live by his clever, erring pen.

Four children have I left to me:
        a widow now, one no more able
        to clothe or feed her brood
        since they're too young to seek for work.
And so I do present to you
        my youngest son James Glencairn Burns,
        now eight years old.

Though young, he has his father's wits
        and may, God willing, on the morrow—
        while he may not write great poetry—
        at least make useful offerings to society
in whatever calling he pursues
        through your good offices,
        your generous guidance.

I pray you therefore, gentle governors,
to hear this distant voice from Scotland:
      for pity's sake to take
      my child into your Hospital in London:
there to be brought up
with other poor men's children.

James Glencairn Burns (1794–1865) was the youngest surviving son of Scottish poet Robbie and his wife Jean. Awarded a place at Christ's Hospital in 1802 after his mother had written to the governors on his behalf, James later travelled to India, where he served in the East India Company, rising to be a Lieutenant Colonel. His picture hangs in the National Portrait Gallery.

Learning Loving-kindness, Horsham, *1972*

'Give, and it shall be given unto you: good measure, pressed down, and shaken together, and running over....For with the same measure that ye mete withal it shall be measured to you again.'
(St Luke's Gospel, 6:38, KJV)

I knew I had my place
at Horsham
through the generosity
of one I'd never met—
he was too old to leave his bed
or look on me,
a missionary's homely child
with not a penny to my name,
and a drought back home
where my parents laboured
under unrelenting sun
for others,
all for love:
and not for gain.

Oxen, my father said,
were what the villagers needed
if they were to grow their grain.
At school we put our heads together,
fellow Grecians and I,
making a plan
to grow a crop of money
here in England
with a sponsored hike:
so strangers could plough
and grow their grain
in famine's ravaged land.
Later I had the chance
to deliver them myself:

a yoke of oxen—
those our money bought
in southern Africa—
to lead them over the border.

As that dear man had done for me
and other Horsham brothers,
so did we
for many others
in a far country.

Sewing in the Sixties: Hertford, *1962*

She who could not hold a tune,
who every year in ward singing contests
was told to mouth the words,

learned to love, instead,
the heavy workhorse
of the dayroom's Singer sewing machine:

to sit with rows of pins between her lips,
needles threaded in her black apron,
and sew her way through yards

and yards of cotton, silk, or linen;
or stand with scissors in her hand and shear
then sew her way to victory through the calico.

Miss Richards held no fears for her.
She would arrive calmly and with confidence
for stitch and seam inspections
at the stern front desk.

Rows of cross-stitch on her tablecloths
marshalled themselves as faultlessly as Horsham boys
marching outside Big School to their lunch.

Without a bulge or pucker, never tight
or ruched in awkward places, her garments
would have rivalled Quant's or Biba's.

It was said of her she had the eyes of a designer:
the colours that she chose clashed startlingly,
unexpectedly, but gloriously.

Juniors with needle-punctured hands and bloodied fingers
came to her in floods of tears,
were kindly helped through seams sewn back

to front
or knots in threads
or sleeves put in the wrong way round.

And in the Upper Sixth she won
(as every Hertford pupil knew she would)
the coveted prize
of the Needlemakers' Worshipful Company.

I never heard what did become of her
but remember her now with head bent over the Singer.
I imagine her dresses, blouses, tailored coats

left trails of broken hearts
and empty corporate pockets
on the catwalk in her working years.

Her needles and her Singer
sang the songs for her
that she could never sing herself.

Cheers: London, *1968*

Victoria Station, and I'm shivering
in unfamiliar English January,
crushing, pushing gladly
(for warmth, if not for friendship's sake)
into the melee of Horsham boys
cheerfully, fearfully, tearfully
bidding goodbye to brothers, sisters, parents,
scrambling through open carriage doors
onto the waiting train:
excited, delighted, on edge,
knowing this time what will lie ahead.

As for me, having said my farewells
four months before to family in Africa,
I'm one of the cheerful ones

until my right shoe takes a notion
to make a journey this side of the ocean—
but separately from my foot:
disappears without ceremony—
oh, what a mishap—
into smut-filled darkness,
down the Dreaded Gap

where there is weeping and wailing
and gnashing of teeth...

'Hopalong!' my fellows joke.
'Where's your peg-leg,
Long John Silver?'
'Where's your parrot?'
'You'll have to walk
one-shoed all the way to Lesotho!'
'Get. On. That. Train!'

the scowling porters roar,
'shoe or no shoe. Yes, you, boy.'
And the guard growls,
'I'm blowing my whistle. NOW.
So are you for Horsham or Victoria,
silly, shilly-shallying child?'

Pandemonium! Boys laughing, cheering,
now they have some entertainment.
It's my turn to be tearful, fearing
no one has the money
for another pair of shoes.
I cannot be a one-shoe wonder
all through the whole spring term.

Enter a man of kind judiciousness
a man of prudence, enterprise.
No frowns, no glares—
just quietly lowers his umbrella
through the Dreaded Gap
and hooks my shoe out;
hands it me
as quick as winking.

No fears.
No tears.
All cheers.

The whistle blows
for the Christ's Hospital Special.
No time to wait.
Away we go into 1968.

A Fairytale for Future Blues: Dark-Eyed Boy and Cat in the Limes, *1986–87*

The morning after the Great Storm of 1987 at Horsham, a school cat called Emma was found perched on the largest branch of her favourite lime tree, now felled by the wind and lying with others along the Avenue.

'She's just a moggy,'
they said.
'A little mongrel cat from the City.'
True, I was a scruff-bag of a kitten
no one wanted, skinny,
skittering down cobbles and alleyways
near the Thames to escape
the drowners with their evil sacks,
bound for the river with kittens in tears.

One walleye and one black eye, I have,
but four neat white paws,
bright whiskers that polish up perfectly.

Yes, I was just a nameless moggy
until a dark-eyed boy rescued me,
wrapped me in his long blue coat,
gave me the name 'Emma'
and carried me, terrified,
on the railway line to Horsham;
smuggled me into a grand brick house
and fed me when Grecians and grown-ups
were busy with Other Important Things.

You did not know that cats
can speak, you say.
Perhaps we do.
Perhaps we don't.
But I can surely wink and watch,
perched high in a favourite lime tree
while my adoptive father, still
hardly more than a kitten himself,
looks out for me.

Last night the greatest storm I ever heard
heaved roots and trees to topple them.
World in uproar.
My mews flew lost in the wind
like battered birds.
Under the warm red bricks
I crept into a grating,
curled up tight.
Sky in tumult.

Today they found me still alive
but with eyes like saucers,
fur bristling,
clinging to my favourite lime tree
because here I'm safe from harm
even though the world has switched
from vertical to horizontal;
even though the sturdy limes
hang weeping in each others' arms.

My kitten-boy finds me shivering,
shocked & full of fears, comforts me as once
he was himself brought comfort by the school.

Difficult Days

On Cheapside, *1552–1560*

My father was a Londoner.
I never knew—
they never told me—
how he came to meet *ma mère.*

She spoke in French to me;
that I do recall. And I remember
how great pestilence took my father,
so she brought me in her arms to Greyfriars
where the poor were welcomed.

Weeping, she said,
'Quand tu es né   When you were born,
'j'écoutais les cloches de Bow   I heard the Bells of Bow,
'les belles, belles cloches avec leur mélodie joyeuse
the lovely, lovely bells with joyful sound

'et votre père m'a dit   and your father said to me,
'Il est un fils de la cité   He's a son of the City.
'Alors, restez ici à Londres   So rest ye here in London,
'quelque soit le sort   whatever shall befall.'

She told me this again, again;
then closed her eyes and slept.

And what befell
was a kindly beadle in his ermine robes
who grieved to see me hungry,
ragged, poor, alone;
who wrapped me in a cloak
that smelled of lavender from France.

He brought me
to Christ's new Hospital,
spoke gentle words,
gave bread to me, and meat.

They taught me à écrire et lire en Anglais
how to read and write in English,
clad me in russet, then in blue and gold,
apprenticed me
to the Worshipful Company of Drapers
in fair and ancient halls on old Throgmorton Street—

all for the love of Edward, King;
for the love of God, their Lord:
true founders of the Hospital.

Caught Between Two Queens
St Edmund Campion: The Tower of London, *1581*

You scarcely speak of me in modern days.
Why would you,
in another time?
But I shall pray for you
and for the scholars of your day,
that truth and goodness will prevail.

A bookish lad on Paternoster Row
where my father kept a bookshop
in the shadow of St Paul's,
I grew up clad with words,
with words, too, as my meat and drink.
I learned to speak from early days
of wisdoms that my father taught me,
and truths I then imbibed
from masters at Christ's Hospital…

In my short life—I tell you now
for I am certain that my days
on earth wind to a close tonight—
I have been caught between two queens:
both childless, both, in latter years,
relentless in their bitterness.

To the first I was to give a loyal address
at Aldgate in the summertime of AD 1553.
Then, I was just thirteen—a child—
when Princess Mary came from Suffolk
to be crowned as queen in London.
She was, I later learned, determined
that the school that Edward founded
would not, could not, be allowed to thrive:
a *Protestant nest*, a *blot on London*.

At the ancient gate she swept along and passed us:
would not vouchsafe one single word,
though we made courtesies
and stood respectfully
in our bluecoats, waiting, waiting
for Mary, destined to be queen...

To the second I was bound to make a speech,
to lead collegiate debate before Elizabeth
in Oxford, AD 1566—at the university
where I'd taken my degrees and holy orders.
She vowed how much she valued me;
replied in kind to welcoming words I offered her,
promising me gladly in glozing words
I should be *provided for* by some
among her friends and loyal followers.

I see now what a strange conceit I've fallen into,
even with the mercy of my Lord
to hold me in his hand...

The first queen spurned me,
would not countenance my approach;
yet would now, were she still alive,
perchance, be pleased to give me words
of thanks for service
to the church she loved so well.

The second had professed delight in me,
yet, soon as I returned to England
as a Roman Catholic priest,
sent men to hunt me out.
And yet, again, I do suppose
she kept her words of promise to me...
in her own way...since, for sure, I am
provided for in this narrow cell of little ease—
also on the morrow's scaffold.

And so it is: tonight I find myself writing final words
fast locked in the Tower: awaiting transport
through London's staring streets
to Tyburn, where tomorrow morn
I'll shed my mortal coil
and rise to life in Christ my Lord.

Yes, I have been caught between two queens.
And yet I choose to follow neither.
Instead, I choose another altogether:
our Lady Mary, Queen of Heaven
mother of our blessed Saviour,
Jesus Christ—the truest Word
God ever spake: he whom first
I came to know at Greyfriars
and on Paternoster Row.

St Edmund Campion (1540–1581) was among the very first pupils at Christ's Hospital: 1552–1558. Ordained as an Anglican priest after his studies at St John's College, Oxford, Campion later converted and was priested as a Catholic in Douai in the 1570s. Returning to England in 1580, Campion preached fearlessly. He was captured by spies of Queen Elizabeth's Privy Council in June 1581; then tried for treason. All his fine oratorical skills notwithstanding, he suffered a grisly martyrdom at Tyburn on 1 December 1581, unwilling to the end to renounce his faith.

The Lamb Who Loved Pork: London, *1782–1789*

Charles Lamb's privileges could not go unnoticed
by his alter ego, Elia,
for Charles Lamb liked good food as much as any child
and was provided for by those who lived close by,
who saw that he should eat much better fare than most.

While others made the best of bluish porridge
gristly mutton-scrags, pease-pottage slops;
or boiled beef tough as leather,
strung with gobs of fat
that made us choke,

Lamb ate the choicest breads
and meats well seasoned
with ginger or with cinnamon
his family brought to him
kind-heartedly each day.

True, we noticed he was shamed
because there was not more to share;
but hunger ruled him, as it ruled us all...
and yet, there came a day
when loving-kindness overruled his hunger.

Coming back to school on London Bridge,
Lamb met a beggar who was starving, destitute.
Wrapped tightly in a pudding cloth, a cake
his aunt had made for him lay in his arms;
he saw the need; he gave away the cake—

yes, every morsel, every crumb.
But in the evening, back at school, we found him
mourning what his heart had prompted him do;
there was no cake to eat: neither for him,
nor for us, his friends.

Years later as he writes so lusciously of succulent roast pork—
the essay you still read so laughingly today—
we hear him smack his lips with glee.
You readers love his comic turn of phrase
but find between the lines of greed
the hunger of small boys in need.

The Bostock Girl, *1918*
At CH Hertford *1907–1911*; in London *1911–1956*

On the Lines

Not for Lilian Ada the work
of munitionettes upon a factory floor,
glamorised by soldiers' songs in Normandy;
not for her a cowering behind closed doors
in housewifery or domestic service,
or knitting socks for tommies in the trenches,
wielding yarn and needle through the cloth,
or tailoring for some unseen master—
for all that she knew how to sew
with the best of Hertford girls.

No, another path had beckoned her:
with brains and deft dexterity in her fingers,
a clever listening ear and tender sympathy
for those in haste, or horror—
those with secret matters on their minds—
or generals with urgent strategies
for regiments in France...where pigeons
and despatch riders had had their day.
This was a modern war—
now on London's own front line—
which called for modern means
and modern women on the lines with men.

Not for her the obvious path from school.
Instead, she chose telephony: returning
willingly to work when daily tasks were done,
staying at her post if enemy airships struck;
racing pell-mell through the streets on foot
with messages for the War Office

when the lines went down
or buildings blazed around her—unsung
in her bravery, her faithfulness to duty
on the lines, the lines of literal fire.

Lilian Ada Bostock, 1895–1988, was originally from Clerkenwell in London. Directly after leaving school, she began serving in the General Post Office as one of the early London telephonists. Years later, she was to become the GPO's Chief Supervisor of Telecommunications, a position she held until her retirement in 1956. The London Gazette *records two medals awarded to her: The British Empire Medal in 1918 (when she was only 22) 'for displaying great courage and devotion to duty during air raids'; and the Imperial Service Medal in 1956. This modest, little-known woman had helped to shape one of the world's foremost telecommunications networks.*

The Ballad of Edward Felix Baxter, VC, *1916*
Ward X, Hertford, *1896–1901*

'Greater love hath no man than this—that a man should lay down his life for his friends.' (John 15:13, KJV)

Edward came from Stourbridge.
Baxter was his name.
He volunteered to fight the war,
to play the patriot game.

They sent him out of Liverpool,
while he was in his prime:
a young man, barely thirty;
to some it seemed a crime.

They drilled them and they dressed them;
they shipped them all to France—
ten thousand men and counting—
left nothing up to chance.

Now carrying a live grenade,
Edward ran through heavy fire:
in sortie after sortie
to cut the enemy wire.

A raid was set for early hours;
they crept to No Man's Land
to slice through any final wires...but
things didn't go as planned:

A luckless lad tripped off a wire.
Edward saw their chances fade.
The lad fell forward, knocked Edward's arm:
he dropped the hand grenade.

The detonator was primed; all men fell still
while dawn birds stopped their singing.
The flower of Lancashire drew their breaths,
and prayers to heaven went winging.

Four seconds, three, then two....
Old soldiers frowned and groaned.
The officers cringed back in fear
and bombardiers moaned.

No thought for self had Edward,
but only for the others.
Without a murmur, scarce a word,
he moved to save his brothers.

The sergeant shook; the privates cried,
but Edward quietly stepped
disarming the weapon before it blew—
as others stood and wept.

The raid went on in belching smoke.
Explosions rocked their world.
The final cables neatly cut,
all hand grenades were hurled.

When all was done they found themselves
in German trenches deep.
'Climb out! Go back!' brave Edward cried;
but trench walls were too steep.

He was the last at the foot of the trench,
the last man there for others.
He was the last at the foot of the trench
who lifted up his brothers.

When all the smoke had cleared away
and April light burned blue,
they looked around for Edward—
but he was missing, nowhere near in view.

They sought him in the trenches;
of him there was no sign.
They sought him through the tangled wires;
news ran up and down the line.

No thought for self had Edward,
but only for his brothers.
Without a murmur, scarce a word,
he gave his life—*his life*—for others.

Sent to France in January 1916 as a second lieutenant, originally with the Liverpool Irish, Baxter died April 1916 at Ransart, near Blairville, France, having saved his fellow soldiers not once but twice in the space of a few hours. In September 1916, he was posthumously awarded the Victoria Cross for his outstanding bravery.

Marching in Our Sleep: Edmund Blunden in Northern France, *1916*

We were singing at the first, not understanding
that we were only leaves tumbling in a stream,
hurrying to our own destruction.

France sweltered, heat throbbing
over dusty fields
and under a weary sky.
Long before the name of Givenchy
meant perfume sweet to the nostrils,
we marched toward guns baying for blood,
toward the growing shout and stink of war.

Its talons came reaching far,
claiming ever more men for its meat.
And on we tramped into its yawning maw:
the stammerers and whistlers,
the mystified and terrified,
the dazed and crazed,
those mangled, masked with blood...

All were marching, heads nodding, marching in their sleep
to the thin beating of the gas tom-toms:
southbound to the Somme.

At Givenchy, bizarrely,
I was told that some of my poetry
would be published soon in London.
We ached for the world left behind us:
for England in its innocence; mourned
lost civility and sense; yearned for words
sweet and full of hope on unblotted pages.

On canal towpaths, by roadside ways,
by mounds of masonry and broken poplars, our advance
was not as we'd marched in schooldays:
no path lit with primroses;
no apple-cheeked orchards,
no beds of perfumed roses—
though wire-thorns grew barbed enough, and deep.

No. We were marching,
marching, hollow-eyed, in sleep.

Note: In Edmund Blunden's memoir, Undertones of War *(Penguin Books, 1928, reprinted 2000), he describes being 'almost mad for sleep' as he and his fellows in the Royal Sussex Regiment endured bombardments and march after march in often terrifying conditions. Lizzie Ballagher is grateful to the Estate of Edmund Blunden (in care of David Higham Associates) for permission to base this poem in part on Blunden's writings.*

Basement Stories: Telling Tales After School, Hertford, *1940*

Away from the Blitz,
we knew we were lucky
to be out of London's bombardment,
bedding down in tiered bunks
below the ward;
below the rooms we used to fill
with laughter and debate
or the clatter of the Singer on the long table,
the shifting coughing fidgeting
lucky-peppermint-sucking
peacefulness of prep.

But we missed the usual patterns of the day: the gossip
as we'd undressed for bed upstairs before the war—
exchanges of news
family stories
shared histories
tales told out of school
of Latin lessons
or the latest disaster in the cooking school
or the explosion in the chemi lab that morning
or that long-awaited lesson on human reproduction...
what a cringing, giggling moment!...
the bio mistress beetroot-faced and blustering
while we pretended nonchalance
as if we knew it all—
that stuff about the birds and bees.

To solve the problems of long silences at night,
Hazel, Mina, Mary and Audrey were always prepared—
as good Girl Guides must be—
had memorised Morse Code.

Assuredly, silences were better than the booms,
the bangs and blazes back in streets at home,
but we were lonely after lights-out
in our sudden war-time stillnesses.

They taught us all
by tapping code on outstretched hands
as we lay on our bunks...
            to wait for sleep to claim us.

Doodlebug, Horsham, *June 1944*

Such an innocent-sounding name:
as if a bumbling dark-winged beetle
had blundered down Barnes' dormitory
bouncing off shuttered windows
crazily confused
circling round and around on itself
spiralling in the air
doodling black curves.

But no.
It wasn't like that at all...

Sun just over the woods at four
when I woke in muted light
to the hesitant,
juddering, *phut-phut* of a V1
overhead... dull clattering
stuttering...then cutting

out.

Summer silence.
No early birdsong
in the trees outside:

just a breath held,
expelled
at the gust, the blast:

ceilings shaken
window-frames shattered
glass broken
plaster cracked and crumbling...

Poor Peter and Richard tumbling under their beds
            —awoken and weeping—
                  too late now to run to the Tube!

Right by the infirmary, nose in splattered dirt,
            the doodlebug had crashed:
                  pieces splintered, scattered...

            earth, grass cast up, wreckage smoking
like a shark-finned cigar...

for sure, the most exciting thing to happen
at the school that year.

© Lizzie Ballagher

Between Times: Horsham, *1944*

Winter evening closes in:
lessons, rugby and tea behind us,
prayers yet to come...
Neither do men light a candle, and put it under a bushel,
but on a candlestick...

Shoes cleaned, inspected, but our trades are still to do:
clearing of changing rooms,
washing of basins...
Let your light so shine before men,
that they may see your good works,
and glorify your Father which is in heaven.

It's that in-between time
between   the sweeping of floors,
                  the sweat of prep:
and that moment between daylight easing
into an uneasy night...
Lighten our darkness, we beseech thee, O Lord,
and by thy great mercy defend us
from all perils and dangers of this night.

It's that in-between time
between   the hours of marching,
                  regimented time,
and quieter hours of reading, prayer and sleep;
of thoughts far-ranging from our London bombsites,
playing fields, or wooded Sussex hills...
The star, which they saw in the east,
went before them, till it came and stood over
where the young child was.

It's that in-between time
between   endless summer light
and high games in Hackney
or digging the allotments with our mother—
and a thin Christmas with our father away at war,
not coming back to London soon
(no matter that they keep on saying:

'All be home by Christmas!')
Then spake Jesus again unto them, saying,
I am the light of the world:
he that followeth me shall not walk in darkness,
but shall have the light of life.

It's that in-between time
between   when war has bubbled, boiled
and branded lives for far too many years,
while peace is still a country lying far ahead
whose border we cannot yet see or cross.

Slam! Smack! The clamour and crack
of black-out boards banged
on wooden window frames marks
that moment
in between.
'No showing any lights, now, boys.'

Boys with Hollow Legs, Horsham *1947*

Hollowed out after hurried days
your stomachs grumble
and you're bending double,
embarrassed by your hunger
but driven by your need
to feed.

Over at Hertford
(or so your little sister says
in teasing letters written dutifully
on Sunday afternoons)
she has it easy.
Her ward is near the buttery.
She knows when bread is baking
by the heavenly smell,
runs fast
to knock the monitresses' study door,
'Please, there's no bread left for tea...'
'Then go and fetch some, silly.'
And away she goes in her pinny,
back in just a tick
with a fat loaf tucked
under one arm
that will all be gone
to the vultures perching
in the kitchen long
before the grace is even said...
Not that it matters, she adds,
for another girl will go again
in twenty minutes
and bring fresh bread a second time:
few questions asked.

While back in Horsham
your stomachs complain
louder and still louder.
'But why be hungry?'
slyly says a Grecian who's
the Red under the Bed
if ever you met one!
'You're juniors, not peasants,
and have just as much right
to the full ration of bread
as we do. You're still growing!
And anyway, haven't you heard
about the starving French?
And what about that tyrant
Marie Antoinette?—
who had the nerve to wave
a languid hand, exclaiming,
'If they have no bread to eat,
then let them eat cake!'
Go on, squit—protest!'

The paper goes from lap to lap
in quiet hours of prep that night—
quiet except the grumbling
of your hollow stomachs.
Silently, the signatures mount.

And then you stand, shaking,
the brave one after all:
present the housemaster your petition
requiring that the monitors
give out fair portions of bread and spuds
to juniors as well as to themselves.

The housemaster frowns,
firmly shuts his door,
holds conference with the senior boys.
You win the argument
and eat your fill—
there's always plenty now.

And when you see
your Hertford sister in the holiday,
she looks at you in loving awe
and says how straight and tall
you've grown.

The Wallis Boy, ***1891***

Born in Derbyshire,
brought up in New Cross,
schooled down on Newgate Street
and later at Horsham:
you remember clearly, even so,
a day when you weren't yet quite four
beside the Butterley Reservoir:

walking gently with your father—
before poliomyelitis took away
his walks for ever—
watching grebes dive for food,
seagulls strafe the water.

And your father choosing smooth,
smooth stones to skip, to skim, to spin
across the mirror
of the reservoir:

to bounce, bounce,
while he made you count
how many bounces
he could create before
the pebble vanished
in the lake.

Then you looked up at him,
marvelled at his magic.

In Jeopardy of Their Lives: The RAF Foundationers' Trust: *1951–52* A Haibun

four centuries gone
wars without ceasing grind on:
orphans left bereft

By 1951, Old Blue Barnes Wallis was already both a fellow
of the Royal Society and serving as a member
of the Christ's Hospital Council
of Almoners. Through his careful work
with the RAF Benevolent Fund,
the school's RAF Foundationers' Trust was first set up
late in 1951.
Previously, Wallis had been encouraged to apply
for the Royal Commission Award to Inventors,
to gain monetary recognition
for his ingenuity and contribution to the war effort.
Deeply saddened by all Bomber Command casualties in the war—
recruited internationally from Allied countries—
he flatly rejected
the notion of profit from the deaths of others,
particularly from those
of the audacious aircrews
who had flown to their deaths
in aircraft he had designed.

opportunities
scarce, women left in mourning:
their husbands missing—

husbands who gave all
at mighty Möhne, Eder, Sorpe—
in breaking of dams—

flooding of valleys
of railways, bridges, factories:
Ruhr industries, towns

Later, however, after hearing an Old Testament sermon about King David's sacrifice for his men ('Is not this the blood of the men that went in jeopardy of their lives?'),* he decided he would after all apply for the Royal Commission Award and, if successful, would use it to set up a trust at Christ's Hospital that would benefit the children of those who had served in Bomber Command between 1939 and 1945.

for the young children
of men of truth, devotion—
courage in duty—

brave airmen's children:
vulnerable, at a loss—
lacking good schooling:

who would benefit:
weak, in need of protection—
without maintenance

The first trust pupils—one girl at Hertford and three boys at Horsham—joined the school in January 1952 and were soon
wearing on their left shoulder
the badges of the trust—designed
by Barnes Wallis himself.

Over the years a hundred and fifty-two children have received
the benefits of the trust's provision.
In itself, this testifies to the ongoing sacrifices made
by aircrews in time of war:

they shall mount up on
angels' wings above the earth:
shall be remembered

** The sermon Barnes Wallis had heard was focused on the Book of Samuel, II, 23:14–17, in which David, battling with his men against the Philistines, is offered a drink from a well in Bethlehem; he refuses it because it seems to him tantamount to drinking the blood of his fellow fighters, and instead pours it out as an offering to God.*

Country Boy, *1953–54*

When the school was marking four centuries
of its august history in 1953,
I was playing in the dusty lanes of Devon
all unaware—a dreamy day-boy
at a local school, without a care
and very little learning
buckled under my belt.

Instead I lived for afternoon readings,
sitting with my grandmother:
tales of derring-do from *Treasure Island,*
Jungle Book, White Fang...
when I listened and dreamed.

'We're disappointed,'
the grown-ups murmured
when I'd met my sponsor
but failed the entrance tests,
and failed the entrance tests again.

I sighed. I tried again.
'I think I can. I think I can.'
So went the motto of the little engine
in one of my favourite nursery tales...

Yet I failed again,
knowing I was somehow
falling far behind,
left to rust on a siding
like some old engine
in one of my railway stories.

Come the spring of 1954
I tried once more—and passed
the entrance test: 'I thought I could.
I thought I could!'

By autumn I was buckling on
the Housey leather belt,
beginning to be equipped
for whatever would come next.

Lessons the first and second:
I think I can...I thought I could;
as well, that even if failure's a trend
it need never be a destiny.

The Religious, Royal & Ancient Spud-Bashing Ceremony, Hertford, *1966*

No chapel Matins yet are sung.
Sunday morning, far too early:
No waking bell has yet been rung;
our sisters lie in easy sleep
while we have got the peeling task
to do before we break our fast.

Paring knives in hand
we talk of Milton's *Samson Agonistes,*
which we should have read by Monday.
There's much we do not understand
and more to read when we should rest
but I shall read it, later, on my knees
while prayers are said and hymns upraised,
hiding the book in the folds of my Sunday best.

With our fingers turning blue in muddy spud-water,
we yank out potatoes one by one,
dutifully cleaning, quartering.

Clumsy at first, I gouge myself,
bleed, mutter, laugh it off
and keep on putting out their little eyes
in sharp revenge—

poor spuds—

so there will be no eyes to glare darkly
O, dark, dark, dark, amid the blaze of noon
irrecoverably dark, total eclipse...
from the mashed and plated mounds
on trestle tables in the dining hall—

O, thanks be to God!

That Cold Spell: Horsham, *1963*

Scraping by—in every sense—
during the Lent term that year:
white avenues cut between piled snow;
no chance to march or do PT.
Big School became another gym
and some intrepid souls went out

running through the fields—cross-country
tougher than we'd ever run again.
North-side lav-ends frozen up by night
were scarcely thawed by day,
and sometimes not enough coal
to heat water for the kitchens.

Sand, sand everywhere, with holes
in our school shoes from skidding in the snow
on paths sculpted from the ice.
And the sicker bursting with boys:
hundreds, feverish and moaning—
so many they had to bring in extra SRNs.

Ah, but we could go tobogganing
on Tower Hill and Sharpenhurst
till our hands turned blue
and our cheeks flamed red
and our teeth ran away with themselves
chattering in the cold.

And Doctor's Lake frozen so thick
that after we had swept the snow away
we could skate on it for hours
each Saturday. We even created
an ice-hockey pitch, eagerly
zipping around on skates till March.

'What about the marching?' we hear you ask.
No, not until a day in the middle of February
when a way was cleared through the quad.
And the band, the band came two abreast
between the banks, the banks of snow:
conquering heroes in the cold.

The Big Freeze, Hertford, *1963*

They lived out that winter
in the frost pocket of England
between banks, tunnels, and arcades of shovel-sculpted
snow.
Even the River Lea was safe to cross without a bridge—
half a yard thick with ice.

The Ashbourne Fields might just as well have lain
in Iceland or Antarctica
for all that they could make it there
to bully off their hockey-balls, hurl netballs.

Every classroom blazed with bleaching light
while, though radiators blasted heat,
girls shivered, longed for spring.

Staff sent them out unsupervised
in groups on polar explorations:
cheeks flaming in the cold,
eyes burning in the frost,
noses pinched, fingers blue.

Sliding in their leather shoes on crusted wedding cakes of snow
they dared new paths they'd never walked in crocodiles:
crunched miles to drink tea, eat teacakes
with newly adopted 'aunties'
over in Ware or Amwell.

Back later on the ward,
after spoonfuls of malt and cod-liver oil to fend off ills,
they bred chilblains on their toes and fingers,
dreading the evening run to unheated lavs,
sometimes scraping snow from inside window-panes.

They thought the thaw would never come.

Letters from home when post got through the snow
told of big sisters having babies in an ambulance,
or snowbound in their living rooms, their flats—
            dramas undreamt before.
All were agog, delighted, excited to be

so old they had suddenly become aunties themselves
while the snow fell,
            and the snow fell more,
                  and the snow fell longer—

all while nobody was really looking.

Emily Shows Some Gumption, Hertford, *1966*

all this after stumbling half-blind with sleep
downstairs to early morning prayers—

time to do our duties
(trades, our London ancestors
had called them...)
and, whether we were wide awake or not,
sweeping, dusting, polishing had to be done:

1. those brass door handles...we learned
to look on them full of dismay—
the smell of ammonia thick in our noses—
if our gusto and the Brasso
pot were running low...

2. the cloakroom basins
daubed with hockey mud,
a couple of sinks with steeping shin-pads
from the 6's match
we'd won on Wednesday...

3. dripping swimming costumes,
hockey socks, blues—navy knickers—
on the drying racks
above our heads, and Sunday's
brown lisle stockings dangling...

Emily once told me she got up early, knotted
the shoelaces of all the girls who'd bullied her—
and strung their shoes up, dripping
mud into the sinks, on the day when the bullies
were on that cloakroom rota...

well, her punishment was swift and apt
though she had breezed it, laughed:

to scrub the sinks—alone,
all eight of them—
with Gumption, till they gleamed…
but Emily loved cleaning anyway…
so whose was the brass, the gumption then?

© Lizzie Ballagher

Tradition

&

Artistic Vision

Blue & Gold: The Crest, *1553*

One generation has passed away, yet still the courtiers
who live on from Henry's days will speak of the sun-bright splendour
of the tents and tournaments, the feasting and the merriment
at the Field of the Cloth of Gold in the Year of Our Lord 1520.

Yet here's a thing outshines all that:
for even the gentle brightness of the child King Edward
cannot eclipse the surety of heaven's azure:
gold *fleurs de lys* on caerulean blue—

a crest of argent, truest silver tried in the crucible
of the boy king's short and doleful life;
a crest of argent, truest silver tried in the fires
of Bishop Ridley's final suffering.

A sword stands straight, gules for the blood
and love of Christ: His Hospital.

Early in the sixteenth century, all western Europe was nervous about Ottoman expansion. Europe's response came in the form of high-profile meetings between three of the great Renaissance princes of the time: Charles V, Holy Roman Emperor and leader of the Hapsburg Empire; Francis I of France; and Henry VIII of England. Henry met twice with Charles V, also in great pomp and circumstance with Francis I in a bid to pre-empt aggression and secure lasting peace. Their magnificent meeting at the Field of the Cloth of Gold in midsummer 1520 was a show of strength and unity, a cleverly choreographed public relations and political coup that sent unambiguous messages to eastern powers. Nothing like it had ever been seen before.

Henry's son Edward was to take a very different approach. Sensing he had not long to live, and moved by the preaching of Bishop Nicholas Ridley in 1552, he founded three great institutions in the City of London, among them, of course, Christ's Hospital.

Blue & Gold: The Clothes, *1553–2020*

Blue for the overarching sanctuary of the school—
    a sky to cover, shine on us.
Gold for saffron dye to keep away the plague
    that raged within the City's gates.

Blue for the badge of apprentices' trades:
    skinners, salters, grocers, drapers.
Gold for the gifts the London liveries gave:
    goldsmiths, founders, clothiers, tailors.

Blue for humility, the garb of servants
    waiting at their Lord's behest.
Gold for the diadem, the bright coronet
    of Christ's own suffering on the Cross.

Blue for the truth of Christ's very words:
    'When I was naked, you did clothe me.'
Gold for the crown of heavenly compassion:
    'When I was a stranger, you took me in.'

Was Shakespeare later making fun
    of yellow stockings (all cross-gartered)
when he dreamed Malvolio for the laughter of the crowds?
    It matters not—

for here's
no sneering, gleeful jeering
at shivering infants left in icy rain;
no widows', poor men's
frightened children
treated with disdain—
nor pleading at a fast-shut door,
neglected for another's gain.

Instead in blue and gold
we have sure welcome here,
a store of kindliness, not tears.

St Matthew Speaks Across More Than Fifteen Hundred Years: London, *1557*

I
Under the judgment of my people Israel,
daily I sat at the gate
of the imperial Roman customs' house,

well known in Capernaum
but hated while I served a puppet king—
cast out of my own synagogue.

Here I consoled myself by grafting
for all the money I could garner
through extortion.

Indeed, because they had so damned me,
I became one who keeps
a scrupulous record:

a running narrative in ledgers
of those who owed me for my pains.
Not one escaped my greedy eye.

II
But all has changed: upon a day
of calling, Christ looked at me—
at me, whose eyes *they* would not meet—

and bid me follow Him.
'My son, you'll write
a newer record, for a holy writ:

'A book whose gospel pages
will turn this world
completely upside down.

'So, like a leprous man, or one once paralysed,
stand up; arise and come with me
to serve the ones with nothing:

'to wash the feet of poor ones,
clothe the naked, visit the sick
and care for little children.

'Those are my commands;
now you shall write them in your record:
good news for all the world.'

III
No word there was of condemnation
from His lips,
no cold dismissal.

And so I left my ledgers
at the cruel customs gate,
and quit my Roman coffers—

those shining coins, the death
that I was labouring so hard to live...
I rose to follow Him.

IV
Therefore, dear people of another time,
I charge you now, who hear these words
when fifteen unkind centuries have slid away:

take up the work that Christ once gave to me—
gave to those He calls His friends
in any land upon this earth.

Stop not to count the cost—
as many times I did when at my post
beside the Roman customs house.

Thus, in giving up yourselves, your wealth,
you shall find health: find more, not less,
find life, not death.

© Lizzie Ballagher

'Then shall the King say to them on his right hand, Come ye blessed... for I was an hungered, and ye gave me meat; I was thirsty, and ye gave me drink; I was a stranger, and ye took me in; naked, and ye clothed me; I was sick, and ye visited me; I was in prison, and ye came unto me.'

Matt 25:34–36 (KJV)

Influenced by the Gospels, King Edward VI's charitable successors met each year by tradition on St Matthew's Day, 21 September. In later centuries, this day came to have many traditions attached to it: gifts of money to pupils, church services; and the band, of course, marching through the City. But their original purpose, from 1557, had been to appoint governors in accordance with the 1553 charter for all the royal hospitals of London, including Christ's; and by edict of the Order of the Hospitals of King Henry VIII and King Edward VI (1557):

'And yearly, upon the day of St Matthew th'apostle, at a general court to be held in Christ's Hospital...shall be elected and chosen new governors to govern the said hospitals...'

Under the Sign of the Bluecoat Boy: William Reeves the Colourman, *1781*

Clever with his fine-drawn fingers
from the first time he put on the cobalt coat
and gamboge-yellow hose, he fed on colour
as his fellows fed on pease-pudding, broth or mutton.

Only a few quick words of praise
from the art-school master
in early weeks of learning
and he knew what trade he would seek.

Dark dreams of hunger, of narrow, shadowed City ways,
yielded to the leaf-greens of trees
beside St Paul's. He drank the light shifting
from sunrise to sunset on the Thames:

carmine and cobalt, vermilion and crimson lake.

Just as the river, the time flowed on.
Soon they apprenticed him in gold and silver:
bending wires to his will, drawing them
through finer, ever finer dies.

Strands of gold and silver shimmered, glittered
in his eyes but never satisfied his heart: meshes
that snatched at and trapped him—bars of a birdcage—
yet he longed to fly free into light, into colour.

With his Christ's Hospital brother, Reeves took
as his motto the Bluecoat Boy: traded, gathered
soft resins, ground pigments of bone, stone and charcoal;
then, under the sign of the Bluecoat Boy, sold

in a crafted mahogany box, worlds
in miniature perfection, small cakes
that others would savour, hunger for,
to devour the banquet of colour that blazed in his vision:

forty colours to paint, to radiate,
forty colours to take: umber, sienna, chrome yellow,
gamboge yellow, viridian and ultramarine,
carmine and cobalt, vermilion and crimson lake....

© Lizzie Ballagher

Susannah Speaks, *1829*

In blue and green, plain
for sake of modesty
        (tokens of their charity),

hair hidden for meekness,
we go about our days under the chimes
        of clocks, the ringing of the bells.

Clumsy girls in our early days with sewing tasks,
we pricked ourselves and bled
        on cloth they gave to us to mend,

yet soon grew cunning with the thread,
skilled in the ways of plonket, darning wool and linsey;
            calm and quick with flashing needles

mending our brothers' saffron hose
stitching caps and aprons for ourselves,
            for juniors yet to enter to our colonnades.

And thus it is you see us in the main
with eyes dipped down,
        coifed hair covered under snowy cotton,

chattering like sparrows in the lime trees out on Fore Street:
used to being watched, for sure—though
        unaccustomed to being noted, marked.

I blush because you stare so, sir,
and I must look away to middle distance
        as you bid me—betraying nothing,

only arching my brows
in confusion, false queenliness, solemnity,
        bemusement,

telling myself that if I could learn to sew, to serve,
surely for this hour I can learn to dwell in silent joy
        on days to come

        when I may conquer *other* hearts?

Susannah Holmes' Legend Debunked, Hertford, *1966*

'A useful member of society
in the humbler walks of life
wherein she would be expected to move.'

She was a beauty,
face so serene,
apple-cheeked with surprise
at being singled out for painting
not just once, but twice.

In Hertford she adorned the dining wall
in spotless cap
and grass-green apron—
badge of honour and of service.

O, Susannah!
Over porridge and cold curled toast
we did not speak
(as rumour says we did)
in hushed Hertfordian tones
of supernatural visitations—
nor did we tell tall tales of soft-soled shoes
meandering down the wards at night.

Forget mad yarns of ghosts alighting from the chimney flues—
stories you might have heard in Horsham's second form.

Why does her picture hold the eye?

Just this: where not a smear of make-up
graced our mouths
or lit our eyes
we spoke instead of *The Eyebrows,*
of hers so perfect, arching over,
not in arrogance; not twisting
in sarcastic gaze.
No, she was just girl of our own age
thinking of a life ahead—

perhaps already sure
she would be loved.

Tall Tales, *2004*

Daily we stared at her picture:
Susannah Holmes.
Her image is burned
on our retinas.
All those years later
she haunts us yet.

An older Old Blue told me once
that when Susannah's painting
hung in Hertford's hallowed halls
she was revered
for her blushing prettiness.
Not so when Susannah came to Horsham!

Some called her the Blue Nun.
They told us tall and fearsome tales
of how she drifted nightly
down infirmary corridors,
frightening poor newbies
in their hallucinating beds.

Innocently—I'm embarrassed to admit—
we believed those tales
and used to lie awake in Leigh Hunt
shivering,
waiting to hear footsteps:
the ghostly wailing on the stairs.

Marching on St Matthew's Day, *1903*

St Matthew's Day, and we have left
the leafy groves of Horsham
for our age-old haunts in London's smoky City.

Here our ancient roots run deep;
this isn't just any marching band;
for forty years already
(a biblical span),
we've marched in time
in tune with City pageantry.
And now we're parading
to the Mansion House once more.

Our heads are high.
Our steps are sure.
We march with drums and an army of children
changing year on year but marching on

for years, decades, and centuries.

Bareheaded, hefting little flags,
the younger pupils follow on.
We move in easy gait, short steps
as we were drilled.
For all our ancient garb so grave and heavy
the pieces that we play are no vainglorious, patriotic puff
but playful, joyful,
all giving listeners delight.
And yet we move with the precision
of a classic Frodsham clock—
musical and mathematical all at once,

following the flashing cuffs,
the twirling batons of the drum major
and his drummers.
Trumpets, trombones, cornets, saxophones,
blaze out brazen notes that ring
like golden coins
on old Dick Whittington's dark pavements.
The Lord Mayor doffs his feathered hat
to honour us:
yes, even us, the *waifs and strays* of London Town.

Brangwyn Reflects, 1923

We knew in 1912 when Dr Upcott called me
to my task that a witches' brew of war
was bubbling on the Continent.
And, when I put pen to paper
for first drawings late that year,
I had the sense that friends in Belgium,
Austria, France and Germany were—
like all of us in Britain—
now facing direst danger.

Crevasses yawned
in the canvas of the Continent—
breaches in the beauty
of a world we thought we knew.
Most of all I grieved
for my beloved Belgium.
What else could I do but agree to the making
of war posters, advertisements for War Bonds,
and postage stamps...?

Yet painting familiar gospel stories,
lives of many saints
in luminous and lustrous colours,
when all around me cascaded
into chaos and despair;
to lift a candle in the darkness—
was to find and hope to mend tears
in history's fabric: yes, even among
war's stains and darkest shadows.

Since the chapel walls could not hold mosaics—
the gorgeous radiance I so craved—
I chose instead most glowing pigments;
blended them as I'd learned
from master craftsmen;
fast-bound them then with egg yolk—
tempera on canvas—
no cracks would I allow to open here...
unless they let new light in.

I wanted a glorious vitreous shimmer:
the gloss and gleam of glass
in blissful hues; the blues of heaven,
golds of truth and treasure—of miracles;
lily-whites of purity—all colours as in dreams.
But I worked, too, for the grind and grasp,
the grit and graft of men, their muscles and their sweat
in labour. And the perseverance of women:
their sharing in a longing for a better world.

Many times critics have said of me:
You don't know who you are
or what you want
or where it is that you belong.
It's true—born in Belgium,
still I am English, yet also son of the Welsh—
a man, too, to serve both lords and leaders...
but also a blunt man whose bluff craft
is not for the elite.

No, for I am a man who chooses
the lame and beggars from the streets
of Hammersmith—market traders,
vagabonds, women at their washing,
and ragged rapscallion children of poverty—
to serve as models for my work: to sit
or stand in for St Paul, or St Augustine;
St Columba or William Caxton, fiery St Peter,
or dogged city preachers in the East End.

Amid the war's profanity,
this work created havens of hope,
harbours of sweetest sanity.

Commissioned by the Ministry of Information during World War I to create war propaganda through a variety of media (something he did without charge) Frank Brangwyn was also recommended to Dr Upcott by Horsham chapel architects, Webb & Bell, as the right artist for Christ's Hospital. Dr Upcott's commission, then—to create sixteen murals for the then bare wall-panels—was something quite different from the work he was to undertake during the war years. At CH he was to depict the spread of the Christian Gospel: from Peter's preaching on the first day of Pentecost two thousand years ago to East End Pentecostal-style ministry in early twentieth-century London.

Brangwyn came to his task with a rich wealth of influences: from William Morris in England to Klimt in Austria—and beyond. Working for more than ten years in his Hammersmith studio, he painted the sixteen canvas panels with all the passion and loving attention to decorative detail of a mediaeval manuscript illuminator.

Arguably, in a time of national anguish (which he portrayed so directly and painfully in some of his work that it was rejected even by those who had commissioned it), these Brangwyn murals are examples of light and hope, as well as lessons in Christian history for the children of Christ's Hospital.

The Davis Boy, Horsham, *1940*

Spellbound,
you could not
move, were rooted, like
Coleridge's listener
when that ancient mariner
commenced his ghastly tale.
Your brother's Beethoven record—
the Eighth—soared, seared,
thundering in your ears.
And music moved you.
Struck by lightning,
you stood.
You raised your arms,
who had never danced before,
or ever thought to dance.
You moved inside the music
allegro vivace, and the music
moved in you, *allegretto*
scherzando.

You could not choose
but hear the thunderclap,
and were compelled to sway
swoop   fly   flow   go
into and under the music as if
in a pool, a waterfall of sound:
white-water rapids
that swept you
scherzando
out and over
and between
the narrow straits
of the day's constraints
then out again and into an ocean

of living joy, *vivace, allegro vivace!*
surging, cresting, with depths
you longed to plumb, to surf
and swim and dive in freedom—
lost, yet found for ever:

lightning conductor.

Conductor Sir Colin Davis 1927–2013 was a CH pupil 1938–1944. He joined the school band in 1941 as a second clarinettist. Clifford Jones in his book Christ's Hospital: The History of the Band *cites Old Blue Bryan Magee (MP)'s remark that as a child Sir Colin 'played the music as though he [were] inside it.'*

Four Hundredth Anniversary, *1953*

Marching in the band to St Paul's,
to the Lord Mayor's Mansion House
on the four hundredth anniversary of the school,
we Horsham boys and Hertford girls—
so many of us from rural backwaters
or rundown city places—
were over-awed by all we saw
in the ancient City
as we stepped out, marking time.

Mine was the tenor drum.
I bore it proudly—
white gloves flashing as I raised the sticks;
head thrown back,
aware of watchers gazing open-mouthed,
at the discord between our modern instruments
and our strange Tudor gear;
at the gleaming brass, our trumpets, timpani—
and hearing loudly, in accord,
the steady beat of drums,
booming drums and marching feet.

But any pride I felt was punctured in a wink.
One twirling stick flew from its string,
went sailing over watchers' heads
into the waiting hands of a star-struck boy
who promptly ran away with it—
vanished in the crowd.
Crestfallen, I fumbled in my pocket for the spare—
it was not there!

But instantly a watchful bobby on the beat
had caught the runaway and wrested from his grasp
the souvenir he'd thought to bear along the street.
Intent, my benefactor followed closely
until he could sidle along
and press into my hand
the errant drumstick—what relief!

So on we marched again.

Leopard on the Loose, ***1953***

Back on the Tube after all the parades,
the pomp and circumstance,
the soaring music in St Paul's,
the haze of glory and the burst of pride,
we clattered through the Underground:
went rattling back to catch our train from London Bridge.

Over my shoulders as tradition then required
I wore the tenor drummer's leopard skin.
The other boys with modest clarinets or flutes
played games in the back-reflecting glass
of train and tunnel as we sped along:
snarling in mockery at the grinning mouth
of this tame leopard draped around my neck.

At last we shrieked into London Bridge.
Awkwardly, I stood with drum upraised
in fear of a crushing in the crowd's crazed surge.

But the drum was unscathed. Instead,
a passing umbrella-point had stabbed
straight through my innocent leopard skin.

A trail of sawdust like the crumbs of biscuits
left by Hansel and Gretel in the ancient tale followed me
along the platform, up the draughty stairs,
all the way back on the Horsham train.
The other boys made fun of me,
and I wished I had a Hertford girl's swift
gift of needlework

to execute a foolproof mend
upon the leaking spotted skin
of my favourite feline friend.

Hertford Crocodiles, *1955*

Away from
the school's
familiar walls,
we straggled
in twos
between shops,
along streets
and out
across fields
where streams
ran slowly,
muddily, to
the Meads.

Lagging behind,
new girls
looked avidly
for crocodiles.
Hopes dashed,
they didn't
even see
an alligator.

Not
a
single
one.

Marching from Four's, Hertford, *1962*

Nearest the bell, we meet its clangour
greet its clamour
stepping *left-right* from the open door
into bell, birds and morning
under the limes
left-right on red tarmac

don't you cut corners
stay in step
don't tred
the heels of one in front...

Heads up
shoulders back
we stride to breakfast.

Thus we march in pairs, wheeling the turns
in neat right angles
over three sides of the square
perhaps out of respect
for royal mathemats
from whom we're severed—

(it's more than eighty miles
from our dusty colonnades to Horsham.)

So, hearing drummers, trumpets, cornets in our heads
we march into the go
and flow:
the rhythm of another day.

Marching to Westminster Abbey, *1966*

Her father had no money for music
so she might learn to play.
But, oh, how she loved to sing.

They went to Westminster in the rain—
nine hundred years since William came
and conquered England.

In the cathedral, Horsham boys
stood proudly in the gallery,
brass trumpets gleaming.

The choristers from Hertford
raised their heads
to watch, to listen and to sing.

When the procession entered in,
trumpets blazed across the nave
resounding to the roof,

the recesses, the distant arches,
lifting the hair
on the back of her neck.

Suddenly those little figures
on the Bayeux tapestry
came riding through her mind—

the roll of drums, shrill cries of men and horses
on the battlefield:
the blood, the wounds, the pity...

yet all that, even that must happen first
for England, for Edward
to come to sovereignty at all.

A sense of history fell on her as once,
four hundred years before,
the weight of destiny fell so hard

on Edward's boyhood shoulders.
The hymns, the words—they taught him how to love
the poor, to see the City's children sheltered.

Poor Princes of Darkness, Horsham, *1970*

Friday, best day for chapel duty.
They wake gleefully
        before the dawn, in darkness.
John's watch proclaims that now it's six—

the quick half-dozen dress in darkness.
They are the ones who rule the school for half an hour,
        who reign while other sleep—
            on whom depends the fresh start of another day.

They have an hour,
        and time slides easy
            for these princes.
                Hush!

            All's silent.
No wind stirs
        in the lime trees.
No light burns in their eyes.

So away they rush
        in twinkling winter air
            below the crackling stars,
with shards of frost beneath their shoes.

Big School's clock-face is mute, in shadow.
        In the close, snuffed-out smell of chapel
            when the doors are opened,
                they light the candles one by one

            to fend off darkness, spectres.

A Friday breeze insinuates itself, whining
between glass and stone, door and lintel,
quenching their early eagerness;
still, when they ring the bell to call

the faithful (and unfaithful) boys
no voice replies.
No chaplain smiling thanks.
Thick darkness reigns until

'It's one a.m.!'
a shocked small voice laments—
'Not seven!'
'Oh, we have woken everyone!'

Feverishly, fearfully,
they kill the lights,
hold breaths
wait for the clap of doom

that surely will befall them:
the flung-back door,
the anger, indignation
of those they've wakened from fast sleep.

But nothing—all stays silent.

One by one they find a place to sleep,
to wait the dawn:
Keith on the altar steps,
David G below the Brangwyn,

Eddie curled in the pulpit,
John, Chris and David B
banked in by the padding
of the masters' pews.

Again: cold air.
They see their breath in grayscale light
and wait the dawn,
the doom.

Sydney's Stomp, *1988*

'I write, not only with my head and hand, but with my feet…all these songs are…dances.' Sydney Carter, In the Present Tense, Book 2, 1969 (two years after he was already famous for 'Lord of the Dance'.

In the late 1980s, Sydney Carter (1915–2004, Christ's Hospital 1926–1933) went to sing and speak to a small gathering of fans in a private home in north Kent. Among the group was a fellow Old Blue and long-time enthusiast for Carter's unique faith-and-folk music. Who knows?—because in true Carter fashion nothing was recorded at the time—perhaps their conversation went something like the one in this poem.

OB	Why do you write songs?
SBC	I always sing before I write.
OB	Then don't the songs change over time?
SBC	Oh, yes, I rearrange them, change them, every night.
OB	You're making a joke?
SBC	No—just defining what is folk!
OB	But you do write the songs down? Or are they recorded differently in every town?

SBC Yes, I write them,
clap them, tap them,
beam them in my glance,
let others play them
on the fiddle or the flute,
on the bugle or the lute,
bouzouki or the saxophone,
on the trumpet or the cornet.
I dance them,
sing them with my feet...

OB Guitars, ever?

SBC No, never.
I'm no instrumentalist.
I think in voices,
in the sound of dancing feet,
devise the way
to spring a question
on the listener—
one with an answer
that comes from the listener.

OB You're a bit of an iconoclast?

SBC A bit! I like to weave a pattern,
in and out
and leap about.

OB And where—
beloved troubadour
whom we adore—
is God the Lord
in all of this?

SBC Beside me, always—
dancing!

GROUP (singing gleefully)
Dance, then, wherever you may be.
I am the Lord of the Dance, said He.

Credits & Acknowledgements

Quotations from the Introductions to In the Present Tense, Books 1 and 2, *1969, together with part of the chorus of 'Lord of the Dance', are reproduced by permission of Stainer & Bell Ltd, London, England www.stainer.co.uk. All rights reserved.*

Lizzie Ballagher is grateful to Stainer & Bell Ltd for permission to use the quotations incorporated into this poem.

Music Unbound: Horsham, *2005*

Please don't think when you learn
we're from some poor inner-city estate
that all we care about is rap or thrash-metal,
or grind or grunge or punk rock.

Or if we're down from northern towns,
cooled by cooling towers or Pennine winds,
kindly don't imagine we sit with fingers in our ears
and sing uncool folksongs all day long.

Or if we've come from far-off war-torn wastes
please don't suppose that we sing only
in our native tongues,
lamenting countries left behind.

And don't presume because we've never had
an instrument to call our own
that we can't hold a tune
or play a note in eight- or twelve-tone.

Nor should you assume because we've never sat
in concert halls or orchestra pits,
or sung *fortissimo* in cathedral choirs
that we can't celebrate with music.

Not so!   For here at school
stage curtains   are swept wide for us.
Walk down the Avenue   some Sunday afternoon
and hear that R&B full volume   from an open window,
or indie anthems blazing   in the background
of our Grecians' studies, folk-   rock roaring in our kitchens.

Lions of music rise   triumphant in our midst,
to shake that golden   mane of sound:
rich and passionate: unbound.

© Lizzie Ballagher

Total Immersion: Horsham, *2009*

Unborrowed voices flower,
and borrowed instruments are tuned:
raised, chimed, tinkled, rung,
        triple-tongued, plucked, bowed, strummed,
            beaten, trumpeted, drummed...

Clocks break down, shards shattering at our feet,
        for here no time has meaning
            with music swelling, unafraid:

        mediaeval masterpieces, plain-chants,
            great roaring, soaring choral works,
                sentimental rousing hymns,
                    rock and pop, folk and jazz and gospel.

The blue-gold waters of the music school grant us
        total immersion in its pool:
            sound waves splashing,
            rolling back in recital room,
                in chapel—sometimes even in the library,
                or on a clattering staircase
                    echoing in song,
                    echoing just for the sheer joy of it.

Music fills each Horsham space that we inhabit:
        smiles shining, spines tingling, ears open,
        eyes locked on the captain, drum major, conductor;
        hearts in tune:
calmed to quieter waters in chapel candlelight,
        where Brangwyn's lilies bloom incandescent;
carried outside in the flashing tides of marching—
        the beat and rhythm and swing of it;

or surfing the glorious breakers
of towering orchestral sound...
while woodwinds
whisper at our backs.

© Lizzie Ballagher

Outdoors

&

Indoors

Elia Goes Swimming at Newington, *1785*

True, in winter I could hide myself
between the shelves of bookshops:
lose myself in magic realms
I'd learned to love so long ago...

but leave-days—
long days when we were granted holiday—
were my grieve-days in dark days of winter
far away from home.

However, in summertime,
save for boys who found
our boisterous water-games disquieting,
we could go quite cheerfully
all the livelong day to play in Newington,
our bluecoats, shoes and yellow stockings
cast off along the riverbank
until the pumpkin sun sank down.

Cooled, with thirsts all slaked,
we joyfully splashed and swam
like otters in the River New,
revelling the day away,
wading in the silky water
that ran—for us alone, it seemed—
all the way from Hertfordshire...

And then in twilight to return to school
as hungry as hunters,
full of tales of our adventures
afloat on sultry seas:
swept into the mouths of monstrous rivers,
or even caught in the mouths of monsters
out beyond the oceans:
those deeps our seafaring fellows
soon should cross.

The Smallest Boy *1950*

Wild on open northern moors,
running amok with Father away
and Mother's mind unhinging
                    in the strain,
I was shipped like a ration parcel—
                    small, at that—
from grandparent to grandparent
until each died. And 'Something
has to be done
about this little boy!'
I overheard the grown-ups say.

A scholarship was found for me
to an unknown country far away—
'Sussex,' they said—
but I wasn't 'foreigner' for long,
surrounded by voices from deepest Devon
or London's rough East-End.

While we could play marbles, cricket, football,
scrap in the playground,
march in the band,
sweet-talk Miss Todd in the art school,
wolf down herrings,
duff and custard,
porridge and jam, as much as we liked,

hunger troubled me no more,
nor where I was to lay my head next night.
I was a bluecoat boy
in a dark blue coat
with yellow stockings
and a peg and settle all my own.

I dreamed I had come
to a holiday camp
where I might live for ever:
stay safe and sate
my avid curiosity.

The Smallest Girl, Hertford, *1961*

Fidgeting to be fitted for new uniform,
I stood knotted
with concern for my mother—
I've been her *big sister as well!*
How will she manage?
What about my brothers?

Around and around me the white tape went:
quick numbers jotted down
for those strange and scratchy clothes—
the blue tunic, pale blouses, striped tie, lisle stockings;
Sunday's dark coat-frock that made me feel as if I looked
like a blue ironing board with gold stripes.

'The Smallest Girl who's ever arrived in Two's,'
Mrs Winstone intoned, tut-tutting.
I frowned and tried to make sense of it all.
So why do I need to leave my mother now?
Are there no others
of eleven or younger?

'And you're such a *thin* child,'
she added severely, knitted eyebrows
emphasising her point before
she turned me once again, muttering, to pin up the hem...
just as if I were somehow to blame
that we'd all been run ragged
looking after my fragile mother,
tending to my younger brothers.

Fitted for uniform that day,
because I was so small
in others' reckoning—
titch, squit, little one—
I did not find my fit in the school
until I settled into lessons.

Blessed with quick eyes and ears,
unafraid to answer if I understood,
willing and used to working hard,
I slowly made my way
from youngest to oldest,
from smallest to one of the tallest.

Gradually I grew to realise
that taking thought
about one's stature isn't,
as words in St Matthew's Gospel taught,
always very wise.

My Naughty Little Sister, *1959*

She'd heard my tales of school
and couldn't wait to bid farewell and thanks
to friends from primary school
before she joined the Hertford ranks.

At home she marched around our cramped bedroom
in a blue tunic I would soon outgrow,
laughed at the soft velour I'd proudly worn
to travel home for holidays—
navy with the crest all red and blue and gold.

She vowed so scornfully, in mockery,
'I'll never be made to wear a hat.
Not one like that!'

But she followed me to Hertford
just a year after I strapped on
brown school shoes, donned
a blue pinafore and
a blue velour hat, myself.

Stuffed in a carriage made for eight
we rode the train in sardine-style
from Liverpool Street
to Hertford East,
ten or twelve of us jammed in tight.
No train would wait—
'Jump on! Or you'll be left behind.'

Pulling the leather strap to drop
the window of the train,
my sister cried sarcastically,
'Oh breathe that fragrant air!'

Her head went out.
She looked about
as the train clacked on and jangled,
clicked and clanked through Seven Sisters.

Off blew her velour school hat.
She shrieked in horror.
Jenny in the corner snapped,
'You witless girl—sit down!'
Red-faced, I raised the window
for my little sister.
Witless, I thought, *and hatless now.*

Just four days later she was summoned
to Miss West's hushed study,
handed a brown paper package half unwrapped,
told to open it properly
and explain herself;
a railwayman from Hertford East
had handed in the hat
and she was in some trouble.

Mutinous, unbowed, she said,
'I didn't mean to let it blow away.
But I *hate* that hat.'

Gently, she was told, she would not want
to lose her head (like two of the wives of King Henry VIII)
by putting it out of a train.
She shed some angry, laughing tears.

Then half a century later
when her daughter married in Australia
hers was the biggest, bluest
velourest hat
in the whole wide church.

Outdoor Boy in the Vale of Evesham: John Snow, *1941–51*

He knew when he was seven—
eight perhaps—what he would do,
though not yet how that ambition
would be brought from dreams
to the light of any summer's day.

By his own admission wild—
freely he ran the fields and lanes
of Worcestershire:
nesting, scrumping, fishing,
testing himself by climbing trees,
gleefully swinging on bell-ropes
in his father's church bell-tower.

His grandfather and father
had dreamed the dream before him:
that John would be a batsman.
A vicarage child, no silver spoon
for him, but he had more:

his father to bowl and show him
how to hold the bat;
three sisters and a patient mother
to play the game with him;
and a willow bat to beguile
the longest days
in the rambling Evesham garden.

Here raspberry canes stood close
as hostile fielders of the ball; the garden roller
sometimes served as wicket,
clanging the 'out!'
with the dullness of a broken bell
when his father was the bowler
and he'd misplayed a stroke.

A kind of craze possessed him
in those early summer days:
a May-time fever when cold winds ceased,
when lawns' first cut was made; when sunlight
and his strength fell on him like a mantle;

when the crease was mown,
green sweetness of grass
and honey pervading any moving air;
when practice nets were hung,
red balls bowled faster,
ever faster, over the top
and sometimes wildly...

Cricket dreams expanded in his mind,
his every waking moment.
But change now wound towards him
fast as an inswinger down the crease:
a place to board at Horsham before he was ten.

Outdoor Man at Horsham: Len Bates, *1935–1963*

Born at Edgbaston
where his father was groundsman,
Len Bates cast aside his soldier's kit
the day that he came home from war;
threw down his rifle, full of joy;
went out to nets to practise.

For Warwickshire he scored
twenty-one hard-fought centuries
and twenty-thousand runs.
Now two years past retirement,
a legend in his time,
Bates came to coach at Horsham.

As Snow much later said of Bates:
he was a brown hawk of a man
eyeing the players shrewdly;
intolerant of lazy, lackadaisical play:
arithmetic, sympathetic in his ability
to measure boys, to know, to calculate
who had the wit to bat, to catch,
to run, to field, to bowl...Under his gaze
they learned to find their rhythm;
he brought the best from every child.

From Bates they learned
quieter confidence, a faster bowl
or shorter run-up;
a neater way with bats;
best placings of young hands and feet;
the will and skill to win.

Had Bates been a spinner of cricket tales,
then the boys he taught
became the poetry he wrote:
the rhymes in their own rights,
epics in their own times,
legends in their own lights.

Outdoor Boy at Horsham: John Snow, *1951–1959*

Bereft as his family drove from the gates,
he spent the first day crying. But then
the sun lit up those acres of sporting fields;
he found he could play games
almost every afternoon.
All homesickness fled.

Here at school it was football, rugby...
and to his delight cricket, cricket,
and more cricket! He played
to boundaries, ever wider boundaries.

Poised like a champion greyhound
in the traps before a race,
he was always first to the field
for nets or practice sessions.

Bates taught him how
to hit the ball with ease, fluidity;
to hold the bat
with just the right grip;

to use the momentum of his lanky legs,
long arms and longer body
to run up powerfully: to bowl
with all the grit and grace of a professional.

Within two years Snow grew
to value all he learned
on Horsham's playing fields;
was transformed into a cricketer:
the fours and sixes others hoped to score were bowled away
before the swiftness of his arm.

John Snow dedicated his book Cricket Rebel *(Hamlyn Publishing, 1976) both to his parents and to Len Bates, then the cricket coach at Christ's Hospital. Lizzie Ballagher is grateful to John Snow, and to his book, for ideas for this three-poem sequence.*

Howzat, Hertford, *1960*

At Hertford in the mid-twentieth century, the greatest cricketing achievement—surpassing even a win in inter-house matches—was, in the games' staff's view, to demonstrate keenness for the game. Sadly, this ethic did not always produce the intended consequences among the girls. While a few genuinely fell in love with cricket, many spent years feigning enthusiasm, day-dreaming (and if they could manage it) sunbathing in quiet moments.

Decked in Ashbourne hats
we form our crocodile, duck
up the long alley
to high open fields,
polishing the ball as sunshine
honeys down on us.

Showing how it's done,
Miss Park lopes to the wicket,
strong-arms the ball—wow!

Sun-dazed like beatniks
at festivals, fielders chew
sweet Ashbourne grasses,
urging each other
to blow on them, make a screech
that sends Miss King quite wild.

Astigmatic, Sue
cannot catch the ball. But mind
if she's fast-bowling—
all this after her
brother spent the Easter hols
teaching her some tricks.

Horsham had coached him:
where all the boys wish they could
fast-bowl like John Snow.

Pippa *sans* her hat
shades her eyes against the sun,
is scorned for missing
easy catches till
a scorcher finds its way straight
into her hot hands.

Howzat!

Hollyburning, Hertford, *1958*

Our favourite winter night on every ward:
lights out, dressing gowns pulled round,
the ward-mistress unfreezing any end-of-term frowns
as she bears in a stout cream candle in a jar,
carrying it as proudly as were she
Florence Nightingale on a dark Crimean ward;
then monitresses come trooping in at last
with lesser candles,
lighting them solemnly in saucers
to flicker on the mantelpiece below the roll of honour.

We range ourselves
around the hearth:
circle of light in the dayroom's December darkness
under the litanies of names
of those who've gone before
and taught this age-old tradition to our seniors
when they were little girls themselves.

For days we've gathered holly on our walks,
and now the grate is piled up high,
nearby baskets overflowing with more to spare,
topped by a Yule log the steward has given.
Orange fire roars, soars in the chimney,
black leaves crackling, red berries sparking:
even the chimney glows scarlet in the dark.

Then carols and old songs until bed-time—
Hosannah! Gloria in Excelsis!
Should Auld Acquaintance Be Forgot—
exams and all old enmities forgotten:
instead, darkness driven from our doors
by holly-fire, by holy fire
and the voices of the angels,
all of us knowing we'd be on the train next day
from Hertford East to Liverpool Street...
            and so to Christmas.

Ascension Day Picnics, Hertford, *1960s*

'O clap your hands, all ye people; shout unto God with the voice of triumph...for God is gone up with a shout, the Lord with the sound of a trumpet' (Ps 47:1, 5, KJV*)*

The psalms are sung,
the Matins done.
Now, babbling, bubbling with excitement
we board coaches
for the traditional day's outing.

Hatfield House, Dunstable Downs
and Epping Forest are likely picnic places—
we don't always know where we're going till we get there—
but where for a change we can roam free
of ward mistresses, monitresses...

The Ilford Film in black and white
tells other truths:
knots of girls camped
on Girl Guide groundsheets
huddle together to stave off late spring's chill

as wind claws at us from below the hill:
though we sit perched
like country princesses
by some muddy path and watch
sheep safely grazing fields beside us.

One year, spiteful rain falls endlessly.
We picnic now in a cattle byre
with mud up to our ankles.
Around us, trees bend double in the wind,
dripping dolefully, hung with water.

None of this matters while we swig
samizdat cider (watered-down)
from a plastic mug—hooch smuggled in
by someone's brother one Long Saturday—
or decorous orange squash;

or munch on greenish hard-boiled eggs and ham,
first carefully undertaking
the obligatory lettuce inspection
for unwanted, wriggling protein.
Then, oh! those glorious sticky buns!

The girl who had the fold-out camera
shoots us all
while we make funny faces,
screwing up our eyes
in May-time mid-day glare

and hearing in our heads the lyrics
of the Beatles' latest tune,
wishing it was indeed
a *good day sunshine*
we could be sitting in.

Then back in the coach and Hertford-bound,
furiously sucking peppermints,
knowing we can get away with things today
that wouldn't be tolerated otherwise. Dutifully
we start with *Unum concentum tollite* and Girl Guide songs...

but soon we switch to a version
of the newest Stones' or Shadows' tunes
from *Pick of the Pops*,
or soppy love-songs, homesick blues
sung uproariously in breathy laughter.

Beyond the coach's steamed up windows
winter's gone up with a merry shout
and leaves are now unfolding by the roadside
in fresh and vivid greens
for summer's true beginning.

Cheers: Horsham, *1973*

We were the privileged, all right:
could drink our three half-pints of beer
each week at the Grecians' Club.
Great stuff
though, surely,
never enough.

We learned to brew our own
in a ramshackle shed near Peele,
smuggled our witches' brew
all through the Tube
where no one thought
to search for us.
Cheers!

The beer was foul
but home-brewed hooch was far more fun
to slurp, far stronger
than the ale we drank more decorously
at the Grecians' Club.
Cheers!

In our study
we hid the crates of beer
behind chairs
and under tables.
If anyone noticed, no one snitched on us.
Cheers!

Summer in my last year,
and in came Lamb's housemaster,
all smiles, to start a plan, he said,
for my stellar future.

The stellar future came to pass
a fraction sooner than we planned
as bottles chose this very time to blow
like fireworks under the furniture.

I caught my breath.
He raised an eyebrow, grinned.
'We'll have that chat,
I think, a little later.
You may have other things to do.
Get that lot binned.'
Looking pointedly at the floor
and calling back, he shut the door,
'*Cheers!*'

Time

&

Change

Science Triptych: *1899–1985*

New Water, London, 1899

Backing away from the front,
we watched with widening eyes
as he demonstrated from the teacher's bench
with hissing hydrogen flame
directed on a flask
how to condense water.

The watchglass filled with H_2O:
pure water in our place
of sometimes dirty water
from the Thames.

Hydrogen Gas at Hertford, 1968

Item one: there, there, at the top
of the periodic table!
That we, like Boyle, could learn to make it…
surely some kind of wonder?

But Chemi T had us feed HCl
down a thistle funnel and into a flask
of granulated zinc;
then watch the fizz—

bubbles rising, rising—
and collect the gas from the tube.

She showed us how to test with splints.
We heard that squeaky pop
she had described for us before.

A Coming Together, Horsham, 1985

More complex now,
the apparatus intrigued us all:
two test tubes full of water
sealed with bungs,
fitted, both, with carbon rods
(one negative, one positive)
and wires connected to a DC battery.

So what should we expect, our teacher asked,
if a current were passed through?

Explosions?
Fizzing bubbles?
Squeaky pops?
Ice cream, sir, and lollipops?
(silly suggestion from the back).

We held our breaths, observing…
bubbles, bubbles in them both.

We turned the tubes:
            unstopped the positive first
no squeaky pop but a glowing splint
that rekindled in a flare of flame—
we'd made pure oxygen!

            unstopped the negative next,
applied a glowing splint
and got that squeaky pop—
we'd made more hydrogen!

Full circle back
to home-made oxygen and hydrogen.

We could go round again, combine them
to create pure water...

Verrio's Views: The Leviathan Moves from London to Horsham, *1901–1902*

Royal Holloway art curator Charles Carey speaks about the painting's move, which began in the spring of 1901 and was accomplished exactly one year later, in April 1902.

When first I saw this painting, my breath
was caught, my heart was stopped
but only for an instant. And not because I loved it
at first sight, but because it is gargantuan!

As if we were charged with moving three great dragons
from the dining hall of Newgate's cloistered walls,
I led men in the building of new stanchions;
supervised the structures that they put in place;
saw pulleys, ladders, levers at the ready
to take full weight—two tons, and half another more:

three panels all neglected, pocked and pitted
by uncouth youth who threw their cabbage,
their greasy mutton gravy, without regard for art
or for the history of their ancient school!

I shuddered when I realised the task ahead;
but having overseen the moving of some mighty pieces
knew it could be done. On my direction,
men hauled upon the ropes.
The leviathan writhed, sagged, twisted,
threatened to descend upon the labourers...

then steadied as I knew it would,
held fast for skilful hoisting,
was gently lowered to the floor
and rolled in cylinders.

With frames and battens,
plates and scaffold poles
the leviathan was moved
to a horse-drawn van and slowly,
slowly carried down the roads and lanes
to a new home here in Horsham...

where I cleaned it, relined it, restained it,
strained it on a newer Oregon pine-tree frame.
Again I led men in the building of stanchions;
supervised the structures that they put in place;

again saw pulleys, ladders, levers at the ready
to take full weight—two tons, and half another more—
hoisted it inch by inch,
groaning and twisting against taut ropes...
but raised it, raised at the last
to the long, long wall of the dining hall.

Voices from the Lime Trees: Last Day, Hertford, *1985*

They lined us up in the square under those lovely lime trees
for a final photograph.

We're all smiling, but look closely and you might catch
the frisson of anxiety behind the shininess.

After a final walk up the curving stairs
to formal graces and the lunch-time gavel

as we'd always known it at Hertford
we felt lost—

glad to know of the opportunities
that Horsham in the autumn would afford,

yet, in a funny sort of way, surrounded
by rumours of coming bulldozers, cheated

because the bulwark of our rituals (however out-of-date,
ridiculous) was what we knew:

what defined and shaped our lives
but would now go under a very different gavel.

Soon we would be learning other languages—
not just Latin, French, or Greek, or German—

but the customs of Horsham in a different dining hall,
with another set of strangers,

starting right from the beginning again under the Verrio painting
that showed our forebears on their knees...

'Love the Brotherhood,' bade the granite inlay
at the foot of Hertford's dining-hall stairs:

but that would be a slow beginning
in a faster time of change.

Voices from the Lime Trees:
First Days at Horsham, *1985*

'But O!
How oft, at school, with most believing mind,
Presageful, have I gazed upon the bars
To watch that fluttering stranger!'

(Lines from S T Coleridge, *Coleridge, Poetical Works* (London: Oxford University Press, 1969, ed.1912 by E H Coleridge), p 240.)

Locked in, hedged in, boxed in
that's how we'd felt in the eighties
living under frankly antiquated rules,
a regime incomprehensible to us—
and sometimes silences too long
and cold to bear

where barbed wire grew on wall-tops,
where girls in 8's could see beyond the gates
to couples kissing on the steps of the local cinema

though none of that for us, of course,
who lived as strangers in our older world,
all out of time and out of step
with people marching not
to the summons of a meal-time bell
or across to a hushed, dim chapel,
but to their own beat
in far wider streets than ours...

To move to our ancient inheritance at Horsham, then,
was novel, nerve-wracking;

what struck us in the early days
was the space, the openness in this new place:
to move and speak and laugh and sing
and be heard—actually listened to at last;
named, finally claimed as part of the larger school...

though the boys were as foreign to us as we to them,
they were kind in their bewildered sort of way;
we were so outnumbered
that at first we kept old silences
and simply watched until, soon,

the pace picked up. We breathed
the free air of Sussex woods and fields;
broad, sunlit vistas spread before us.

The Naming of Names, Horsham, *1985*

'O be some other name
Belonging to a man.
What's in a name? That which we call a rose
by any other name would smell as sweet.'
Shakespeare's Romeo & Juliet, *II:2:41–44*

After the Hertford invasion:
startling changes—
not all obvious...

never mind the shock and strangeness
of girls sitting eagle-eyed in science labs,
or racing on the playing fields,
or singing in the choir:

young women with clear voices, minds of their own,
who told us they felt they'd been let out of gaol
coming to all this space,
this open place...

no, what had altered most
for those of us who noticed such a thing
was how the masters changed the way
they spoke to us by name:

no longer were we Smith or Shufflebottom,
Kwame, Hardwick, or O'Doherty:
but John or Peter,
Jamal, Richard, Daniel...

suddenly we were selved again,
humanised and honoured for our own beings—
not just for our family name
but for who we knew ourselves to be...

since there was little honey in the rapped out,
snapped out surname summoning us;
so it was sweet to hear
upon the tongues of those who taught us

the names bestowed so lovingly from the start,
our titles and entitlement:
the names we knew as birthright.

Sunday at the Cenotaph, ***2018***

I haven't seen you since the summer.
You've grown: your hair though tied in wispy plaits
still drifts in the Whitehall breeze,
        but you are carried forward
        on the cloud of music and remembrance
        marching with all your friends
        as you lead the People's Procession past the Cenotaph:

black shoes gleam from under bluecoats
on the scuffed November pavements;
        ahead of you the whirl and flail of drumsticks,
        the white-gloved precision of the drum major.

How upright you are,
shining eyes so fixed on the sheet-music
that you don't see me in the crowd,
your proud grandmother
here to remember her own grandfather,
        the one she never knew,
        your twice great-grandfather
        who lost his life on the Somme
        among so many more—

the grandmother who watches now with swelling pride
        that strange mix of solemnity and cheek
        that seems to mark the children of Christ's Hospital.

Your band is a rainbow of defiance,
        dazzling against the steel-grey streets of London's winter,
a loud shout of dissent
        in the face of a murderous century of war.

Exhilarated, bright with joy and hope,
you march past a hundred strong
behind the flail and whirl of drumsticks,
the giggles of the piccolos,
the sonorous tones of saxophones
and pompous boom of the big bass drum...

while you with your wispy plaits and unwavering eyes,
with all your gentle innocence of war,
push out the glittering slide of your trombone—
it's almost as long as you are tall—
and pass me—your proud granny in the crowd—
in your bright cloud of music.

Full Circle

'In my beginning is my end.' *T S Eliot, East Coker, The Four Quartets.*

I

Field trip: trained now to begin with a null hypothesis
we record our dull premise
that between gastropods
on the sedimentary shore
and gastropods on the rocky shore
there would be no
differences in population.

Gathering, gathering data for a whole day:
tide in, tide out,
tide in again…

searching for signs of predation,
drilling shells for traces of parasitic invasion,
we weigh, we count, we measure,
gather, gather data

until we have a heap,
much as the tide heaves up
shingle and pebbles from that longshore bar,
depositing them again…
but only until ebb tide…

and what we find
on this field trip / beach trip
blows our first hypothesis
straight out to sea with mounting waves:
no simple picture, this—
so many variables in our investigations,
so many beyond our imaginations.

Now trained to begin with a null hypothesis
(what use is any dull hypothesis?)
we begin again when the tide sweeps out:
gathering, gathering shells once more:
beach trip.

II
In Sussex by the sea
on, on, in 4/4 time
marching as if
there's no other way to move
in Sussex by the sea.

'Sussex by the Sea'—
CH's marching song—
goes in and out, tide-like,
with verse, refrain and chorus:
left, right and left, right,
with boots in time
to booming drums
and cheery bugles.

So if the newbies don't know
the song when they start
they'll surely know it by the time we end
in Sussex by the sea
with 'Sussex by the Sea'.

III
That poet knew a thing or two.
The journey we begin at school
already has an end in view—
despite a truth we may not yet see
as pupils of promise,
in a place full of promise,
and of promises kept fast for centuries.

Thus I began with loose yarn-ends,
with the prayers of a prince in London,
with the visions of a swimming boy,
and now, here, I end with the same.

Or do I end with the Hertford beginnings,
beginning again at the end
of all the themes and variations
looping full circle
with beating retreat in Sussex by sea?
with Hertford's lost ends, its loose ends?
with the prayers of a prince who began with a premise
and lived out his promise in London?

A Bronze for Christ's Hospital

In 2017 a public sculpture in bronze by Andrew F Brown was erected in Greyfriars, Newgate Street. This work was to commemorate the presence of Christ's Hospital in the City of London between 1552 and 1902—350 years—a time during which the school lodged, fed, clad, and taught over 45,000 children through the kindness of many London benefactors and donors.

From the City's dismal shadows,
from the hungry streets of Bow or Newgate Market;
from pestilential haunts on Cheapside
          where Chaucer's shade must surely still be shifting

          ran, helter-skelter, children of the City:
without bed, without bread,
without mothers, without fathers,
without clothes, starving with the cold,
sickly with lack of food and honest air—
          many without shelter save low bridges, alleyways.

To Greyfriars first they arrived,
often in twos or threes.
Some brought a brother, some a sister or another:
daughters, sons of friendless ones;
children of travellers and strangers; the dispossessed;
          urchins, waifs and strays.

          Yet, now, all step to the inner music,
the beat on the street of a march into their future days:
some serving others as once they first were served;
unashamed in bluecoats, yellow hose;
confident, not arrogant;
          original, unapologetic...

marching from long-past Tudor days,
they are the ones coming to be
tomorrow's hopes, those finding newer ways—
daughters and sons of Christ's Hospital.

Endings & Beginnings: Horsham

Out through the east cloister
    the band marches crisply on
      while leavers drift or dance or march
        into their lives
          with eyes to the fore, the fore....

          If music echoes behind them
        in ears and minds and hearts
      it is music to carry them onwards:
        on the wave of summer air
          on the swell of satisfaction
          on the rush of joy
            for investigations just begun
              art and craft hard-won
                a race well run
                  a work well done....

Drums in perfect synchronicity
    mark time, mark time:
      sashes, maces, flashing gloves,
        brass uplifted, glinting back
          July's yellow blaze....

Where hopes flare like beacons
    smiles break more radiantly,
      even, than this summer sun...

while out across the quad
    the band marches crisply on
      and leavers drift or dance or march
        into their lives
          with eyes forward, forever forward.

Credits & Acknowledgements

In the poem 'Sydney's Stomp', quotations from the Introductions to *In the Present Tense*, Books 1 and 2, 1969, together with part of the chorus of 'Lord of the Dance', are reproduced by permission of Stainer & Bell Ltd, London, England www.stainer.co.uk. All rights reserved.

Without the support, scholarship and good sense of the following people, this collection of poetry could never have been written. I am indebted to them all: family, friends, fellow members of the Poetry Society and Society of Authors; to the staff of the Christ's Hospital Museum and of the City of London Museum; to the families of Old Blues celebrated and remembered here; to editors of *The Blue*; to historians, librarians, biographers, researchers and the keepers of the literary estates of some Old Blues. Above all, I am indebted to Old Blues of the last seventy years who have showered me with ideas, stories, memories, and suggestions for the poems gathered here. Please forgive me if I have through some oversight omitted any of you.

Mel Anderson
David Arnold
Jane Bailey
John Ballagher
Mark Barley
Terence Bate
Pete and Carole Batty
Chris Blewett
Rosie Brave
Diana Cant
Simon Chadwick
Yvonne Chapman
Rohan Dale
Helen Davis
Fiona Dodd

Jules and Vanessa Dussek
Desi Elizabeth
Estate of Edmund Blunden (David Higham Associates)
Estate of Sydney Carter (Stainer & Bell Ltd)
Allison Fahy
Nick Gibson
Clorinda Goodman
Chris Grady
Stephanie Graves
Rennie Halstead
Simon Hardwick
Mac and Jenny Hawkins
Elizabeth Haylett Clark at the Society of Authors
Bruce Heywood
Libby Horner
Liz Jay
Wendy Jones
Amy Lonton
Jane Lovell
Guylène Marchard-Green
Angela Martin
Clare Messenger
David Miller
Susan Mitchell
Caron Nadal
Caroline Payne
Alicia Pentin
Julie Poole
Stephen Poole
Myrna Reader
Graham Riches
Alun Robert
John Snow
Richard Stenning, Philip Whyte, and Simon Frodsham
at Charles Frodsham & Co Ltd
Lesley Stone

David Taplin
Jackie Trinder
Zac Thraves
Lindsay Usher
Maria Van Vatanen
The families of Barnes Wallis and Mary Stopes-Roe
Philippa White
Victoria Wilson
Kate Young

Bibliography of Sources for Christ's Hospital Poetry

David Arnold, *From Hackney to Horsham: A Schoolmaster's Life* (Grosvenor House Publishing Limited: Tolworth, 2018).

Gerald Atkinson, *A Book of Housey Slang* (Christ's Hospital Enterprises Ltd, Horsham, 1994).

Mike Barford, *Badges, Prizes & Tokens: Christ's Hospital Heritage No 7* (Christ's Hospital: Horsham, 2013).

Mike Barford, *Cartoons: Christ's Hospital Heritage No 5* (Christ's Hospital: Horsham, 2012).

Mike Barford, *Engravings: Christ's Hospital Heritage No 2* (Christ's Hospital: Horsham, 2010).

Mike Barford, Diana Gould, Clifford Jones, Ken Mansell et al, *Memorabilia: Christ's Hospital Heritage No 3* (Christ's Hospital: Horsham, 2011).

Edmund Blunden, *Undertones of War* (Penguin Books: London, 1928, reprinted 2000 by Penguin Classics).

Sydney Carter, *In the Present Tense* Books 1 and 2 (Galliard/ Stainer & Bell Ltd, London: 1969).

Samuel Taylor Coleridge, *Biographia Literaria*, Ed George Watson (J M Dent & Sons, Everyman Editions no. 11: London, 1956).

Samuel Taylor Coleridge, *Coleridge, Poetical Works*, Ed Hartley Coleridge (Oxford University Press: London, 1969).

Bob Finch, 'Lodging and learning for children cast adrift' (letter to *The Telegraph,* 27 January 2016).

Audrey Griggs, *Away from the Bombs and the Boys: Christ's Hospital Girls' School in Wartime* (The Book Guild: Lewes, 2004).

Clifford Jones, *Customs Traditions: Christ's Hospital Heritage No 4* (Christ's Hospital: Horsham, 2011).

Clifford Jones, *Postcards: Christ's Hospital Heritage No 1* (Christ's Hospital: Horsham, 2010).

Clifford Jones, *School Life: Christ's Hospital Heritage No 6* (Christ's Hospital: Horsham, 2012).

Clifford Jones, *Christ's Hospital: The History of the Band* (Christ's Hospital: Horsham, 2017).

Clifford Jones, *The Sea & the Sky: The History of the Royal Mathematical School of Christ's Hospital* (Christ's Hospital: Horsham, 2015).

James Henry Leigh Hunt, *The Autobiography* (Smith, Elder & Co, London, 1850).

James Henry Leigh Hunt, *Studies at Christ's Hospital,* 1828.

Charles Lamb, *The Essays of Elia* (J M Dent & Sons, Everyman Editions no 14: London, 1947).

David Miller, compiler, *In Their Own Words: Christ's Hospital & the Great War 1914–1918* (© Multiple authors 1914–1998).

David Miller, *Sir Barnes Wallis & the RAF Foundationers' Trust 1951–2003* (Christ's Hospital Club: Horsham, 2003).

Ed Smith, 'Room at the Top' (*Times Modern, The Times,* 11 July 2011).

John Snow, *Cricket Rebel, An Autobiography* (Hamlyn: London, 1976).

Anon, *Christ's Hospital: A Short History* (Christ's Hospital: Horsham, 2018).

Anon, *Christ's Hospital Girls' School, Hertford* (Daniel Edelman Ltd: London, ca 1980).

Anon, 'Lessons for Life: Hearts and Minds' (*Daily Mail Magazine,* 18 February 2006).

Anon, 'Night hundreds of trees fell at Christ's Hospital' (*Country Times*, October, 2017).

Holy Bible, King James (Authorised) Version, 1611.

Multiple contributors, *The Blue* (Christ's Hospital, 1950 onwards).

The Book of Common Prayer, 1548.

VII

Old Blues in Canada

Between 1617 and 1778, an astonishing 967 students were sent from Christ's Hospital to work in the American colonies.(1) There was just one Canadian child, Thomas Gant, a five-year old, taken by a ship's captain to an unidentified person in Quebec City. He was shown as an enrolled student. In the 160 year period, this meant an average of six students per year.

The first significant mention of students being sent to Canada is noted in an article published in the house magazine of the Hudson's Bay Company.(2) This company was founded in London, England, in 1670, to develop trade and commerce (principally fur) in the territory comprising the Hudson Bay watershed known as 'Rupert's Land' after Prince Rupert, the Governor of the Hudson's Bay Company. The Company embarked upon a policy of recruitment of well-educated young men (typically 13 to 18 years of age), these to be hired as indentured apprentices for periods of up to eight years. Pupils were chosen from London charity schools, with suitability in such fields as navigation, surveying/mapping, and trade.(3)

Two such schools were selected – Christ's Hospital, founded in 1552 ('Blues'); and The Gray Hospital, a Royal Foundation of Queen Anne, founded in 1695 ('Grays'). In the period 1680–1806, the Hudson's Bay Company took 22 apprentices – 11 came from The Grays, and 11 from The Blues. The students from Christ's Hospital were rated as better educated in reading, writing, and grammar, and showed desirable emphasis in mathematics, navigation, and cartography. (The school even had two full-scale model ships at its Newgate Street site.)

One of the apprentices, Joseph Beioley, who arrived in 1800, became a chief factor (in charge of a fur trading post) of the Hudson's Bay Company in 1821. Later, he was governor and president of the Amicable Society of Blues and a life governor of the Benevolent Society of Blues.(3)

In the 20th century, four more boys were hired as trainee factors. This brought the Hudson's Bay Company's programme to an end, with 15 persons hired from Christ's Hospital in the period 1670–1930.(3)

There were of course other Old Blues who made their own way to Canada, of whom several made a significant contribution. Thomas Wright (1740–1812), Old Blue, was a surveyor, politician, and judge. He arrived in North America in 1758, where he furthered his education with practical work under the surveyor general of Georgia. The following year, as deputy to the surveyor general of the Northern District of North America, Wright assisted in the survey of St John's Island and Cape Breton Island. In 1769, St John's Island was made a separate colony from Nova Scotia, and in the following year Wright was appointed a member of the Council. Wright was appointed Surveyor General of the colony in 1773. The following year, he became a judge of the Supreme Court. At the time of his death in 1812, Wright had been active in surveying and mapping the Atlantic shore of North America for almost 50 years. After his death, the post of Surveyor General went in turn to his sons, Charles and George, and to his grandson, George, who held the position until 1854. For an 80-year period, then, the island's only Surveyors General were members of the Wright family.(4)

Also of interest, although he was not an Old Blue, William Wales was sent to Hudson Bay by the Royal Society, to observe the transit of Venus in 1769. He later became Master of the Royal Mathematical School at Christ's Hospital. Wales Point in British Columbia was named in 1793 after William Wales by Captain Vancouver. In his journal, Vancouver remarks:

'The west point of Observatory inlet I distinguished by calling it Point Wales, after my much-esteemed friend, Mr Wales of Christ's Hospital to whose kind instructions in the early part of my life I am indebted for that information which has enabled me to traverse and delineate these lonely regions.'[(5)]

Presumably, the concluding portion of this remark refers to the voyage Vancouver made in James Cook's ship *Resolution*, when he was one of the junior officers while William Wales served as the astronomer.

John Colborne (1778–1863), Old Blue, was a career army officer. He fought in the Peninsular War, where he commanded the 52nd Regiment of Oxfordshire Light Infantry. He commanded the same regiment at the Battle of Waterloo, where he distinguished himself. In 1828, he was appointed lieutenant-governor of Upper Canada. In this position he greatly increased the population of the province by initiating a system of immigration to bring settlers from Britain. In 1836, he became commander-in-chief of all the armed forces in British North America. He returned to England in 1839, where he was elevated to the peerage as Baron Seaton. In 1860, he was promoted to Field Marshal.[(6)]

Hamnett Kirkes Pinhey (1784–1857), Old Blue, was a successful businessman and landowner. He left Christ's Hospital in 1799 to go into trade, and appears to have prospered. In 1819, he was a liveryman of the Company of Grocers and a governor of Christ's Hospital. The following year, he left for British North America. He had been given a land grant north of Ottawa, where, eventually, his estate amounted to more than 2,000 acres. He served as local reeve, warden of Dalhousie District Council, deputy superintendent of schools for Carleton County, and eventually in 1847 as legislative councillor – a position he held until his death in March 1857. He was a philanthropist, and appears to have considered education most significant as his philanthropy included sustaining Christ's Hospital. (He used his governorship in the school to sponsor the education of young Canadians and Englishmen.)(7)

In 1858, Robert Burnaby (1828–1878), Old Blue, arrived in Victoria as an experienced civil servant from Her Majesty's Customs Office in London, and with a personal introduction to Governor James Douglas. Through this recommendation, he spent a short time as private secretary to Richard Clement Moody, the founder and first lieutenant-governor of British Columbia. During his first year, he founded a firm of commission merchants, in partnership with Edward Henderson, an old school friend from Christ's Hospital who managed the London office. Before the end of his second year in Victoria, he was elected to the legislative assembly of Vancouver Island, a post in which he served his constituents for five years. He was one of the founders of the Victoria Chamber of Commerce. Burnaby has been fittingly commemorated in a number of place-names in British Columbia, including a lake, a strait, an island, a municipality, two mountain ranges, and finally Burnaby Mountain, the seat of Simon Fraser University. He returned to England in 1874, where he died four years later.(8)

The Canadian Pacific Railway (CPR) started various programmes in the 1880s to help settle and develop Western Canada with emphasis on trade and agriculture. This was under their Canada Colonisation Association and later Department of Immigration and Colonisation. An important thrust of the association was to encourage bright, young, well-educated Englishmen to emigrate and form an integral part of the developments taking place. Of the many schemes developed by the CPR's Immigration and Colonisation Department, 'the CPR/Macdonald College Plan' started in 1925 and lasted well into the 1950s. Part of the Plan was

'The Old Country Farm Scheme' – an arrangement for students from English Public Schools who demonstrated a desire to farm in Canada to enroll in Macdonald College. This included several Old Blues.(9)

At this point, it is appropriate to mention William Hamilton Fyfe who was Headmaster at CH from 1919 to1930. An Old Blue in Vancouver found out in March 1930 that Mr. Fyfe was in Canada with a group of British headmasters and intended to visit Vancouver. (Subsequent to his visit, he was invited to take up the position of Principal at Queen's University, Kingston. This he accepted; he remained in Kingston until 1936 and was knighted.)

Through notices placed in local newspapers, a few Old Blues arranged for a dinner in Mr. Fyfe's honour. At that dinner, a resolution was made to form a local branch of the Christ's Hospital Club. Thus was founded the BC Old Blues section (BCOB), which has met to celebrate Founder's Day every year since, except during the Second World War.(10)

No records were kept of the first two dinners, but at the third dinner in 1932, there were 14 Old Blues present. Word got out about the annual dinner, and the number of Old Blues increased, with 20 being present in 1933. During the 1930s, the number of Old Blues attending the annual dinner remained around 15, as many of the members, having been at Christ's Hospital in the 19th century, were elderly or had died.

At the first dinner in 1930, the youngest Old Blue was Gerry Lancaster (Coleridge B 1912–20). Also at that dinner was Commander Archibald Reed (2's, 1882–88). Commander Reed went on to become the Vancouver harbourmaster for 32 years, and was followed by Captain Gerry Lancaster; so that, between them, the office of Vancouver harbourmaster was occupied by an Old Blue for over 50 years.

In 2000, Susan Mitchell, Old Blue (then treasurer of Christ's Hospital), travelled to the USA and Canada to encourage Old Blue activities in those areas. In Canada, she visited Toronto and spoke to a number of Old Blues. As a result, the Eastern Canadian section (ECOB) was formed; it has met every year since. It is known that there were many previous meetings in Quebec (mainly Montreal) and Ontario (mainly Waterloo), but few records were kept.

The records show that 140 known Old Blues came to British Columbia from the end of the 19th century to the present, and 128 known Old Blues came to eastern Canada in the period 1921–1994.[11]

Chris Johnson, Nanaimo, BC, May 2019

b1941; 1952–59 CH; 1960–64 Trinity College, Dublin; 1964–67 geologist with California Standard Company, Alberta; 1967–69 UBC; 1969–72 market research analyst with Imperial Oil; 1972–74 partner in a trading company in Greece; 1975–2001 various management positions with Macmillan Bloedel, Canada; Secretary-Treasurer BCOB 1997-present.

End Notes

1) 'Child Apprenticeships in America from Christ's Hospital, London 1617–1778', by Peter Wilson Coldham
2) 'The Beaver', 1977, Hudson Bay Company magazine, by R.I. Ruggles,
3) Notes from J.R. Reynolds, Old Blue
4) *Dictionary of Canadian Biography*, vol.5
5) 'British Columbia Coast Names, 1592–1906', by Captain John T. Walbran
6) *Dictionary of Canadian Biography*, vol.9
7) *Dictionary of Canadian Biography*, vol.8
8) *Dictionary of Canadian Biography*, vol. 10
9) DVD, 'Through the Ages' - Macdonald College 1906–2006
10) BCOB records, 1930–2019
11) CHOBA Directories, 1997, 1999, and 2003.

VIII

A Heuristic Success Story

I will always remember my first chemistry lesson at Christ's Hospital School in 1959. The master entered the laboratory in the Old Science School, and we hushed our idle chatter. Without saying a word, Mr. Potts walked to the front of the class where there was a laboratory table, took a piece of polished copper metal about two inches square with a pair of tongs, and heated it in a flame very deliberately in front of the whole class. After a few minutes, it had turned black. He turned off the Bunsen burner and looked at us. What did we think had happened? Why had it turned black? What was the black substance? One by one, each of us in the class had to submit an idea, and these were listed on the chalk board. Then one by one the ideas were discarded after a discussion guided by Mr. Potts (who took the role of co-enquirer) in a critical spirit which was rigorously based on simple logic that could be obtained only from our observations. Subsequent experiments were designed to discover the nature of the black powder: that it was copper oxide and not soot, as some of us had suggested. Later still, we transformed the black copper oxide into beautiful blue copper sulfate crystals with sulfuric acid. Magic! I was hooked! I loved the simple logic that was used to explain the observations. I wanted to be a chemist in the big world and transform things using chemical reactions that I could explain with equations! Equally important, we were taught to write up experiments in a clean and concise way that was totally unambiguous; the conclusions were not allowed to wander or be over-extrapolated from the data or observations.

We had been taught how to think! Little did I know that I was on the receiving end of the heuristic method of teaching science by discovery: test, observe, deduce.

Later on, my chemistry teachers were 'Pop' Beaven (with a glass pop-eye that wandered around the class independently from his good eye); and C F Kirby, who ran a wonderful large laboratory with tree trunks to sit on, an ancient dog named after the element chlorine, bones boiling up in a cauldron, a batch of mead brewing, old WWII radios squeaking, batteries in wire circuits with electric motors, a dissected fish and frog and rabbit side by side, a huge wall picture of a cow under a tree surrounded by the biological life cycle of carbon dioxide, and a hive of bees outside against a window pane. Drummed into us was the difference between precision and accuracy (terms that are much misused by the public and politicians today). On free Sunday afternoons in his lab, we boys would be allowed and encouraged to set up our own experiments and tinker with batteries and bulbs and ammeters and chemicals, to find out things for ourselves, to DO things using simple and inexpensive home-made apparatus. Natural curiosity of the boys was encouraged. I still have my old notebooks, and when I show them today to my three boys in a far-off land nearly 60 years later, they are always impressed with the factual way they were written up and the neat diagrams showing the apparatus.

The other person that always impressed me was the psychiatrist Dr Matthews, a visiting elderly lecturer who would hold our attention for three periods in our time at CH: the first when we were about ten years old and new to the boarding school; the second when we were about 14; and the third when we were about to leave school at 17 or so. His lectures lasted about four hours, and focused on the human body and mind; how 'the tribe' functioned as a team of hunters/gatherers, and different types of people would contribute to the survival of the tribe. For instance, how even an unpopular member of the tribe (for instance, a hoarder who had obsessive-compulsive habits) could on occasion supply clothing or food when the tribe had to escape a predator. Dr Matthews also gave insight on how the male human mind might differ from that of the female. Most interestingly, I can recall the contents of these lectures vividly even today, 60 years later.

Curiously, I ended up being top of every chemistry class, but near bottom in algebra, history, Latin, French, Greek, music, and all the other subjects except English and the Manual School (where we learned how to plane wood and make simple furniture, weld metals, and print programs). So, I left Christ's Hospital ignominiously in 1963 from the fifth form with just two 'O' Levels. I landed a job as an apprentice research technician with the Reed Paper Group in Kent, attending Maidstone Technical College one day and three evenings a week in a programme called day release, which led three years later to the Ordinary National Certificate (ONC) in chemistry. My weekly pay barely covered the cost of my digs. I rode through the rain to work on an old BSA B31 motorbike.

Later, I worked for ICI Plant Protection in Yalding as a junior analytical chemist; then I took a big step and worked as a chemist at the large international pharmaceutical company Burroughs-Wellcome (B-W) in their radioactive synthesis laboratory in Beckenham in south-east London, helping determine the metabolism of some new drugs for malaria. In the basement of the lab building was a huge (25ft) working model of the floating laboratory that Sir Henry Wellcome had built, and used by his company to study malaria and its mosquito larvae parasite in tropical countries a hundred years before. I would gaze at it and admire the way Wellcome's research team had discovered that if you could spread a very thin film of oil on the surface of standing water, you could prevent the mosquito larvae from developing into adults and infecting humans with malaria when they sting.

I became experienced in liquid scintillation counting for measuring C-14 radioactive metabolites in samples of blood from human studies. In the meantime, I finally attained Higher National Certificate (HNC) in chemistry from Woolwich Polytechnic in 1968. Day release was a very efficient way to obtain a technical degree whilst still working at a job.

Not convinced I was getting on in my career as fast as I wanted, I felt frustrated. One day in 1970, however, quite by chance, I bumped into Dr Goodford, the head of research, who invited me into his office. He asked me if I would like to work in America with the USA branch of Burroughs-Wellcome, who were relocating from old New York City labs to a new research building in the research triangle in North Carolina, where the company would be short of scientific staff. He arranged for me to be interviewed by Dr Gertrude B. Elion, his counterpart in B-W USA. I was interviewed by her a month later when she came over on a business trip. She was keen to use a new analytical technique called high pressure liquid chromatography. Happily, I had been learning to use HPLC a week before the interview! At the end of the interview, Dr Elion offered me a research position and I said 'yes!' without realising the huge step this would be. She had the legal people in B-W arrange all the paperwork for work permits and visa, while I looked in an atlas to find out where North Carolina was! My parents encouraged me to go, and I emigrated to the USA in November 1970 to work in Burroughs-Wellcome for Dr Elion in the experimental therapy department. Here, I became quite skillful in using HPLC to study pharmacokinetics of the new anti-gout drug Allopurinol and its analogues. We also worked on 6-mercapto-purine for leukemia; Acyclovir for HIV; AZT for aids; Trimethoprim, or Septra, for meningitis; and pyramethamine for malaria, using rational drug design. I grew to be a good chemist using HPLC, and was sought after to fix instrument problems in adjacent laboratories.

I enjoyed working in the research triangle in the brand new ultra-modern building, and I rented an old farmhouse with a big garden near Chapel Hill. I would come home each day after work, harvest corn and tomatoes, dig for potatoes, and retrieve eggs from my chickens; I played rugby at the local rugby fields at UNC; and I learned to ride horses; also to play Appalachian mountain music on my 5-string banjo. A great life!

After eight wonderful years, I moved to New Jersey to work at Hoffman-La Roche, where I did research on Etretinate and its related compounds, and even invented and synthesised a novel retinoid. Then after another seven years, I moved to Austin, Texas and in 1990 co-founded with another chemist a small research company called CEDRA Corporation, which we grew from six people to 400 over 17 years. We were basically a contract bioanalytical laboratory and a clinic quantifying drugs in blood and urine from human subjects in clinical trials of new pharmaceuticals from major drug companies which were undergoing safety, efficacy, and pharmacokinetic testing. These experiments must be done with great care and properly documented, as all the results are scrutinised by the USA Food and Drug Administration. The blood concentrations of some of these drugs were in the femtogram-per-millilitre range (as an example, this would be equivalent to accurately determining the concentration of a single aspirin dissolved in 500 interconnected Olympic-sized swimming pools!) and special equipment had to be used, called HPLC-MS-MS, which combines the separating power of a High Pressure Liquid Chromatograph with the specificity and sensitivity of a Triple Quadrupole Mass Spectrometer. On a normal day, there would be half a dozen people chasing me down to ask an opinion on why some assay was not working, or to review data and reports for accuracy. I would simply apply the heuristic method and cause-and-effect logic that I had learnt at Christ's Hospital to set them straight, or to suggest a possible solution to the problem. The variables and trends would have to be identified, and a simple experiment devised to determine which condition was out of control. For reports, I would recommend a simple unambiguous sentence instead of a complicated paragraph with unnecessarily long words.

My business partner and I sold CEDRA in 2007, six months before the stock market crash. I was asked to continue working as Director of Scientific Affairs of Worldwide Clinical Trials (as it had been renamed by the new owners). It has grown now to be a large international clinical testing lab, and I remain working there as consultant radiation safety officer. I spend more time with my three sons, Colin, Travis, and Dominic, and my lovely wife, Susan. I enjoy restoring antique cars (a 1959 Heinkel Bubblecar, a 1953 MG TD, a 1934 Bentley, and a 1935 Rolls Royce); and motorcycles (a 1924 BSA with acetylene gas lights (!), a 1929 Sunbeam, and a 1950 Ariel Square Four); playing the 5-string banjo; cooking for my boys; and refereeing rugby around Austin, Texas. In 2007, I purchased 34 acres of land to build playing fields for the local rugby club, Austin Huns, similar to what Jack Doyle has done at Stanford. And in 2009, I planned and had built a log home equipped with solar electric panels on my Lake Austin waterfront property – where we have lived ever since.

Some time ago, I reviewed all my publications over the years and found that I had co-authored six pharmaceutical research papers with Gertrude Elion, who had been awarded the Nobel Prize in 1988; also I had either authored, or co-authored, or had presented at research meetings about 80 times in the pharmaceutical area; and I have three patents. Not bad for a boy who left school after the fifth form unable to conjugate Latin verbs! My daily goal is to determine something that can be improved, or to rectify a problem, big or small. My most creative time is about 3am, when my mind is relaxed and can 'look outside the box'. The subconscious part of the human brain is the most creative.

Several years ago, I became a donation governor of the school, and I found that choosing a presentee is not an easy task. I also donated some funds that have been used to remodel and consolidate the science school buildings into a centre of excellence for teaching science at Christ's Hospital. I also helped design a new lab in the science school, called the Chromatography Lab, where students could do practical experiments using HPLC. The idea in my head was that students who were perhaps not necessarily of university level but were good with their hands could gain experience separating mixtures of chemicals using HPLC. This experience would really give them a great advantage when interviewing for science-oriented jobs when they left CH. I want others to enjoy being taught practical science.

Thank you, patient science masters at CH who taught me; and Professsor Henry Armstrong, Charles Browne, and Dr Gordon Van Praagh, who championed the heuristic method of learning science by discovery! Long may we have teachers who make use of children's instincts to explore and discover, for this is how we learn.

'I hear and forget,
I see and remember,
I do and understand.'

*'A child's mind is not a vessel to be filled,
but a fire to be kindled'*

Christopher Bugge, Texas, June 2019

b1946 Wandsworth, London; CH 1956–63; 1963–65 Jnr. chemist at Reed Paper Group, Kent; 1965–67 Jnr. analytical chemist at ICI Plant Protection, Kent; Ordinary National Certificate in Chemistry, Maidstone Technical College; 1967–70 Analytical chemist at Burroughs-Wellcome, Dept. of Tropical Medicine, Beckenham; Higher National Certificate in

Chemistry, Woolwich Polytechnic; 1970–79 Transferred to Dept. Drug Metabolism, Burroughs-Wellcome, Research Triangle, North Carolina; 1979–85 Senior analytical chemist at Hoffman-La-Roche, New Jersey; 1985–2007 Co-Founder and Director of Scientific Affairs, CEDRA Corporation, Austin, Texas; 2007-present: Consultant and Radiation Safety Officer, Worldwide Clinical Trials, Austin, Texas.

IX

Fighter Pilot to Media Entrepreneur

It seems that my conception took place out of wedlock, late in October or early November 1932. The marriage of my parents took place at a registry office the following January 1933, as a matter of some urgency, since the shame of an unmarried pregnancy in those days was total. They moved into the house of my paternal grandfather on Victoria Road in Northwich, which is where I was born. The house was two rooms and a back kitchen on the ground floor; two bedrooms and a box-room on the top floor. I shared a bedroom with my parents, while Granddad had a bedroom, and his lodger, Mr. Comerford, slept in the box room. There was just a cold water tap in the back scullery and an outhouse at the bottom of a small yard.

My father, Thomas, always known as 'Tommy', was a professional footballer, playing for Preston North End of the First Division, as it was in those days. He was 24 years old when I was born and had been a professional footballer since he was 17. He turned professional with Northwich Victoria of the Cheshire League, was transferred to Stockport County of the Third Division North, and then on to the big-time with Preston. His wage was £8 a week – big money then. His father, my granddad, worked as fitter for Cheshire Railways, earning 30 shillings a week – less than 20% of what my father earned. However, professional footballers only got paid for a maximum of about 30 weeks, since wages were paid for pre-season training and the football season itself. During the summer, my dad got nothing, since unemployment pay (the 'dole') was not paid to seasonal workers, which included footballers. Come the beginning of the season, he was always broke. I was born on 3rd August, so there was very little money in the house!

Prior to the shotgun marriage, my father had lived at home with his parents and four or more brothers in a terraced house on Peter Street in Northwich. My father's mother was a very stern, tall woman. My mother was a bundle of energy, never stopped moving, and always with jobs to do, not only for herself but for everyone else around her. She was very intelligent, and at age 11 had won a scholarship to Sir John Deane's Grammar School, the best school in Cheshire. Much to her chagrin, however, she was forced to leave school at age 16 and put to work, for the large family needed money and she was the second eldest. She resented this for her entire life, and was determined that her child was going to get a great education, whatever the cost.

When I was three, she would sit with me in the early morning and teach me to read and write by the light of the fire. I started school proper at the early age of four, by which time I could read and write extremely well. At age nine, I won a foundation scholarship to her old school, Sir John Deane's, which meant there were no fees to pay; my education was free. I did well at the grammar school, where my best subject by far was mathematics, taught by Nick Turner. When I was 11, he approached my parents with an idea that changed my life. He had discovered a link between Sir John Deane's and a famous English public school called Christ's Hospital.

Christ's Hospital was founded in 1552 by the boy king Edward VI. Edward's church of choice in London was St. Bartholomew's, where the rector was Sir John Deane, native of Northwich, Cheshire. When Edward VI discovered that his rector had founded a grammar school, he gave him the right to send one boy per year to sit a competitive exam in London, the winner of which would receive a full scholarship to his new charity school, Christ's Hospital. As far as we could discover, no-one from Sir John Deane's had ever taken up that challenge, but Nick Turner was suggesting that I should go to London and sit the exam, with the possibility of winning a place at Christ's Hospital.

So, off we went to a London being bombed daily by the Luftwaffe. We stayed at a small hotel in Russell Square near the examination hall. As I remember it, this huge hall held more than 1000 desks and more than 1000 boys sat an examination for ten places at Christ's Hospital. I won one of those places. My mother told everyone that I came fourth out of the 1000-plus, though I don't know how she could possibly have known that! As it was, a letter arrived offering me a place at Christ's Hospital, starting the following September, just after my eleventh birthday. Needless to say, my mother accepted with alacrity. The fact that I would be leaving home and going off to boarding school was never even discussed.

I thoroughly enjoyed my years at Christ's Hospital and could not wait for the holidays to end so that I could get back to school. After a bright scholastic start, I discovered all the sports and played rugby, cricket, and fives for the house and school at all ages, almost certainly to the detriment of my schoolwork. I passed all the exams and got good results, but not as good as they might have been with the same commitment that I put into sports. My school captain at all levels was Dennis Silk, who went on to become an outstanding head of one of Britain's greatest schools, Radley. He died just a few weeks ago (as I write in 2019), and we remained friends until that day, 70 years on.

I wasn't good enough to win a university scholarship, which left me with two alternatives on leaving school: the civil service, or the armed forces. I chose the latter and obtained a permanent commission in the RAF, which put me in for life. After six years, my last squadron was a night-fighter squadron based in Malta.

During my last few weeks in Malta, I had decided to resign my commission and leave the Air Force. After Cranwell, a year in Canada, Masirah Island (Oman), and a night-fighter tour in Suez and Malta, I decided that grown-ups should be doing other things than flying; hence my resignation, and my decision to emigrate to Vancouver, Canada. Why Vancouver? Thereby hangs the tale that fashioned my future.

In Canada, 1952, I had taken leave of six weeks and, with my best RAF friend, Alex Trotman, had hitchhiked around North America. Our first 'hitch' was aboard an RCAF North Star from Winnipeg to Vancouver – a ride that we obtained on condition that we acted as co-pilots in the crew. We left Winnipeg around midnight, with an ETA for Vancouver of 06.30 hours. We had military passengers in the back and were therefore limited to a maximum altitude of 10,000 feet, since the aircraft was not pressurised and did not have oxygen stations for all the passengers.

Leaving Alberta, we were picking our way carefully through the Rockies at 10,000 feet. The sun was rising directly behind, and as we dropped down to the coast, there was Vancouver laid out before us in all its glory! Snow-capped mountains all around, green forest, Vancouver Island, and the sparkling blue Pacific beyond. I will never forget that magical sight. At that moment, without thinking, I said excitedly that I would come back to live there at some time. And I did: in October of 1956.

In London, I was interviewed by a rather sombre air vice-marshal, whose initial discussions centred around persuading me to stay in the RAF, his main point being the hundreds of thousands of pounds that the Air Force had spent training me and how I was about to waste it! When he finally got the point that I was determined to resign my commission, he reluctantly agreed. He then briefly took me through all my quarterly squadron reports, written by my various squadron and station commanders of the period of my service. Overall, the reports were pretty positive, but two points which could be taken negatively came through consistently. Firstly, I was described as aggressive, which I pointed out to the air marshal was perhaps not a bad characteristic for a member of Fighter

Command of the Royal Air Force. (I thought that was what we were being paid for!) Secondly, I was described as a loner, mainly because I didn't drink in the officers' mess and hang around with the boys. (Actually, I didn't drink at all.) One station commander went so far as to justify the 'loner' tag by pointing out the paucity of my mess bills – one month in Malta amounting to the grand total of sixpence! Responding to this 'loner' point, I did point out to the air marshal that I was a team player, having played rugby and cricket for the RAF and its squadrons wherever I had been posted during my service. He also mentioned that my mother had written to Air Ministry, asking them to refuse my resignation and keep me in the Air Force. (Thanks, Mum!)

After arriving home in Prestatyn, North Wales, I booked passage on the *RMS Saxonia* of the Cunard Line, from Liverpool to Montreal, sailing 13 days later. Vancouver had always been my ultimate destination, so I also bought a train ticket from Montreal to Vancouver, with a stop in Winnipeg, where I intended to see a young lady of my acquaintance. How this was accomplished in such a short time I do not remember, but I was obviously in a hurry to get to Canada and start the new life! I would board the *Saxonia* with £10 pocket money and £315 to start me off in Vancouver. It must be fairly rare that anyone can be absolutely precise about their money and possessions at any moment in time, but I certainly was at the moment when I boarded the ship in Liverpool on 17th October, 1956! In addition to the £325, I had one suit, one blazer, two pairs of grey slacks, shirts, ties, underwear, rugby and cricket boots; plus, my cricket bat, which I was awarded in the Middle East RAF team for scoring a century; and a Remington portable typewriter.

On that typewriter there hangs a tale. The day before I was due to sail from Liverpool, I read an advertisement in the local Rhyl paper for a Remington portable typewriter for sale at an address in Mostyn, a town on the Welsh coast, which was on the road to Liverpool. As my parents drove me to

Liverpool the next day, we stopped in Mostyn on the way. They gave me £10, and I bought the typewriter to take with me to Canada. I had learned to type on Masirah Island, and that typewriter turned out to be the beginning of another career in Canada. I bought the typewriter, and arrived in Liverpool around lunchtime. The goodbyes with my parents was a pretty unemotional affair, since we were not a family given to emotion. I don't remember hugs and kisses, and there were certainly no tears – probably a handshake with my dad, but even that was not a given! The truth was that I probably couldn't wait to get aboard.

The *RMS Saxonia* of the Cunard Line had an overall length of 608 feet, a beam of 80 feet, and a gross registered tonnage of 21,631. As I boarded via a gangplank, the ship seemed enormous, although I never did get an overview of the actual ship, but rather through photographs. Obviously, for the princely fee of £72, I had booked a humble tourist-class passage. Imagine my surprise, after boarding, when I was allocated a berth in a first-class cabin! In today's language, I was 'upgraded', but I had no idea why. The cabin had two berths and I was sharing with another gentleman, whom I viewed as being much older, but in truth he was probably about thirty years old. After introductions, he told me that we must visit the chief purser without delay, since the ship was due to sail in less than three hours and the two of us had business to transact; and would I please give him a one-pound note! *A bit cheeky*, I thought, but I liked him.

My cabin companion was obviously a very experienced trans-Atlantic traveller and knew precisely where to find the chief purser. I did not pick up most of the conversation, but he and the purser nodded and smiled at me, and I saw my companion slip something into the purser's hand. When I enquired what that was all about, he smiled wisely and told me that I would find out shortly. The ship sailed at 18.00 hours, and as the Mersey disappeared astern, around 20.00 hours, we both went down to dinner. We were in the first-class dining room, where the tables were set for six, four, or two. We were shown to a table set for six, and were shortly joined by four of the most gorgeous young ladies I had ever seen! The penny dropped! My cabin friend had slipped the chief purser two pounds to set us up for the entire voyage! Needless to say, dinner was great, and then the six of us finished up in the ballroom.

The voyage was to last six days and on such a relatively small ship, daytime activities were pretty limited to reading, chasing the girls around the ship (only in the interest of keeping fit!), or playing cards. On the first day out from Liverpool, I was reading in the lounge, desperately trying to stay awake after half a night spent walking a lovely around the bridge deck, when an elderly gentleman approached and asked if I played cribbage, which of course I did. We met every day around ten in the lounge and played cribbage for a couple of hours. It was at his suggestion that we played for money. Fortunately, he wasn't a very good player and was obviously a man of some means, because over the course of the voyage I won more than £100 and disembarked in Montreal with £435 in my pocket!

There were many more single ladies on board than single gents, and there was great competition for attention! Katherine was a great attention-grabber, but she surpassed herself on the third day out when she asked me for help in getting her costume together for the newly-announced fancy-dress competition. The *Saxonia* had been running into heavy weather, and as a result the six-day voyage was now going to take seven days. And since dancing on a heavily tilting deck was dangerous, a fancy-dress competition offered a new diversion for the passengers.

She had obtained from the ship's butcher shop some lengths of muslin, used in those days for wrapping meat. She had laundered several lengths of the muslin and was preparing to enter the fancy-dress contest as 'A Leg of Lamb'. Wearing just underwear, she wanted me to wrap her in the freshly laundered muslin, which concealed a little, but not a lot. It was a task that I undertook not the least reluctantly. With added high heels, Katherine looked really great and won first prize.

Following the fancy-dress evening, with rough seas still all around, it was announced that since there was no dancing, there would be a singing contest – or at least, a reward for any passenger that would stand up and sing with the band. I have no idea where my nerve came from, but that evening I sang with the band. The song was *Mountain Greenery*, and for my performance, I was awarded a three-pound box of chocolates. I had never seen such a large box of chocolates before, and shared them with my five dining companions. My cabin companion, whose name has been forgotten for years, turned out to be something of a real character. He was about 30, good-looking, minor public school educated, well-spoken and well-dressed, with a real eye for the ladies. We really did get along pretty well, and when he heard I was heading for Vancouver, he even tried to persuade me to join him at his destination, Palm Beach, Florida.

I remember the whole seven days as being slightly surreal and something that I, and everyone else, I assume, knew was going to end and disappear in a few days' time, as if it had never happened. Confirmation of this unreality came the night before we docked in Montreal, when one young lady, in the midst of a mad, passionate embrace, asked that I wouldn't see her off the ship since her fiancé was meeting her at the dock in Montreal! She was emigrating from England to get married. I guess I was the last – or lost – fling!

After disembarking, the immigration formalities were fast and easy, and I must have taken a cab to the railroad station, since I don't remember staying overnight in Montreal. A boring train journey of two days and two nights to Winnipeg later, I got off and checked into the YMCA. Here, I met Dolores, who took me home to meet her mother. I only vaguely remember the house and her mother, but I do remember that Dolores was pretty cool! I told her I'd had enough of the train and intended to buy a car and drive the rest of the way to Vancouver, and that if she wanted to come with me, she was welcome. I don't think that at that moment she had any intention of coming with me.

The next day, I went out looking at used cars and fixed on a Ford Fairlane. The night I bought the car, Dolores announced that she would be coming out to Vancouver with me and had told her mother so. From being totally opposed to the idea, she had done a complete 180-degree turn; I didn't know why. On the drive, we shared the motel room, and she paid half the room cost.

We drove out of Winnipeg on the morning of 29th October, 1956, and, as I remember, took three nights and four days to reach Vancouver. In Vancouver, Dolores moved into the apartment of an old radio friend, Teri Clarke and her sisters, and I went to the YMCA. The next day, I rented a room in the house of an old lady around 15th and Cambie, for which I paid the princely sum of $16 per month. My landlady also, on the odd occasion, invited me down for breakfast!

I settled into a routine that saw me having dinner at the White Spot at 13th and Cambie pretty well daily: always chicken and fries in a basket, for very little money. I joined the Vancouver Rowing Club and was immediately also employed in their first rugby team, playing either centre or scrum half.

For the next year, I barely saw Dolores. She took a job as a copywriter at CFUN, and I ambled around Vancouver, not really looking for work, but rather looking for a direction. At the same time, I spent a few hours a day at my typewriter, composing, creating what I don't remember, but I do remember that I still had dreams of becoming a writer.

The other person I knew in Vancouver was another girl who had hitched a ride with us in Northern Italy that previous May. Her name was Jocelyn, and she lived with her parents in a fashionable part of Vancouver, to where I was constantly invited for dinner. At the end of November, her father, who was personnel director of the Hudson's Bay Company, suggested that I might be interested in temporary employment during the Christmas season, working at the Bay.

I started in the sporting goods department at the Bay at the beginning of December, and worked there until the middle of January, when the sales were finished. I thoroughly enjoyed the experience and was flattered when, at the beginning of January, I was offered permanent employment, starting with their six-week executive training programme! I refused in the nicest possible way, with the reasoning that I had other unspecified plans. The other plans were non-existent, and when I left the Hudson's Bay Company in the middle of January, it was back to the typewriter and the search.

At the Rowing Club, one member of the rugby XV that I befriended was a guy by the name of Rod McCallum. His father owned a Ford dealership in Edmonton, and he was working for the Ford Motor Company at their western HQ in Burnaby. He evidently mentioned me to the district manager, Bill Wilson, who asked that I go out and talk to him about going to work for Ford. Bill was a really good guy, an excellent manager; we really got along. Within thirty minutes of my walking into his office, he offered me a job running the import desk for all the English-made Fords that were coming into Vancouver by ship for distribution throughout Western Canada. He seemed to think that I would have no problem handling the logistics and the abundant paperwork – and I didn't. With a starting salary of $250 per month, I worked at Ford in Burnaby for three months: February, March, and April, 1957. I received a raise of $25 at the end of the first month! Looking back, I did not apply for or seek out either of those first two jobs in Canada, and it was a pattern that has stayed with me for my whole life. I have never applied for any job anywhere, which was never a deliberate personal policy, but rather something that just happened. My next move in Vancouver, however, was not exactly to apply for a job, but rather to create one for myself.

It was in the spring of 1957 that my rambling ideas of what to do for a career/living, started to crystallise. I'd had enough of the Ford Motor Company, even though I'd enjoyed my time there. I was even awarded a bonus for saving them thousands of dollars by spotting that duty was being paid on the crates that the cars were imported in – crates that were subsequently burned! Value nil!

At the end of April, early in the morning, I went to see the radio division of the Canadian Broadcasting Corporation, not looking for a job, but rather to see if I could sell them some of my writing. At the reception desk, I told them that I wished to speak with someone who commissioned any form of writing. Without batting an eye, the lady picked up the phone, and within five minutes I was sitting across the desk from a gentleman called Bob Orchard. He introduced himself as the head of the talks department, and asked what he could do for me.

I explained that I had just arrived from England, and that I was a writer who was looking for work. Did he have any need for a freelance writer? We chatted for a few minutes about the sort of thing I could write (much liberty with the truth on my part!) and then, consulting various schedules, he told me that he had a seven-and-a-half minute slot in Trans Canada Matinee (a two-hour, nationally-broadcast magazine show that ran every afternoon) the following week. Would I be interested in writing a piece for it? Yes, I certainly would, and could I meet with him again the following morning? Meeting set, I went off to create a piece about my friend Ali Osman, the trader of Khartoum, as a seven-and-a-half minute talk.

Back at eleven the next morning, I delivered my piece to Bob Orchard. He read it only once, looked up, laughed, said he loved it, and would buy it for $50! Fifty dollars – a fortune! 'Sold,' I said, standing up, at which point Bob asked where I was going. 'Home, to write something else,' was the answer. 'Not so fast, you now have to voice the talk, for which I will pay you an extra ten dollars.' Still in shock, 30 minutes later, I found myself in a radio studio.

The only semblance of a microphone that I had experienced before was the upright telephone that we had used as a microphone for our clandestine/pirate radio station on Masirah Island a few years earlier. This, however, was the proper thing in a proper recording studio, so I read my Ali Osman piece, evidently to everyone's satisfaction.

Over a subsequent coffee with Bob Orchard, I asked what else he might like to commission/buy, and after consulting his schedules, he told me that he had a 15-minute slot coming up at 10.15pm, once per week for twenty weeks. He said that he would be interested in 20 15-minute talks to be written and voiced by me, if I thought I had the material! The fee for writing and voicing would be $75 per talk. I told him that I would love to do it, and would bring him some finished talks and outlines for the complete series of 20 within the next few days.

Back in my solitary room, I bashed away solidly at my Remington portable for hours on end, and within a few days had two talks written, and comprehensive outlines for the remaining 18. The series was titled 'King of an Island' and, yes, was all about my time spent on Masirah Island. I had absolutely no problem in filling the time with all the adventures, big and small. The CBC news magazine printed an article about the series, even including a photograph of me in khaki tropical uniform, holding a goat kid, taken on Masirah.

A few sample titles:

1. The Ghost of the Headless Camel
2. The Clothesline and the Six-Foot Sandshark
3. Census Time
4. Building the Distillation Plant
5. Sea Water Coffee and Arab Manners
6. The Sheikh and His Daughter.
7. Goat, Chicken, Shark and Crayfish – All Curried.
8. The Wreck of the Baron Inverdale

I wrote and recorded all 20 talks over a period of three weeks, and was delighted with my cheque for $1500. With my monthly expenditure of about $100, I had enough to live on for a year. Even more exciting was my description on the CBC pay slip – 'Freelance Writer and Broadcaster'! With my newfound wealth, I decided that I could afford to move to better accommodation and left my $16 room for an apartment that cost me $40 a month.

This move was also prompted by the fact that my father was coming out to Vancouver for the summer – an exploratory trip to see if he and my mother could move to Vancouver. He got a job immediately with the Canadian National Railways at the main station on Main Street. He worked shifts – some at night, which he enjoyed, since he could then wander around Vancouver during the day. He obviously spent very little, and sent most of his pay-cheque home to my mother every two weeks. He spent about four months in Vancouver, more than paid his airfare to come out, and saved a pile beside. He was desperate for my mother to join him, since Canadian National kept offering him very well-paid (in comparison with England) permanent jobs, but she wanted none of it, and in the end, he reluctantly returned to England. In the following years, he reminisced about his time in Vancouver and wondered what his life would have been like had he stayed in Canada.

After selling 20 talks to the CBC, I assumed, correctly, that I had exhausted the talks market and sought advice from Bob Orchard about what I might write next. He suggested that I write a radio play – a novel idea, but I had not a clue as to what a radio drama script looked like. Bob gave me a couple of copies of radio plays, and I went away to write my first radio drama.

It took me two non-stop days of ten hours a day, and on the third day I presented my finished script to Bob, who read it in front of me, said nothing, and walked out of the room. He came back in five minutes, told me that he had given it to the Head of Radio Drama, and he would let me know what he thought in the near future. I thanked him and was finishing my coffee when the gentleman in question arrived, announced that he loved my play, and would buy it! He did not, however, like the title, which was 'The Colonel Offered a Drink'.

I thought it was an extremely clever title, referring to the bribe offered to a squadron pilot who would shoot down one of his friends returning to base with an atomic weapon hung up on his aircraft. (Yes, that was the basis of the plot, all about flying!) I started to explain my reasoning, when a look from my friend Bob Orchard brought me to an abrupt halt. I asked the Head of Radio Drama what he thought was a good title. Thus it was that my first radio drama went out under the title 'H-Bomb'.

The fee for a 30-minute radio drama was $200, but that was not just for the writing; for that fee I also had to attend the recording of the play. I wasn't sure why, but on the appointed day I attended the CBC recording studio where I met the director of my play, Ray Whitehouse, who, I subsequently learnt, was the top radio director of the CBC. All the actors were assembled in the studio below us, and the recording engineers with Ray and me were in the control room above. Another startling new experience!

After a directorial briefing, the recording started. I was astonished to be consulted by the director at various intervals as to my feelings about the delivery of a certain line, or was the mood right, etc, etc. I finally understood that as I was the author of the piece, the director valued my opinion as to whether we were translating my script into sound in the way that I had envisioned it. On the odd occasion, I changed a line of dialogue here and there, and was consulted regularly regarding the sound effects of jet fighters taking-off and other flying sounds.

We had recorded about the first 20 minutes, when Ray called a halt in the recording and gave the actors a break. During the break, he told me that we were going to be about

90 seconds short of the half-hour, and he needed me to write another couple of pages into the script. So, I found myself in a recording studio, scribbling furiously during the actors' break. I cracked it in ten minutes and Ray thought my added dialogue gave an extra dimension, he said! Talk about pressure on a retired RAF officer of six months – but I didn't think about that at the time.

With the recording finished, we adjourned for a brief post-mortem. The director was very satisfied with the final recording, and assured me that he would ask for the transmission to go out at a peak radio time. Both he and Bob Orchard then asked what I was going to do next, suggesting that I might write another radio drama, since they had a continual need for scripts and my writing was apparently new and different. I didn't say so, but I thought that was because I was also new at the game; since I didn't quite know what I was doing, there were no established boundaries to my thoughts.

I wrote another radio play in the next week, which Ray Whitehouse liked, and it was bought. He then suggested that I should join a series of summer workshops which were being staged by the CBC, titled 'Actors' and Playwrights' Workshop'. The workshop would be attended by a dozen actors and actresses, two writers and two directors, and would take place in one of the main CBC studios. I had no idea what was involved, but readily agreed, since it was obviously going to be great experience.

On the first day, I was astonished to discover that one of the invited actresses was Dolores, whom I had not seen at all over the previous six months, but who was working as a copywriter for CFUN. The other writer was a guy by the name of Paul Power, probably five years older than me, but who had also been making a living as a freelance writer, although I don't think that he did any voicing of his material.

The first session was an hour of modern dance and movement led by a fantastic instructor/dancer. The actors and actresses were right into it, swinging and swaying away in the front of the class. The two directors and we two writers, not actually being performers, lurked at the back of the studio, desperately trying to hide from all the gyrations!

Before lunch, there were further lessons in elocution, accents, delivery, etc, and then we were all initiated into some of the mysteries of television which, at that point, remember, was still a very new medium. (In fact, CBC Television did not go coast-to-coast until July 1958, the following summer.) After lunch, we were all told to go out into the streets of Vancouver, pick out a target person, and follow them for at least an hour. We could, if we wished, engage them in conversation, but that was not exactly encouraged. We then all gathered in the studio and each of us had a couple of minutes to act out and recreate the character we had been following.

Paul and I, in addition to recreating our characters, had to make notes and then, in concert with the two directors, had to produce a plot line based on the characters we had just seen. The directors then briefed the actors and actresses, and we all produced a play. The result was, in turns, chaotic, hilarious, dramatic, exciting, and sometimes all of the above at the same time. It was, however, overall, an extremely satisfying and creative exercise for all participants. By the fourth and final week, we were producing amazing stuff; the pity was that none of it was recorded.

Apart from being a great learning experience, two very specific things came out of the Actors' and Playwrights' Workshop. Firstly, the CBC offered Paul Power and me full-time employment as staff writers – positions that had never existed previously. We would be paid a salary of $300 per month, and everything that we wrote would be owned by the Corporation. There were absolutely no strings attached as to what we would write, or even how much we would write or where we would write it. Paul Power accepted immediately. I took a brief time thinking about this unique offer and then turned it down – really not on the basis of money, since

I could make a lot more freelance, but rather that I didn't want to be tied down.

After my brief introduction to television via the workshop, in addition to still writing for radio, I started an hour-long television play. I found writing for television much harder than for radio. I took about four weeks, not full-time, but still many hours, to finish an hour-long television play. It was fantasy called 'Pins for the People' and was based on the fantasy that the viewing audience could be armed with a mild electronic weapon ('Pin') with which they could register their disapproval of their television fare.

I took it in to Bob Orchard and Ray Whitehouse. They thought it was a good original drama with a unique plot, but unfortunately it had to be sent to the CBC Drama Department in Toronto, since that was the only centre in Canada producing hour-long television plays. It went off with their strong recommendation that it be produced, and we heard nothing for four weeks. The Bob phoned to tell me that my script had been returned and that Toronto was not interested. He was livid that they had written some comments on the script that were totally inappropriate and that he took personally. When I went to pick up the script, he showed me that the head of television drama in Toronto had written on the title page 'This would make a good ten-minute sketch for Wayne and Shuster'. (Two slapstick comics with a half-hour weekly show on the network.) He advised me not to write any more stuff that had to go to Toronto – the inference being that they would only buy material produced in the East. So, I never did!

From freelance writing and broadcasting with the CBC, I was offered a job as promotion manager at CKNW, Western Canada's largest commercial radio station. Looking at a new challenge, I accepted immediately and thus moved into commercial broadcasting. From CKNW Vancouver, I moved into the big-time in Toronto, and from Toronto was offered the job and partial ownership of two pirate radio ships off the British coast.

The Radio Caroline ships, when I arrived, had a combined audience of eight million listeners a week and were losing money rapidly. After one year, they had a deficit of more than a million pounds! The man who convinced me to move to the UK and go into the pirate radio business was Jocelyn Stevens, owner of *Queen Magazine*, friend of the Royal Family, and a leading member of London society. He was the largest individual shareholder in Radio Caroline.

Over a Saturday lunch at the Savoy Grill, he asked what deal I wanted to take over the Caroline operation. Without hesitation, I told him that I must have complete control and 30% of all income that I brought in. That percentage was outrageous – exactly double the commission that we worked for in Canada! He agreed without a second's hesitation, I went directly back to Toronto on Saturday evening and was back in London on Monday morning.

Over the next two years, we took the Caroline audience to more than 26 million a week, paid off the million-pound deficit, and brought in millions more. Personally, I obviously did extremely well on my percentage, which was delivered to the penny. On August 15th, 1967, the Radio Caroline adventure came to an end with the passage of the Marine Broadcasting Act, which made it illegal for British businesses to spend advertising monies with us. It had been a very fruitful exercise, but more than that it had been fun, fun, fun! I was immediately offered a contract by Radio Luxembourg, which entailed one long day a week and paid a fortune… and so it went until 1972 when the British Government introduced local commercial radio stations, and I finished up with a big share in seven of the first eight.

By 1979, I had amassed quite a broadcasting empire with shares in eight highly profitable commercial stations and a sales and marketing operation that sold well over half of all the national advertising on British radio. There was, however, a big downside to the personal profit. The UK government of Harold Wilson had set very high personal taxation levels and

I decided to sell all my UK broadcast interests to the largest commercial broadcaster in Canada, and retire happily back to Vancouver.

One pirate radio anecdote stands out. A movie was made in 2009, called either *Pirate* Radio or *The Boat That Rocked*, depending on the country, and starring Bill Nighy. I happened to see the movie whilst on a trans-Atlantic flight to Boston, and a few weeks later was having tea at Fortnum and Mason in Jermyn Street, London (as one does!) and there at the next table was Bill Nighy.

I went over, introduced myself, and congratulated him on the movie, telling him I had been involved with Caroline. He was most intrigued and wanted to know how accurate the movie had been. I truthfully told him that the movie was nothing like the real thing. He then enquired what I did at Radio Caroline... and I told him, to his amusement, that in the movie, he had played me!

I totally credit my education, experience, and years at Christ's Hospital with giving me the confidence to handle anything and everything that came my way. I must particularly credit Len Bates, the cricket professional, who coached me into becoming quite a good fast bowler; good enough to earn a few pounds as a professional in the Lancashire League during the summer holidays of my 16th and 17th years. Len told all-comers that I was his best 'quickie' in years! More importantly, I credit Len with giving me that absolute self-confidence. This poetry by William Wordsworth seems to provide a fitting last word.

Terry Bate, Gozo, Malta, July 2019

From 'Childhood & School-time', Book 1, lines 270ff:

The Prelude, by William Wordsworth

—Was it for this
That one, the fairest of all rivers, loved
To blend his murmurs with my nurse's song,
And, from his alder shades and rocky falls,
And from his fords and shallows, sent a voice
That flowed along my dreams? For this, didst thou,
O Derwent! travelling over the green plains
Near my sweet birthplace, didst thou, beauteous stream
Make ceaseless music through the night and day
Which with its steady cadence, tempering
Our human waywardness, composed my thoughts
To more than infant softness, giving me,
Among the fretful dwellings of mankind,
A foretaste, a dim earnest, of the calm
That Nature breathes among the hills and groves.

When, having left the mountains, to the towers
Of Cockermouth that beauteous river came,
Behind my father's house he passed, close by,
Along the margin of our terrace walk.
He was a playmate whom we dearly loved.
Oh! many a time have I, a five years' child,
A naked boy, in one delightful rill,
A little mill-race severed from his stream,
Made one long bathing of a summer's day;
Basked in the sun, and plunged, and basked again
Alternate, all a summer's day, or scoured
The sandy fields, leaping through groves
Of yellow ragwort; or when crag and hill,
The woods, and distant Skiddaw's lofty height,
Were bronzed with a deep radiance, stood alone
Beneath the sky, as if I had been born
On Indian plains, and from my mother's hut
Had run abroad in wantonness, to sport,
A naked savage, in the thunder shower.

X

Schoolboy to Oceanographer

The school years

In 1942, at the age of ten, I was transported from my quiet and beautiful home in Bude, Cornwall, to Christ's Hospital, 40 miles south of London. The school was located on the main aircraft route for German bombers travelling across the Channel from Europe to London. And so, suddenly, my whole life was changed when I registered with other boys, aged ten to 17, in this ancient school located partially in a war zone. The school had a history dating back to 1552, when it was founded to occupy the site of Greyfriars monastery which had been vacated by Henry VIII under his dissolution of monasteries act. With a strong disciplinary structure allowing caning for punishment, the school at the same time offered generally efficient teaching methods. To enter the school, one had to have either a scholarship or a 'presentation' made by some wealthy donor. My mother, whose husband had died in a traffic accident, was devoted to the idea that I should go to CH in order to get what she called a 'proper education'. I was given a presentation by a family friend, Mrs. C. Spurgin, who became very interested in my progress through life.

A typical school day consisted of arising to the school bell at 7am, followed by a cold shower, dressing up in the same clothing a student wore in the 1500s – a white shirt, black knee breeches, yellow stockings, and large bluecoat with silver buttons. Next, we were marched off to the dining room for breakfast, which varied with our wartime ration allowance. Lessons started at 9am, generally with some sort of sport in the afternoon. Among the sports were cricket, rugby, swimming, athletics, or fives, depending on season. I enjoyed all of these but only made the school team in swimming. Lunches and dinners were also a parade of marching students, about 50 per squad, the lunch parade generally being accompanied by the school band, in which I played the bass drum. The evenings could be given over to an hour or two of homework, or on weekends, an hour or two of concert, an invited speaker, indoor games, or free time. We marched to the dining hall for all our meals and also twice on Sunday for a service in the chapel. This general regimen was entertaining, but could be marred by incidents of bullying, disciplinary 'handouts', and disruptions due to air raids. Under the threat of a random air attack, the school had been equipped earlier with underground bunkers and in fact was only hit once by a doodlebug (a pilotless bomber) with no casualties. The wartime food was highly variable, but just sufficient if one was prepared to eat the occasional whale or vast quantities of stale bread.

On the academic side, my interest had always been biology: what made this beautiful world function so well? In biology, I was extremely fortunate to be placed in a class with a particular teacher, Mr. Kirby, whose whole perspective of biology was as an integrated subject involving the interaction of species with each other. Instead of learning only names of individual species of plants and animals, he made us observe their integrated function with each other. One example of his unique teaching method at my time was for me to have to observe and record how a patch of grassy ground changed over several months. This gave me a delight in biology that I had never had before! I was not alone in recognising Mr. Kirby's teaching ability. After I left school and met up with other Old Blues, several commented on the unique methodology used by this particular teacher.

In other subjects, I was happy to learn by memory, but I had difficulty with certain details, for example, learning to spell. I recall that my keenness on biology led me to amass the largest butterfly collection in the school. However, when I enthusiastically put my collection on exhibit, the evaluator's comment on my exhibit was: 'The most singular feature of this exhibitor's presentation is his spelling.' I had labelled one butterfly as being a 'taught-us-shell' instead of a tortoiseshell. (Something like this must also have happened to one of my relations, Robert Stephen Hawker, who wrote in his 'Introduction and Farewell Address':

> 'Hard is the task, ill fit for youthful days,
> To gain from judgement's voice the meed of praise,
> And deep the pain that youthful souls must feel,
> When censure damps the glow of early zeal.'
>
> (*The Poetical Works of Robert Stephen Hawker*, C.Kegan Paul and Co. London 1879)

Becoming a scientist

When I left CH, I was devoted to the idea that I wanted to continue my studies in biology. As far as I was aware at that time, there were only two professions in biology: one in agriculture, and the other in medicine. I soon realised that the easier of these two for me to get into was agriculture. By a set of extremely favourable circumstances, the Headmaster, Mr. Flecker, had arranged for some CH students to study agriculture at Macdonald College of McGill University in Montreal, Canada. The circumstance which made this available was financial support that had been arranged by Mr. Flecker as part of a bilateral aid scheme between Britain and Canada. Thus, I emigrated to Canada and took my BSc. in agricultural chemistry. I then went on in the same system to take an MSc. However, it was after completing an MSc in this programme that I decided I should really switch to medicine as a more exact science. So, I enrolled in the Faculty of Medicine at McGill where, after four years, I obtained a PhD. The waves of change did not end there, because informing my interest in biology was a strong fascination with marine biology, though at the time I was unaware that there were any jobs in professional biology. However, from an advertisement in *Nature*, I discovered a job-offering for a biochemist to study the plankton of the sea. This was a subject that had received very little scientific attention, but a group at Nanaimo, BC, with the Fisheries Research of Canada, had decided that the probability theories being used for fish abundance estimations had not worked; their suggestion, then, was to found a whole new school of biologists who would examine food chains in the sea, starting with plankton. When my application for this position was received and accepted, I never looked back!

I soon became involved in a number of joint exercises run by my mentor at Nanaimo BC., Dr. John Strickland. These experiments included studying the plankton community for a couple of months at an ocean station, approximately 1,000 miles off the coast. The purpose of this study was to see how the plankton community of the ocean waters differed from plankton near the coast. Another was a unique study in which a large volume of seawater was enclosed in a plastic sphere; we then followed the time sequence of a plankton bloom. Both these experiments taught us a lot about the time events of plankton blooms. At this point, Dr. Strickland started a manual for the measurement of plankton and nutrients in the sea, so that our results could be safely compared with other scientists using a uniform methodology.

I went away after this early work to become a member of a UNESCO group located in Paris. This group was designed to bring together scientists of different nations so that they could study the oceans together, where a single nation studying the Indian or Pacific Oceans would have a very limited chance of success. My work with UNESCO introduced me to many international scientists, but after a couple of years I wanted to organise some experiments directly related to the dynamics of plankton and the relationship of this food source to fish populations.

Practising my own science

I returned from Paris to Nanaimo, and was encouraged to start my own research group to further investigate the relationship between plankton and fish. The most obvious question to ask was whether one could enhance fish production by increasing its food source. After all, this was very much the basis for agriculture, where increased grass production produced more food for herbivores, such as dairy and beef cattle.

We could carry out a fertilisation experiment by adding nutrients either to a large lake or to the sea, and then looking for increased fish production. The difficulty in either lakes or the sea, however, was that the plants (phytoplankton) were not directly fed on by fish. This was because they were too small, but a large population of zooplankton grazed the tiny phytoplankton, which in turn presented a reasonable sized food that fish could eat. So, in planning an experiment on adding fertiliser to water to increase fish production, one had to go through two steps in the food chain of aquatic animals, compared to their terrestrial equivalents.

I organised a group of scientists with whom we had worked previously. We chose to carry out a fertilisation experiment on a large lake where sockeye salmon spent their first year of life, before going to sea. An initial danger in such an experiment on a lake is that if you add too much fertiliser, phytoplankton would grow too rapidly and cause eutrophication of the lake system, with a resulting loss of oxygen to the whole lake. The experiment was eventually carried out in a lake 35km long and 2km wide (Great Central

Lake, Vancouver Island). Our calculated amount of fertiliser was ten tons, repeated ten times, over ten weeks. The salmon growing for their first year in this lake increased in size by about 30 percent before going to sea. As a result of their increased weight, the ocean survival recorded a return of adult salmon amounting to ca. 373,000, compared with ca. 52,000 before fertilisation. This approximate increase has been maintained over the following 25 years with the continual application of fertiliser. If this kind of result could be applied directly to the oceans, it would probably also decrease the carbon dioxide in the ocean waters – a beneficial effect on pH in the sea, which has been decreasing to the detriment of many creatures, especially corals. Unfortunately, such an experiment has been legally banned as being geo-physically unpredictable.

Food webs in the oceans

Fisheries management has in the past been based largely on the idea of stock recruitment. That is, if you know the number of adult fish and you assume certain losses in their young due to environmental and other events, then you can predict the number of fish in the following year based on probability. This general technique had not worked as a good prediction, and it was our task, started by Dr. Strickland, to come up with an alternative way of predicting the harvest of fish. This gave us the incentive to look at food webs in the oceans to see what the alternatives were for feeding fish. The food web is a more complicated representation of the flow of energy in an aquatic system than the concept of a food chain, such as we studied on Great Central Lake. Dr W Greve and I pointed out that, for example, jellyfish blooms were mostly accompanied by very small plankton food particles. On the other hand, it has been known for some time that the feeding of baleen whales is accompanied by very large plankton. This observation is easier to understand by analogy, if one considers how a loaf of bread might be consumed if it was presented either as breadcrumbs or as a whole loaf. In the former case, only small predators such as mice or insects could possibly expend the time or energy picking up the particles. Given a whole loaf, however, large animals as big as humans could feed on the much bigger prey. So, in the oceans, when very small phytoplankton are present, the food chain tends towards smaller predators, such as jellyfish having a tentacle system for gathering small food items, while even the same biomass in large prey could feed much larger predators. Since the phytoplankton of the sea range in size from a micron to a thousand microns (the cubic dimensions ranging over billion units of size), it is logical to suggest that the larger phytoplankton (e.g. diatoms) could be the source of food for large zooplankton (e.g. krill), while smaller phytoplankton could not support such large predators. I presented this simple summary of a divergent food web at a conference of the Scientific Committee on Ocean Research (SCOR) in South Africa, and a detailed scientific summary of the presentation was published in the *South African Journal of Science*, Vol. 75. p.536–540, 1979. One of my colleagues at the time (Dr. Ray Sheldon) wrote an additional paper giving mathematical equations linking various parts of food webs, which was essential to making the concept ecologically useful.

The Japan Prize

In the autumn of 2001, I was surprised to be the recipient of one of the greatest prizes in science, the Japan Prize. The award had been given to scientists and engineers throughout the world for the advancement of science. Two awards are made per year in different categories, and the presentation consists of a commemorative gold medal and Y50 million. My ceremony took place in Tokyo in the presence of the Emperor. The actual reason for my award has been summarised as follows in my book *The Sea's Enthrall* (Trafford Publ: Victoria, Canada, 2004, p 178):

'Through his research devoted to obtaining a holistic understanding of how pelagic organisms are interconnected in the trophodynamic food web of the sea, he has made a great contribution to the development of biological oceanography. His goal has been to present and alternative method for the management of fisheries, based on measuring the dynamic relationship between fish and their physical, chemical and biological environments.'

The ceremony lasted one week and included my wife, Dr. Carol Lalli, and I having dinner and a concert with the Emperor and his wife; and finally, dinner with the grandson of the man who had originally financed the award, Mr. Konosuke Matsushita.

My distribution of the prize money for the award was difficult, for I had so many people to thank in my career. I decided to honour my family for their support over many years. Next, I wanted to honour my school, Christ's Hospital, by making a pupil presentation available. I became a governor of the school and supported a building fund. Also, I supported a number of oceanographic institutions, including a far-ranging programme at the University of Conception in Chile, for oceanographic research in the southern hemisphere.

Finally...

When one suggests some new approach to a science, it is logical that this may be protested or ignored until it is thoroughly tested. In my case, for example, the fertilisation of Great Central Lake described above has not been duplicated in spite of being run successfully for 25 years. This kind of experiment is very large compared with something that might be done in a laboratory, and there are a number of examples in science which have been treated the same way. However, over longer time periods, new ideas become more acceptable to new generations of scientists. *To look* is good, as the poet George Herbert knew well in the 17th century; but *vision* carries us farther:

> 'A man that looks on glasse,
> On it may stay his eye;
> Or if he pleaseth, through it passe,
> And then the heav'n espie.'

My own summary of being a student, and then spending many years in science, is that my school years were very helpful to my career. It was satisfying to have been able to bring forward some new understandings of the biology of aquatic systems, much of it through experiments, but also even more through writing textbooks that have been translated into Russian, Chinese, and Japanese, and have been among the best sellers on a world market. In my scientific work, I also wish to acknowledge the role of my wife, Dr. C.M. Lalli, who is an oceanographer.

Tim Parsons, Nanaimo, BC, 2019

Professor Timothy R Parsons PhD, FRSC, OC, DSc (Hon) b.1932; 1942–1949 CH; 1958–1971 Fisheries Research Board of Canada (1962–1964 UNESCO Paris); 1971–1992, Department of Oceanography, UBC; 1992 to present. Honorary Scientist, Institute of Ocean Sciences, Sidney, BC; and Honorary Professor Emeritus Department of Earth and Ocean Sciences, UBC.

XI

Inspiring Generations: Quincentenary Questions

We benefit often in our lives from inspiration: as we choose an education; build the relationships that will last our lifetime; select a career path; or simply continue with whatever we are doing at difficult times. Crucially, inspiration affects us most in our secondary school years – as the themed essays in this book demonstrate. And Christ's Hospital is fundamentally concerned with inspiring future generations.

Five thoughtful books – Stephen Hawking in his *Brief Answers to the Big Questions*; Brian Cox in his *Wonders of the Universe*; Steven Pinker in his *Enlightenment Now: The Case for Reason, Science, Humanism & Progress*; Noah Harari in his *21 Lessons for the 21st Century*; David Christian in his *Origin Story* – have been influential in informing our thinking about Christ's Hospital in the 21st century; not because these books provide answers, but because they may help us arrive at the big questions most crucial for CH – the questions I'll refer to as 'quincentenary questions'. As David Christian writes,

'Things are happening so fast that… the details of what we do in the next few decades will have huge consequences for us and for the biosphere on scales of thousands of years… we are now managing an entire biosphere, and we can do it well or badly.'

Fundamental questions have been raised by Old Blues worldwide in an internet-based debate over the past five years, following the consequences of the 2007 global financial crisis. The chapters in this book by committed Old Blues – a young healthcare professional setting out on her career; a skilled, established farmer since the mid-20th century; a systemic therapist near the start of her 21st century career; a distinguished schoolteacher and author; an eminent theologian; a leading medical/nuclear physics researcher; an award-winning poet, inspired by CH to write an extraordinary poetry collection; a geologist who has been for nearly a quarter century the committed Secretary/Treasurer of BCOB; an outstanding technological entrepreneur; a radically successful broadcast media entrepreneur; a world laureate environmental research scientist and oceanographer – all provide an intellectual landscape for these 'big' questions.

Seven initial questions are thus posed for consideration and comprehensive debate by the Christ's Hospital community with aspirations for an ever-improving school 'like no other' towards the great quincentenary of 2052. Yes, that year and those 500-year celebrations for Christ's Hospital are some 30 years in the future, but looking back today, we see that much of what has changed over the past 30 years was reasonably predictable. Some 30 years ago, we already had the Berners-Lee internet (1989), the Apple Macintosh computer (1984), Sputnik (1957), the Moon Landing (1969), and Moore's Law (1965) regarding the trend of computing/transistor capacity doubling about every two years – a theory that has been confirmed and still generally holds true (perhaps slowing a bit) in 2019. Accordingly, intelligent predictions in the realm of science and engineering through to the middle of this century may well be feasible in preparing for the changes ahead.

Much harder, as Stephen Hawking explores, is making predictions about science and engineering in the longer term, as was expressed in the poetic eulogy for Hawking by Kip Thorne (Nobel 2017) during Hawking's interment in Westminster Abbey in 2018, between Isaac Newton and Charles Darwin:

'Newton gave us answers. Hawking gave us questions. And Hawking's questions keep on giving, generating breakthroughs decades later. When ultimately we master the quantum gravity laws and comprehend fully the birth of our universe, it may largely be by standing on the shoulders of Hawking.'

Accordingly, we can reasonably prepare for the quincentenary in 2052 by posing these seven initial questions:

(1) A consortium of schools to promote equality?

Christ's Hospital could create and lead a group of ten committed independent schools – coupled to a group of ten state sixth-form colleges involving some 20,000 students: to advance the 1552 mission and ethos, and to combat social and educational inequities amongst disadvantaged children in a 'mega-school' consortium. This could be named the 'Christ's Hospital Group' of schools, complementing the elitist 'Eton Group' and 'Rugby Group'. This overall consortium idea could be advocated by CH as a sea change towards a new UK government cross-party policy for integrating the independent and state sectors. India, for example, now encourages its private schools to admit a quarter of their students from the poorest children in the local area, and Finland has reformed and integrated its whole secondary school structure.

The work of such a consortium could additionally involve the development of new distance-learning technology with a global reach. Overall, this could lead to an opening up of independent schools to everyone. The ten original independents in this CH consortium could become 100. As with Attlee's conclusion about social engineering in London's pre-WWI East End, this would require cross-party government incentives and support beyond private charity to succeed. Christ's Hospital could be in the vanguard of a great new transformation, applying 21st century teaching methods including open distance learning in a world-class secondary 'Education for All' (EFA) mega-enterprise in a new, post-imperial, consensus UK.

One outcome of this first quincentenary question could be the advocacy of a new Bill in the UK Parliament on independent schools, whereby such schools would be required to admit 25% poor students on zero (or minimal) means-tested fees in order to retain charitable (tax advantageous) status. After all, it was a Conservative prime minister during WWII (Winston Churchill) who promised to flood the public schools with bursary children.

(2) A green Christ's Hospital?

Christ's Hospital has made useful steps towards becoming 'green' (via solar energy panels, for example), but CH could become a beacon of educational responsibility in the context of radically reducing the environmental footprint of the school in order to inspire the tackling of anthropogenic climate change and loss of bio-diversity. This would firstly involve a comprehensive environmental-impact study of Christ's Hospital and, later, progressive environmental and sustainability/industrial ecology policies of the school and the Foundation through to the middle of the century and beyond.

Humanity has evolved to be able to arrest human-induced climate change. Now we must surely act – globally and locally. The movement for tackling the climate emergency by the UK Student Climate Network, as part of the school-children-led global climate-change emergency, represents a passionate movement initiated in 2018 by Greta Thunberg and, developed in 2019, could be built upon at CH:

'We're young, we're students and we're calling for change. Our movement started in February 2019 when tens of thousands of young people took to the streets in towns and cities around Britain, in an unprecedented emergence of

a youth climate justice movement. We've joined a movement that's spreading rapidly across the world, catalysed by the actions of one individual in taking a stand in August 2018. Greta Thunberg may have been the spark, but we're the wildfire and we're fuelled by the necessity for action. The climate is in crisis ... scientists have been giving increasingly dire warnings about the state of our planet for years, with the urgency and severity of their message escalating in recent times. It's abundantly clear: change is needed, and it's needed now!'

Importantly, this new policy should not be naïve; nor should it simply address the more obvious issues, but be founded on hard climate science including carbon sequestration and geo-engineering, as well as reduced reliance on fossil-fuel energy. Geo-engineering as a complement to reducing CO_2 emissions represents a promising way forward, with now the likely temperature overshoot scenario requiring revisions to the existing international agreements on climate change. As the United Nations Secretary-General Antonio Guterres said at a recent summit:

'Climate Change is the defining issue of our time and we are at a defining moment. From shifting weather patterns that threaten food production, to rising sea levels that increase the risk of catastrophic flooding, the impacts of climate change are global in scope and unprecedented in scale.'

This urgent call to international political action occurs at a time when the commitment of governments to this defining issue is waning, especially in the world's biggest economy, USA. A recurring goal of science is to help us live more sustainable lives – whether it's growing enough food to ensure nobody goes hungry (one billion of us lack adequate food security), or making our chemical processes cleaner and greener. Surely it is within the scope of Christ's Hospital to contribute beneficially as a committed voice in this growing UN-Thunberg-led debate – in this anthropocene age.

(3) A Royal School of Science, Technology, Engineering, Entrepreneurship, Materials & Mathematics (STEEMM-Ahead)?

Christ's Hospital has a very good foundation in the STEEMM arena and could now inspire a new, world-class focus on STEEMM, building from the inspiration of the Great Verrio painting of the founding of the Royal School of Mathematics and Navigational Engineering, and research in STEEMM teaching in, for example, Singapore. This would build especially on the tradition of evidence-based heuristic teaching of science by discovery as a comprehensive teaching philosophy towards informed decision-making in all realms.

The UK public spend in the STEEMM area of education in state schools has been significantly cut of late, and CH could lead a national 'STEEMM-Ahead' grand challenge initiative in secondary education towards digitalisation and artificial intelligence (AI). The US National Academy of Engineering has focused on a series of grand challenges as follows: making solar energy economical; developing carbon sequestration methods; managing the nitrogen cycle; providing access to clean water; the development of enhanced virtual reality; advanced public health informatics; restoring and improving urban infrastructure; and engineering better medicines – as well as preventing nuclear terror; securing cyberspace; reverse-engineering the brain; advancing personalised learning; engineering the tools of scientific discovery; and providing energy from fusion.

In September 2019, the UK Royal Academy of Engineering organised a grand challenges summit (www.ggcs2019.com) in London with the engineering academies of China and USA: 'Engineering in an Unpredictable World'. Humanity is facing unprecedented challenges from a population growing to 10 billion by 2050, with accelerating degradation of the planet and its resources. At the same time, exponential technological changes are making the world smarter, faster, and more connected, but with unanticipated consequences.

Engineers are crucial to the international effort to address these rapidly evolving, unpredictable challenges. We need to embed collaboration, diversity, and global responsibility into the solutions we create, transforming the way engineers work, think, and are taught. Engineers have the power to help make a better world for the citizens of 2050, but only if we transform engineering and embrace that responsibility today. Under this, the summit had two sub-themes:

- 'Will AI and other transformational technologies change humanity for the better?'
    - Example topics: equitable access; ethics; healthcare; neuroscience; extending life; engineering education; automation; employment; genetics; robotics; mental health; unintended consequences; AI bias; secure cyberspace
- 'Can we sustain 10 billion people?'
    - Example topics: food; water; energy; waste; circular economy; urbanisation; China's mega-cities; transport; resources; economic development; VR; health provision; digital enablement for rural dwellers

This was a timely world summit for Christ's Hospital in STEEMM education, and might well help foster CH's opportunity to enter the vanguard of sustainable change.

(4) A Christ's Hospital press?

Christ's Hospital already regularly publishes books written by Old Blues, and could establish a specialist publishing arm as Christ's Hospital Press (CHP). (Arguably, the first major book actually published by CH is *Christ's Hospital in the Year 2000.)* The formal creation of CHP could, for example, result in an integrated book series on new technology-based secondary education and policies in consortia/mega schools, and in other specialist CH areas. The present book could perhaps be the first in a series published quadrennially through to the quincentenary – with future volumes sponsored by other branches of CHOBA. CHP could be structured as an umbrella organisation, with each book project undertaken in a financially autonomous fashion – possibly in association with a major academic publisher like OUP, beneficially encompassing all CH Museum book projects. We still need hard-backed books and 'real' libraries in this new digital age, and CHP could be a new voice for promulgating the CH ethos.

(5) An international school?

CH could evolve as a global mega-school inspired by aspirations for a better world, with the ideal of uniting peoples and advancing equality of opportunity. Global integrity and understanding depends on those with the knowledge to stand up for internationalism and evidence-based decision-making. Christ's Hospital could play an increasing leadership role in this realm for the common good – globally.

A suitable link with schools for poor children in India might be one aspect of this initiative. A worthwhile link, in accord with the 1552 ethos, could be with Vivekananda Public School (VPS) in Hyderabad, India (www.vpsngo.org). VPS is a non-government charity school, founded in 1982 for the utterly poorest children, providing VPS students from kindergarten to high school with three full school uniforms, free – as well as free school meals, free text books, school materials, and free education. One could envisage new Old Blues spending a gap semester teaching at VPS; VPS students being admitted to CH at (especially) 16 years; involvement of CH in curriculum and facilities development with VPS; teacher exchanges. An initial step might involve a group of Blues/staff making a fact-finding visit to VPS and reporting on potential CH-VPS collaboration over an ongoing period.

CH has had close academic links with India for centuries, with a vast Indian heritage in 21st century UK. Two Old Blues who lived in India in the 19th century might be particularly noted in this regard: Thomas Middleton, who was Anglican Bishop of India, and in 1820 founded Bishop's College in Kolkata; and especially Sir Alexander Cunningham, who was an engineer with the East India Company, and who then became the founding director-general of the Archeological Survey of India. Cunningham's pioneering and scholarly archeological and geographical contributions (1861–1885) are still much appreciated in India. (Cunningham's son, A J C Cunningham, born in Delhi, is well-known in mathematics for the 'Cunningham Number'.)

The VPS leadership is considering establishing an international steering committee and possibly a 'Vivekananda/Christ's Hospital Conference' in Hyderabad to advance the mission of VPS building on the *sui generis* model of CH – and, indeed, on various long-standing links of CH with India, as delineated above.

Other CH links already exist, with schools in the USA having a closely similar ethos and mission – Oxford Day Academy (www.oxforddayacademy.org) in Palto Alto, California (ODA), and Milton Hershey School in Harrisburg, PA (MHS). ODA is a school co-created with underprivileged young people and their families as a public charter high school for the Sequoia Union High School District of San Mateo County, California. At the core of the ODA model is the notion of students being responsible for identifying and addressing the issues they care most about. Teachers use Oxford-style tutorials to help students connect this service focus with academic content, bringing student agency and personalisation to new levels through five key design elements. Meanwhile, MHS (www.mhs-pa.org) was founded in 1909 by Milton & Catherine Hershey, originally for orphaned boys. Milton Hershey (1857–1945), after the death of his wife, later bequeathed his entire chocolate fortune to the school. MHS continues today as a top-notch coeducational school for approximately 2,000 girls and boys – all from low-income families – as a beacon of social engineering. Perhaps VPS might also be linked with ODA & MHS beneficially through a CH initiative in a consortium of internationally-oriented schools?

(6) 1552–2052: An assessment of success?

Christ's Hospital could establish a new system of yardsticks of success in the context, explicitly, of the charitable mission in regard to admissions and the value-added educational progression for Blues from admission onwards – indeed, tracing the career trajectories of Old Blues life-long. This would be a unique system of life-long performance analysis, one which could take place alongside the academic and sporting achievement metrics and league tables. CH seems to be a much happier, kinder, more psychologically empathetic institution in 2020 than it was in 1950 – and this is one very important metric to address alongside traditional measures. An ongoing key metric is the proportion of students admitted via means-tested zero fees. The vision of linking CH with charity schools for critically poor children in India and elsewhere would build on *Le Cordon Bleu* and could be a new approach to performance success.

(7) A quadrennial conference series

Christ's Hospital has an established tradition of forthright, inspirational debate, and could establish a regular quadrennial conference series. Debate on progress within a formal conference structure amongst Old Blues should also help facilitate continuing support and evolution for both school and foundation. A starting point in this respect has been the conversation between those involved in this book about the future direction of Christ's Hospital. Every four years, such structured conversations might take place in a conference format, perhaps involving a new book every four years along the lines of this present volume.

This book is in many ways a 'proto-conference' on the forward vision for Christ's Hospital towards the great quincentenary; this book is, if you will, an offering of papers, poetry, and essays, as new starting points for discussing ideas for CH in the forthright forum of the wide-ranging and unique, global CHOBA community – as the school moves towards 2052: the quincentenary.

In the context of this vision, it is appropriate to give a final word to the Hertford Old Blue Lizzie Ballagher:

…while out across the quad
the band marches crisply on
and leavers drift or dance or march
into their lives
with eyes forward, forever forward.

From 'Endings & Beginnings'

David Taplin,
Vancouver, BC, Autumn 2019
www.dmrtaplin.ca

Epilogue

Christ's Hospital has done many things for its many children over the almost five centuries of its history; among them, of course, to teach us – but not only in the obvious ways. For it drew us into questioning the world around us; prompted us into resourcefulness and creativity in so many fields of endeavour: from oceanography to aeronautics; from navigation and chronometry to historical writing and poetry; from the engineering wizardry effected in large structures to the finesse of mathematics, micro-processing, pharmacology, and molecular-level chemistry; from concert halls to the halls of academia and commerce; and, crucially, it has also prompted us into lifetime careers in education, mission, medicine, and the church.

Above all, Christ's Hospital showed us the richness of giving service to others; more, it has given Blues and Old Blues alike skills in navigating through difficult times, both real and metaphorical:

It is a world I never thought
        to hear of save in broadsides
        bawled on Cheapside, or in tales
        we read before we fall asleep;
never dreamed of: not even to look upon a king
        who helps to make more possible
        the numbering, charting of the stars;
        the sailing of the tall-ships
        into sunset's storybooks.

From *Verrio's Views: The Hands That Rock the Cradles*

Lizzie Ballagher
Kent, England, Autumn 2019
https://www.lizzieballagherpoetry.wordpress.com/

Acknowledgements

In addition to those already acknowledged at the end of Chapter VI of this volume, the authors acknowledge with gratitude the kindness of various publishers during the preparation of this book: those, as follows, who have granted permission for the use of extracts from the work of the poets listed here:

For use of 'The Lake Isle of Innisfree' and 'The Song of Wandering Aengus' by **W B Yeats**: The Estate of W B Yeats, and United Agents / A P Watts. For use of three poems by Old Blue **Keith Douglas**: 'Aristocrats', 'How To Kill', and '*Vergissmeinicht*' from *Keith Douglas, Complete Poems*, Faber & Faber Ltd. For use of lines from the poem 'Unteachable' by Old Blue **Edmund Blunden**, the Estate of Edmund Blunden, and David Higham Associates. For the use of ten lines from *T S Eliot's Four Quartets*, Faber & Faber Ltd.

The support and involvement of over one thousand Old Blues, since this project was first mooted in 2014, is very warmly acknowledged, including the great cadre of authors of remarkable books, monographs, biographies, autobiographies on Christ's Hospital from Trollope in 1834 onwards by Old Blues. Individuals, too many to record here, have been thanked privately. There are indeed 65,000 stories within the archives of CH of lives and careers of Old Blues; and here are related just a very small, in some perhaps idiosyncratic way, representative fraction. With the connected digital age and the resources of CHOBA, very many stories can be made accessible in the future through websites on the beneficial impact and developments of the CH ethos – and indeed on the place of CH in the linked world of charity schools for the poor and disadvantaged.